# Cape May County

*A Pictorial History by Herb Beitel and Vance Enck*

*Herb Beitel*

*Vance Enck*

This limited edition volume celebrates close to three hundred years of Cape May County.

*Cape Savings Bank has been pleased to sponsor this limited edition of* Cape May County: A Pictorial History. *As one of the oldest and most respected financial institutions in the county, our history has been closely intertwined with the county's development and growth. We take great pride in the confidence and trust placed in us by its citizens and hope that this volume of rare photographs, maps and narrative text will contribute to preserving Cape May County's proud heritage.*

*Special recognition and thanks to Herbert Beitel and Vance Enck for their tireless efforts in making this volume the masterpiece of carefully documented and beautifully illustrated history that it is.*

*The officers and directors of Cape Savings Bank hope that we will all benefit from this look at the past, and that it will serve as a guide for the future.*

Herbert L. Hornsby, Jr.
*President*

225 North Main Street
Cape May Court House, NJ 08210
(609) 465-5600

*A picture of the Wildwood boardwalk along Atlantic Avenue, taken in 1912. This was Wildwood's first boardwalk, where the planks were placed directly on the sand. The walk was not elevated until later. Courtesy of Wildwood Museum*

# Cape May County
## *A Pictorial History*

*by* **Herbert M. Beitel** *and* **Vance C. Enck**

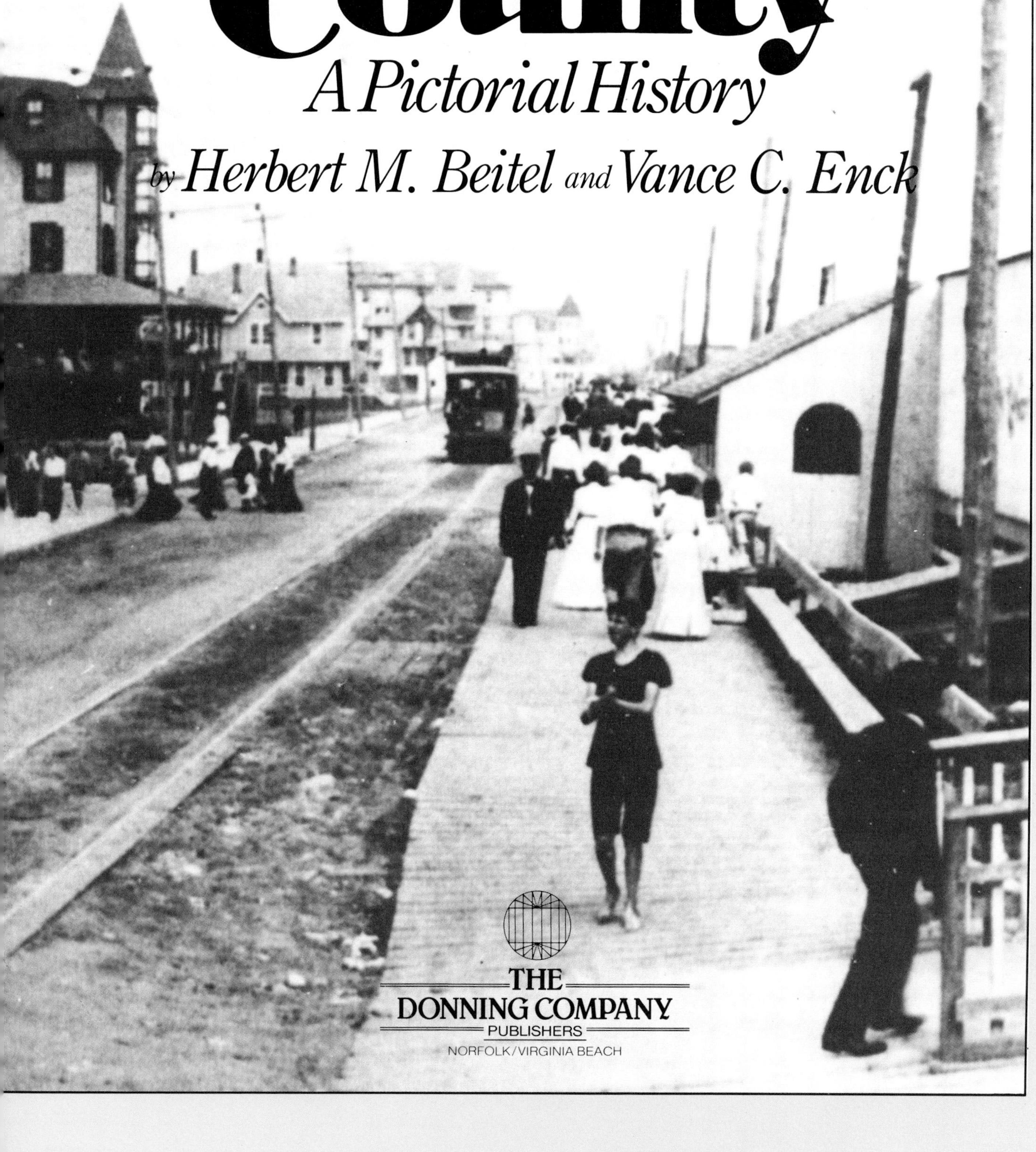

THE
DONNING COMPANY
PUBLISHERS
NORFOLK/VIRGINIA BEACH

The Donning Company/Publishers
Norfolk/Virginia Beach

Copyright © 1988 by Herbert M. Beitel and Vance C. Enck

All rights reserved, including the right to reproduce this work in any form whatsoever without permission in writing from the publisher, except for brief passages in connection with a review. For information, write:

    The Donning Company/Publishers
    5659 Virginia Beach Boulevard
    Norfolk, Virginia 23502

Edited by Veronica Kirk
Richard A. Horwege, Senior Editor

**Library of Congress Cataloging-in-Publication Data**

Beitel, Herbert M., 1925-
  Cape May county.

  Bibliography: p.
  Includes index.
  1. Cape May County (N.J.)—History—Pictorial works.
2. Cape May County (N.J.)—Description and travel—Views.
I. Enck, Vance C., 1931-  . II. Title.
F142.C2B44    1988    974.9'88    88-33451
ISBN 0-89865-749-0 (lim. ed.)

**Printed in the United States of America**

# Contents

| | |
|---|---|
| Foreword | 6 |
| Acknowledgments | 7 |
| Introduction | 9 |
| The Kechemeches and the Tuckahoes | 10 |
| They Found New Jersey Instead | 12 |
| "Thar She Blows!" | 14 |
| Town Bank | 16 |
| Pirates, Privateers, and Patriots | 18 |
| Who Will Be Sovereign? | 20 |
| Tillers, Toilers, Travelers, Government, and Taxes | 22 |
| Patriotism and Rugged Individualism Defeat England | 26 |
| Paths to Progress | 28 |
| **Upper Township** | 32 |
|   *Lester C. McNamara Wildlife Management Area* | 33 |
|   *Beesley's Point* | 34 |
|   *Marmora* | 36 |
|   *Palermo* | 38 |
|   *Seaville* | 40 |
|   *Tuckahoe* | 42 |
|   *Marshallville* | 44 |
|   *Petersburg* | 48 |
| **Dennis Township** | 50 |
|   *Belleplain* | 53 |
|   *Belleplain State Forest* | 53 |
|   *Ocean View* | 54 |
|   *Clermont* | 56 |
|   *South Seaville* | 56 |
|   *Eldora* | 60 |
|   *Woodbine* | 61 |
|   *Dennisville* | 65 |
| **Middle Township** | 72 |
|   *Crest Haven* | 72 |
|   *Burdette Tomlin Hospital* | 74 |
|   *Cape May County Historical Museum* | 75 |
|   *Cape May County Park and Zoo* | 76 |
|   *Swainton* | 78 |
|   *Cape May Court House* | 79 |
|   *Burleigh* | 88 |
|   *Rio Grande* | 90 |
|   *Dias Creek, Reeds Beach, Pierces Point, Kimbles Beach, High Beach, and Del Haven* | 92 |
|   *Goshen* | 92 |
|   *Whitesboro* | 96 |
| **Lower Township** | 98 |
|   *Erma* | 104 |
|   *Cold Spring* | 105 |
|   *Cold Spring Academy* | 106 |
|   *Cold Spring Presbyterian Church* | 106 |
|   *Historic Cold Spring Village* | 108 |
|   *Villas and Fishing Creek* | 110 |
|   *North Cape May* | 111 |
|   *Semper Paratus* | 112 |
| **Trails to Destiny** | 116 |
| **The Jersey Shore and the Barrier Islands** | 140 |
|   *Cape May Point* | 142 |
|   *West Cape May* | 153 |
|   *Cape May City* | 156 |
|   *The Wildwoods* | 180 |
|   *Stone Harbor* | 186 |
|   *Avalon* | 190 |
|   *Sea Isle City and Strathmere* | 193 |
|   *Ocean City* | 200 |
| **A Moving Experience** | 206 |
| **Fishing—the First Industry** | 209 |
| **Mother Nature's Realm** | 212 |
| **Into the Future** | 216 |
| **Bibliography** | 219 |
| **Index** | 221 |
| **About the Authors** | 224 |

# Foreword

Cape May County is blessed with several dedicated and active historians whose cooperation and assistance made the path to assembling this work much easier. However, Cape May does not have an extensive heritage of paintings, engravings, tintypes, daguerreotypes, or other graphics to illustrate its history. Remarkably lacking are any likenesses of the most important leaders and shapers of the county's development. It was not until the birth of the tourist industry, in the late 1800s, that any volume of photos and graphics were generated to aid our efforts, a century later, in compiling a "pictorial history" of the county.

Edward Wheeler, in his preface to *Scheyichbi and the Strand* or *Early Days Along the Delaware*, published by J. B. Lippincott and Company in 1876, wrote in part (we have changed "I" to "we" throughout):

> Every work should be justified by its usefulness and recommended by the manner of its performance.
>
> Criticism of literary style is averted from this little book, since nice elaboration of details, and smooth, consistent unity of parts, with a high degree of literary finish, are impossible in a volume made diverse by the requirements of its purpose and desultory by needful brevity. We have been...left entirely free to follow our own taste and judgment in regard to matter and manner, being bound in agreement with those concerned only that we should serve their purpose by "truthful representations" alone.
>
> Although observers of things we have described so far as they exist in the present, it would be absurd to put forward any claim to original discovery. We have gathered from many sources, but think a display of authorities would be out of place; yet, it is true, we have been more inquisitive than the results may indicate. Errors are possible, even when care is taken to be accurate, and mistakes are not at all inconsistent with an honest purpose; still, if misrepresentations exist in this work they are unknown, and as the motive has been conscientious, and the effort earnest. We believe the consideration due reliability is deserved by all herein published.
>
> But whatever discrepancies may mar the printed pages, there is no occasion to criticise the illustrations for misrepresentation. They are mostly drawn from photographic views, taken on the spot, with microscopic fidelity, and have been faithfully reproduced....They may, therefore, be looked upon as giving a correct idea of the physical features of the beautiful locality in which they were taken, and the varied structures which utilize and decorate the neighborhood.
>
> Neither the artist's pencil nor the photographer's skill can reproduce all that presented itself before the delighted vision. No art can imitate the tenderness of the dawn across the sea, or do justice to the resplendence with which the sun sank among the western waves on quiet Sabbath evenings, but all this may be suggested to the sense, and with many memories, will fill the picture with colors true to nature...
>
> Trusting that these ends may be fully served to the common benefit, and that something of instruction and refined gratification may be incidental thereto, the authors, with pleasure, present their work to an enlightened public.

We concur and adopt Mr. Wheeler's historic purpose and prose.

*Courtesy of Virginia Walsh*

# Acknowledgments

We are indebted to numerous people whose cooperation and support have made this work possible. Most of their names appear in picture credits throughout the book. We wish to express our special appreciation to Jane Dixon for her assistance and encouragement from the very start of this project. We also extend our appreciation of the time and assistance given us by John Merrill; Virginia Walsh; Dr. Irving Tenenbaum; Cornelia Corson Brown; H. Gerald MacDonald; Dr. John Siliquini; Tony Bevivino; Harry Folger; the Cape May County Historical and Genealogy Society President, Virginia Wilson, and staff members, Somers Corson, Hannah Swain and Barbara Arenberg; the Cape May County Library staff, especially Tom Leonard; and the managers and staff of the Cape Savings Bank branches for their patience and assistance during our photo gathering sessions.

*The Great Cedar Swamp, extending seventeen miles across the northern part of the county, divides the county into two sections. The southern part of the county was, for centuries, only accessible by water or by foot. The Lenni-Lenape Indians blazed traces through the forbidding swamp and the thick cedar and oak forests beyond.*

*Wild game in great numbers roamed the county, making it the "happy hunting ground" for the Lenapes. For centuries, only the Indians crossed the natural barriers to enjoy the cooling ocean breezes, lush vegetation, and ample game.*

*Pictured here is a view of the Great Cedar Swamp.*
*Photo by Vance Enck*

## Introduction

The history of Cape May County contains few chapters filled with adventure, excitement, glamour or gore. There are no fateful pitched wartime battles to report. What does emerge is a saga of inexorable steady growth through the innovative pioneering instincts, rugged individualism, deep-seated religious convictions, and fierce patriotic pride of its residents.

Almost entirely surrounded by natural water boundaries, Cape May County is virtually an island that thrusts over thirty miles into the Atlantic Ocean and the adjoining Delaware Bay. The ocean shoreline is lined with alluvial barrier islands separated from the mainland by tidal thoroughfares, inlets, and marshes that are up to three miles wide. The Delaware Bay is made hazardous by forbidding shoals. The Tuckahoe River and West Creek are difficult to navigate in many areas. The nearly ten miles of overland boundary with Cumberland County cuts through the dense cedar forest and the seventeen-mile-wide Great Cedar Swamp which divides the northern part of the county. Although the Indians traced paths through the forbidding swamp in order to enjoy the equable climate, abundant wildlife, and lush vegetation of the rest of the county, settlers were slow to tackle the natural obstacles.

# THE KECHEMECHES AND THE TUCKAHOES

Indians crossed the Bering Land Mass some twenty thousand to one hundred thousand years ago and slowly migrated east and south. The Algonquins were the main tribe to settle the Northeast and the Mid-Atlantic coast. The Lenni-Lenapes, a subtribe, often called the Delawares by explorers and settlers, made New Jersey their home. Other subtribes, the Kechemeches and the Tuckahoes, crossed the swamp to locate their encampments in Cape May County.

Their campgrounds were located inland and were moved frequently. At various times, they were located in the areas of what are now Dias Creek, Cape May Court House, Fishing Creek, Mayville, Cold Spring, Wildwood, Tuckahoe, and, the most important one, at Nummytown. Each summer Indian families from several other areas in the Mid-Atlantic region, as well as the Kechemeches and the Tuckahoes, resorted to the shoreline to feast on the abundant seafood and to bask in the cooling breezes. Attesting to their habits are the numerous artifacts and mounds of broken mollusk shells (broken in making wampum) found in these areas.

Resorting Indians came by foot, single-file, over centuries-old traces through the forests and swamps, to reach the happy feasting grounds. There were many summer campgrounds covering much of the county.

To navigate the waterways in search of the bountiful wildlife and seafood, Indians made canoes on-site. These were fashioned from cut or fallen logs. Covering parts that were to become the bow and stern with mud to protect them, the center was burned and the resulting charcoal was cleaned out with stone axes. These light, portable canoes were often buried in the mud at the end of the season to preserve them until the builder returned the next year (specifically marked trees identified the location). One such canoe was unearthed in 1933 by CCC workers developing Lake Nummy. It was cleaned, restored, and given to the state museum in Trenton where it is on permanent display.

The Indians were a handsome, peaceful people who took from their environment only what they needed. In earlier days there was a teeming bird population that included swans, ducks, geese, and bustards. Freely roaming the area were bison, deer, panthers, foxes, black bears, and minks. Combined with the food from the sea and ample forests, there was a ready supply of everything the Lenapes needed.

The Indians befriended foreign settlers and helped them erect their buildings. It is a matter of record that none of the lands occupied by foreign settlers were fraudulently or forcefully taken from the Indians. Unfortunately, the Indians did not understand the foreign settlers' philosophy of title. The Indians felt free to roam, hunt, and harvest on lands they sold. In fact, they saw no problem in selling the lands more than once. This led to confusing land ownership—confusion and squabbling that took nearly a century to sort out.

The number of Lenape inhabitants was never very large. It is variously estimated that the populations aggregated three hundred to five hundred, with some one hundred braves. These numbers were greatly reduced by diseases brought by the foreign settlers and from the complications resulting from the arrival of "demon rum."

With shrinking numbers and mounting dismay at the restrictions on their freedom, almost overnight the Lenapes moved away in 1735. Their final destination is in doubt. Some reportedly moved to Indian Mills in Burlington County. The Quakers established this as the first Indian reservation in North America in 1758 and called it Brotherton. Others of the tribe reportedly migrated to the Wabash River Valley in what is now Indiana.

Some of the Lenapes intermarried with settlers and remained behind with their new families. Snowflower, sister of the tribe's leader, King Nummy, married Benijah Thompson, a minister. She died after bearing twelve children. The aging King Nummy decided not to join his tribe's migration and stayed behind to care for his sister's children. The date of his death and burial site are uncertain. Snowflower's descendants are still living in the county.

*Kechemeches had enormous appetites for seafood, as attested by the large mounds of shells found near their campsites. They were not a very aggressive people, doing only what was necessary to enjoy life and survive. Their population in the county was always small and was soon outnumbered by the arriving settlers.*

*There are almost no incidents of violence in their chapter of Cape May County history. A handsome, friendly people, their assistance contributed to the establishment and survival of "foreign" settlements in the county.*

*Unfortunately, the Indians who roamed the county produced very little distinctive lore, art, or crafts by which to be remembered. Numerous relics have been found but they are of little historical significance.*

*Etching by Peter Lindstrum used to illustrate maps of the 1600s is presented through the courtesy of the New Jersey State Museum.*

During their summer migration to the seashore, the Lenni-Lenapes industriously made wampum from the shells of the mollusks consumed in their feasting. Indians used the wampum for barter and decoration, such as the necklaces pictured here. Pieces of wampum were about the size of a quarter and were heavier than silver. Because of the shortage of coins and currency, wampum was, for many decades, the main medium of exchange.

Black wampum, made from blue clam shells, was the most valuable. Large transactions in wampum were measured in "fathoms." A fathom was a string of wampum measured by the length of an Indian's arm from the elbow to the tip of his little finger.

Several mounds of broken shells (never whole ones) scattered throughout the county at known Indian campsites attest to their industry in making wampum—and their appetite for mollusks.

Settlers quickly learned to make wampum pieces because of their barter value. Jacob Spicer, an enterprising Cold Spring merchant, actively traded in wampum. In 1756 he offered a prize of five pounds to the person who manufactured the most wampum. This apparently led to overproduction, because he later complained, "Wampum will not sell. Before the Oswego, it was in great demand, equal, if not superior, to silver in value." Oswego referred to a wampum manufacturing center in the New York colony which, along with similar operations in northern New Jersey, had flooded the market.
*Courtesy of Cape May County Library*

*Mary Powell (seated center) was a descendant of Snowflower (Prudence Townsend), sister of King Nummy. She is flanked by her two sons, Josiah and George. The young girl on the left is Lydia, the Powells' adopted daughter. Abigail Ludlam is standing on the right. This picture was taken at the Chester Studio in 1890 when Mary Powell was thirty-four.*

*The picture above is a daguerreotype of Mary Powell, taken when she was ten years old. She was born in Dennisville in 1856.
Courtesy of Mary Brown Callahan*

# THEY FOUND NEW JERSEY INSTEAD!

Explorers seeking the northwest passage to India kept venturing onto the shoreline of a vast, unexplored continent. The first to venture into New Jersey coastal waters were Italians John Cabot and his son, Sebastian, sailing under the English flag. In 1498, they explored much of the coastline and established the basis for England's claim of sovereignty over the area, including New Jersey.

John Verazzano, a Florentine, sailing under the French flag, explored the coast in 1524 and christened the area New France.

Henry Hudson, an Englishman, sailing under the Dutch flag, sailed into the Delaware Bay on August 26, 1609. His ship *De Halve Maan* (Half Moon) anchored overnight in the vicinity of what is now Town Bank. Because of the treacherous shoals, Hudson decided not to fully explore the Delaware. He weighed anchor the next morning, sailed into the Atlantic and north, and explored the more placid river that still bears his name.

Next in the procession of Dutch flag bearers was Capt. Cornelius Hendrickson, who, in 1616, named the area New Netherlands. He stopped long enough to drop off a lookout at Cape May Point. For unknown reasons the unidentified lookout was left to languish there for seven years until he was retrieved by Captain Mey.

In the summer of 1623, Dutchman Capt. Cornelius Jacobsen Mey, in his ship *Blyde Broodschap* (Glad Tidings), led a flotilla of three ships around the cape (which he christened Cape Mey) into the bay (which he also named after himself). Sailing further up the river, he established a settlement near what is now Camden. He then returned to the Atlantic and sailed north to New York to assume his duties as director general of the Dutch colonies. Captain Mey is reported to have been a firm, compassionate, and fair leader. Although he bestowed his name on several areas, the only one that has survived is the now anglicized Cape May where there is no record of his having ever stepped ashore.

*John Cabot made several voyages to the New World beginning in 1496 and extending to 1516. On the second voyage in 1498, with his son, Sebastian, joining him in command, he sailed south from Labrador. They were the first Europeans to visit the New Jersey coast. It is not recorded that anyone from the expedition ever set foot on New Jersey land. However, it is probable that landings were made in search of water and provisions. The Cabots' voyages were the basis of the English claims to most of the North American continent. This engraving depicts John and his son Sebastian landing, probably on the Newfoundland coast, judging by the mountains and large bears.*
*Photographs courtesy Cape May County Library*

Sir Henry Hudson had sailed under the English flag twice to the New World in search of a northwest passage. In 1609 he was retained by the powerful East India Company of the Netherlands to undertake exploration of the newly discovered continent. In his ship De Halve Maan a two-masted, eighty ton ship with a crew of twenty-one, he set sail on April 6 for the northern coast of Norway. When icebergs forced him south, he made landfall at Newfoundland in July. He explored the coast of Maine and continued south as far as the Chesapeake Bay. He then sailed north, entered the Delaware Bay, and anchored off what is now Town Bank. His chronicler wrote, "The Bay of the South River was the first place of which the men of the Halve Maan took possession before any Christian had been there." In attempting to explore the bay further, Hudson encountered "flats" (sand bars) and headed back into the Atlantic and up to "North River" which still bears his name as the Hudson River.

While anchored off Sandy Hook, the first European casualty occurred in the New Jersey area when attacking Indians shot an arrow through sailor John Coleman's throat.

Hudson's glowing accounts of the new land prompted the East India Company to send three more expeditions to the area. Among them was Capt. Cornelius Jacobsen Mey who, during his voyage in 1623, bestowed his name on the point where the Delaware River and the Atlantic Ocean meet. With these voyages, the race for settlements and territory began.
*Courtesy Cape May County Library*

Ships like this replica, used by the early explorers were quite small by today's standards. They weighed-in at a paltry 80 to 120 tons, and carried a small crew of eighty to one hundred men.

Covering vast expanses of open tumultuous water in such frail crafts called for courage, derring-do, and faith. But men braved the elements and endured the rigors, loneliness, and tasteless menus of dried foods to discover, explore, and open-up the New World.

A replica of the Half Moon, about two-thirds the size of the original, was built to celebrate the 250th anniversary of Hudson's voyage. On July 18, 1959, squalls and rough seas broke the masts, which were then replaced with Cape May County cedar masts. Repaired and proudly anchored off the Cape May beach, she was once again attacked by storms on August 1, and driven, with her five hundred-pound anchor dragging, to the edge of McCries Shoals twelve miles south-southwest of Cape May where she was taken in tow by a coast guard cutter. These travails dramatically illustrated the skills and courage required of the early explorers.
*Courtesy Cape May County Library*

# "THAR SHE BLOWS!"

Whaling was Cape May County's first industry. As early as 1631, the Dutch established a whaling settlement at Cape Henlopen in Delaware. From 1840 on, there were sheltering and resting places for whalers on the twenty-foot-high banks at Town Bank in Cape May, about four miles northwest of Cape May Point. Initially, the whalers followed their prey down the coast from New England and Long Island. As the industry flourished, more whalers came. The Cape May whaling season ran from February through April. Some of the whalers built permanent residences in the county. By 1685 there were twenty log cabins and a fifty-foot lookout tower at Town Bank. William Penn wrote in 1683 that two companies of whalers, equipped with boats, would soon be in operation at Town Bank.

Whaling along the Jersey coast was not as immortalized in *Moby Dick*. When lookouts on the shore sounded the alarm—"Thar she blows!"—whalers ran to launch their boats in pursuit of their prey. Harpooners, precariously perched in the small tossing boats, hurled harpoons into the "Right" whale. A wild and dangerous ride usually ensued until the exhausted or dead whale could be towed ashore or, in some cases, harvested at sea.

So profitable was the whaling industry that the West Jersey Assembly approved, in 1693, a tax of 10 percent on the value of whale products extracted by non-residents. This may have been America's first protective tariff.

Whaling continued as a successful industry through the early 1700s. Indiscriminate killing, including cows and their calves, along with advanced hunting weapons, thinned the once teeming herds and drove them further out to sea. Whaling in Cape May County died out to become an almost forgotten part of the county's history.

During the decades that whaling dominated the county's economic life, many ancestral lines, whose names have permeated Cape May's history, were established. Lemying (Leaming), Osborne, Hews (Hughes), Hand, Stites, Eldredge, Skellens (Schellenger), Swain, Corson, and many others.

Among the very early whaler arrivals were John Whilden and his wife, Hannah. Hannah was the granddaughter of John Howland who arrived, at age eighteen, on the *Mayflower*, despite having fallen overboard during his voyage to America. The Whilden family played a leading role in the county's early development and laid the foundation for the claim that there are more *Mayflower* descendants in and emanating from Cape May County than Massachusetts.

*The whaling period for Cape May County began in 1648 and lasted nearly a century.*

*Whaling off the shores of Cape May was a dangerous and risky business. The whales were pursued and killed from small boats in waters near the shoreline. Survival for the whalers was a constant test of boating skills, nerve, bravery, and luck. However, as long as the whale migrations stayed near the coast, a steady stream of whaling men followed them.*

*The average whaler's life expectancy was about six years. Many of the whalers earned enough from their trade during that time to stake new careers as farmers or merchants before the law of averages caught up with them. Most of the whalers who stayed in the county between whale seasons became farmers to support their families. The majority of the early settlements away from the coasts started as a result of these migrations.*

*Illustration courtesy of Cape May County Library*

*Harvesting all the useful products from a beached dead whale was an organized and sophisticated activity. Blubber was cut from the carcasses in huge "blanket pieces" as the whale was rotated to facilitate the stripping, as shown below in an early artist's sketch. These large hunks were then cut two or three times to produce smaller "horse pieces," about two or three feet square. The smaller chunks were then cooked in 250 gallon kettles to render the valuable whale oil. Note the fireplace with kettle in the right foreground of the drawing.*
*Illustration courtesy of Cape May County Library*

*Shown in this picture is a large stripped carcass. The cooper's wagon, upper left, has brought barrels to carry away the whale oil. Whalebone, actually baleen, a cartilage from the mouth of the whale, was cut out for later use as corset and umbrella stays, or as whips, canes, and helmet frames. The residue, after all the other products were stripped, was often used to make fertilizer. Nothing was wasted—only the skeleton was left behind.*
*Illustration courtesy of Cape May County Library*

*One of the few reminders of the important role of whaling in Cape May County's history is this partial skull bone of a whale, located at the entrance of the New Jersey Marine Sciences Consortium Station at Seaville.*

*Whalers were the first foreign settlers of the county. Descendants of the whalers' families account for nearly all of the county's early development. There are still thousands of their descendants living in the county today, making contributions for future history of Cape May County.*

*The whaling centers have disappeared underwater. The whales departed the local waters nearly three centuries ago. But the legacy of this epoch remains.*
*Courtesy of Vance Enck*

# TOWN BANK

Originally called Portsmouth and New England Village by the whalers that settled there, the name Town Bank bestowed by William Penn has survived. It was the first and only settlement in the county for a time, and became the first county seat when the county was officially formed in 1692.

Storms destroyed the landing docks for whaling boats. Tides washed away the high banks that had given the town its name. The original Town Bank is today under water about three hundred feet out in the Delaware Bay. Some of the homes were moved to other areas before the waters moved in. Many of the headstones from the cemetery were moved to the Old Brick Church burial grounds in Cold Spring. The actual graves, however, were not moved.

The Town Bank of today is a residential community sharing the area with North Cape May as a part of Lower Township.

*New England Town (later Portsmouth, finally Town Bank) was a prosperous village from 1675 to about 1700. There were fifteen to twenty crude homes, most built by settlers from New Haven, and a tall observation tower (not shown in this artist's conception of the town). As the whales disappeared from the water off Cape May, whalers turned to other occupations and deserted the town.*

*The relentless erosion of tides and storms gradually washed Town Bank away. If any remnants of the town were to be found today, they would be about three hundred feet offshore in the Delaware Bay.*
*Painting courtesy of Jane Dixon*

*This painting depicts the Town Bank coast with whaling ships offshore.
Courtesy of Jane Dixon*

# PIRATES, PRIVATEERS, AND PATRIOTS

The ocean coastline with its Barrier Islands and treacherous shoals were respectfully skirted by regular merchant vessels. The Barrier Islands, numerous inlets, hidden bays, and wandering rivers so close to regular shipping lanes were, however, the answer to a pirate's dream. The area provided a safe haven from stalking pursuers as well as provisions and fresh water. The few settlers around were friendly with the buccaneers for protection as well as profit. Many of the marauders were English who began as privateers commissioned by the king as the British pushed for naval supremacy. However, when they turned to personal profit they became outlaws. Most famous of these was Capt. William Kidd, who roamed the Jersey coast in the 1600s, mostly along the Atlantic shoreline. Kidd was a wealthy, respected British citizen before turning from privateering to piracy. He was finally captured in Connecticut in 1699 after fleeing from the Cape May area where some of his crew had been arrested earlier. He was hanged in England on a Thames dock in 1701. Kidd was reportedly planning to marry an Absecon girl and to have buried treasure to start his new life. However, the hangman's noose intervened.

Blackbeard (Capt. Edward Teach), a much more typical pirate than the gentlemanly Kidd, occasionally roamed the Cape May coastal shipping routes, but mostly he terrorized the southern coasts. He was finally killed off North Carolina and his severed head carried on the bowsprit of the victorious British man-of-war.

Both Kidd and Blackbeard were reported to have buried some of their hoards of treasure in Cape May areas from Egg Harbor to Cape May Point. In spite of extensive non-archeological excavations over the years, none of the legendary treasure has been found—of record. A large tree, called Kidd's Tree, at Cape May Point, was the site of a favorite digging area. This same tree, at one time, sported a block and tackle that was purported to be pirates' equipment.

French, Spanish, and African pirates in great numbers were reported in Cape May waters until the mid-1700s. The West Jersey Society warned residents of the Cape that allowing pirates to rest and obtain provisions would no longer be tolerated. This was greeted with the settlers' usual disdain for authority.

For a time "wreckers" operated along the cape shores. This unique type of pirating used misleading light signals to trick unwary ships into running aground where the wreckers quickly plundered the hulks.

Privateering was officially sanctioned by the rebellious colonies during the Revolution and the War of 1812 as a means to combat British naval supremacy and disrupt their supply lines. The privateers were most effective in achieving these goals.

Cape May men, especially, were in great demand during these wars because they were experienced sailors and accomplished shipbuilders. Their contributions to the war effort were vital in keeping the supply lines open to Philadelphia and diverting much needed supplies to beleaguered Continental troops.

During the War of 1812 the Colonial naval operations outwitted the British by smuggling supplies past the Delaware blockade.

*The "Jolly Roger" often waved along the Cape May County coast, striking terror in the hearts of regular seamen and hapless passengers. Most of the pirate ships were of Spanish, French, or African origin. Privateers producing patriotic profits from piracy multiplied in wartime to harass the British but reverted back to legitimate activities when the wars ended. A few unscrupulous American captains resorted to piracy as a good way to make a living. The pirates gradually disappeared from American shores. After the 1750s, there were almost no pirates or privateers, except during wartime, along the Cape May coast. Courtesy of Cape May County Library*

*Modern-day pirates appear annually on several Cape May County beaches to celebrate the colorful period of history when real ones roamed the local waters. Note this live replica is a "preppie Pirate," complete with a Yale lock on his chest.
Courtesy of Virginia Walsh*

# WHO WILL BE SOVEREIGN?

For much of the seventeenth century, diplomatic war raged between England, the Netherlands, and Sweden over title to the territory. There were a few face-to-face confrontations but no pitched battles. Finally, in 1664, England asserted sovereignty over the entire region. With the exception of a few months hiatus with the Dutch in 1674-1675, British dominion remained unchallenged until the Revolution.

In 1664 the Duke of York sold the region to Lord John Berkeley and Sir John Carteret with the stipulation that the area by named Nova Caesarea (New Jersey) after the Isle of Jersey where Lord Berkeley had been governor. The new owners partitioned the land into East Jersey and West Jersey, with West Jersey going to Berkeley. In a short time, Berkeley lost his enthusiasm for developing the area and sold his interests in 1673 to Edward Byllynge, a Quaker. Byllynge, shortly thereafter, went bankrupt. William Penn, Gawan Laurie, and Nicholas Lucas, also Quakers, became trustees for Byllynge's interests. The land was divided into one hundred proprietaries, with ten going to John Fenwich and the rest in trust for Edward Byllynge. A proprietary government was established in 1677.

Dr. Daniel Coxe, a court physician to Queen Anne and King Charles II, by the late 1680s had purchased from Byllynge's heirs all of his estate's interests in the land, including Cape May County. At one time, Dr. Coxe owned over one million acres of land in New Jersey, in addition to extensive holdings in many other areas of the continent. He had great plans for developing a proprietary fiefdom with his holdings. In keeping with these plans, Coxe Hall was built on Coxhall Creek near Town Bank with space for his personal residence and for business operations. A whaling facility was built nearby. Although he never saw or used the facility himself, the large two-story edifice with an impressive observation tower was used as the center for the administration of the doctor's holdings, as well as for religious services by several church groups. As Coxe's difficulties in realizing his dreams increased, his interest waned. He sold off some parcels of land to settlers. On March 4, 1691, Dr. Coxe sold the balance of his holdings to the forty-eight members of the West Jersey Society. Coxe Hall was used as quarters for laborers for some time. Finally, it was cut into sections and moved to various sites.

*Edward Hyde, Lord Viscount Cornbury, a cousin of the English Queen Anne, was appointed by her as governor of New York and New Jersey in 1703. Very soon after succeeding King William to the throne, the Queen united the bickering provinces of East Jersey and West Jersey by royal decree. Cornbury replaced the popular George Hamilton who had twice served as governor of both the East and West provinces by consent of the proprietors. Hamilton had first been ousted by an act of Parliament that prohibited Scots from holding any public office or position of trust. The second ouster came with his replacement by Cornbury.*

*A new constitution was promulgated during Cornbury's tenure that provided, among other things, that only those who owned one hundred acres of land or more and were worth at least fifty pounds could vote; that all religious creeds were granted "freedom of conscience," except for Catholics whose freedoms were restricted; and that all printing presses had to be specially licensed. Cornbury was a profligate, vain man. His demands for a very large salary were refused by the Legislative Council and Queen Anne was finally forced to remove him as governor in 1709.*
*Courtesy of Cape May County Library*

*Although Dr. Daniel Coxe never came to America, his son, Daniel Coxe, did. He arrived in 1701, and became actively engaged in his father's affairs. He was commissioned a colonel and placed in command of the Provincial Militia. He moved to Burlington, the capital of West Jersey, married a Quaker, Sara Eickley, and remained there until his death in 1739. An active man, he started an iron forge operation near Burlington and a pottery plant in Burlington. He was a justice of the Colonial Court, a member of the Governor's Council and the first Masonic Grand Master in America. His plan for uniting the colonies was presented, in its entirety, by Benjamin Franklin at the Albany Convention in 1747.*
*Courtesy of Cape May County Historical Museum*

*Part of this house on Jonathon Hoffman Road, near North Cape May, is reputed to have been a part of Coxe Hall, built in 1690 and moved to this site sometime between 1870 and 1890. Coxe Hall was a large structure, with an observation tower, constructed on Coxe Hall Creek at the original Town Bank. Dr. Coxe built it as a headquarters for his holdings in West Jersey. He never came to America, but the building was used by his overseers. For some time after Dr. Coxe sold his properties to William Penn and the West Jersey Company, the building was used to house laborers. The house was reportedly disassembled and one section is said to have been moved to the Daniel Hughes' house on Old Bay Shore Road.*

*There is no record of the eventual site of the third section. A shed at the rear of this present house is said by some to have been part of the original observation tower of Coxe Hall. There is no verification of either of these claims.*
*Photograph by Vance Enck*

# TILLERS, TOILERS, TRAVELERS, GOVERNMENT, AND TAXES

For the eight or nine months that whales were not available off the shores, the original whalers turned to farming and trapping for a livelihood. As whaling was dying out, the whalers were able to purchase land through Dr. Coxe and the West Jersey Society. They moved inland to make farming, lumbering, and trapping the mainstays of the economy. New settlements were created: Goshen, Green Creek, Dennisville, Cape May Court House, Seaville, Clermont, Reeds Beach, Pierces Point, Petersburg, and Swainton.

Early land purchases set the stage for the county's development. Among those from Dr. Coxe were 340 acres purchased by William Jacoks in 1689, and 340 acres by Humphrey Hughes in 1689. Hughes also secured 180 in 1699, from the West Jersey Society. Other early purchases from the West Jersey Society included: 204 acres by Christopher Leaman (Leaming) in 1694; 400 acres by Jacob Spicer in 1696; 50 acres by Thomas Gandy in 1699; 150 acres by Joseph Whelden (Whildin) in 1695; 400 acres by John Canson (Corson) in 1695; 400 acres by Peter Canson (Corson) in 1695; two tracts of 600 acres and 240 acres by John Townsend in 1695; two tracts of 500 acres and 15 acres by Shamgar Hand in 1695; and 255 acres by John and Caleb Carman in 1695.

An orderly government structure, which had heretofore been a nuisance, became a necessity. Clear land titles had to be sorted out of the confused and overlapping claims. The growing commerce demanded courts and roads, and all of this, of course, led to the inevitable *sine qua non* of government, taxes, and politicians.

By 1700 there were 500 residents in Cape May County, and the first official census in 1726 listed 668 inhabitants. A West Jersey Assembly was created. Andrew Hamilton, governor of East Jersey, was appointed governor in April 1692, and, with the consent of the West Jersey Society and the proprietors, became the first governor of all New Jersey. Cape May County was officially created on November 12, 1692, to become the state's second county, following Burlington. The new county's boundaries encompassed 267 square miles of territory in a triangular shape, 30 miles long and 15 miles wide on its northern end. The present boundary lines were finally established in 1878 to include 257 square miles.

Transportation and communication with other areas became essential for the expanding economy. The first ferry began operation in 1692, running from Beesley's Point across Egg Harbor to Somers Point in Atlantic County. In 1704, Shamgar Hand, John Townsend, and William Goldin were appointed by Territorial Governor Cornbury to build roads providing access to the county. The first, the Queen's Highway (named for Queen Anne, and later renamed the King's Highway for King George) was completed in 1707, extending from Egg Harbor Bay to Town Bank and Cold Spring. Today's U.S. Route 9 generally follows this original turnpike's course. Following this, a turnpike was quickly planned and built extending from the Queen's Highway across the Great Cedar Swamp to the Cumberland County line. Today's state highway routes 83 and 47 generally follow the path of this road. With these connections to the outside world, stage coaches began regular operations in the early 1800s. Settlements gravitated to the roads and grew as they were nourished by the growing commercial traffic.

The Barrier Islands were purchased by early settlers but were used only for grazing cattle. The Corsons, Townsends, Swains, and Cresses, among other settlers, swam their cattle across the bays and thoroughfares in the spring. The cattle were left to graze on the plentiful vegetation until the beginning of winter when they were returned and slaughtered for winter stores or sold.

Forerunner of the western "branding" identification, Cape May cattlemen devised "earmarks" to identify their cattle. These were registered with the county offices and enforced. The first recorded earmark was that of Arthur Cresse on July 13, 1692. Rustling did occur, but mostly by those whalers who used the ocean beaches for their harvesting activities.

An epidemic decimated the county in 1714. The disease is not identified in any records. Many of the early leaders succumbed to the mysterious malady, including Nicholas Stillwell, Arthur Cresse, Sr., and Jr., Samuel Garretson, Reuben Joseph Hewitt, William Shaw, John Stillwell, Return Hand, Jedediah Hughes, and Timothy Brandeth.

The population rebuilt and grew to 668 in 1726, including 209 men and 156 women over age sixteen and 149 male and 141 female children. The census listed fourteen Negroes, including 1 male child, 8 men, and 5 women.

By 1772, the county population had reached 1,648 living in a total of 273 dwellings.

Government had become increasingly important to the county residents. Growing commerce, increasing contact with the outside world, and the need for government services ended the casual indifference to authority that existed during the diplomatic struggles for control over the area. Mounting arrogance of the British Crown, in its greed to finance foreign forays and other development ventures, was slowly but surely nurturing the seeds of revolution in the colonies. Oppressive taxation measures in the early 1700s made the Revolution a certainty.

Licensed public houses dotted the landscape of the county. Then, as now, these taverns served as local meeting sites more than places to slake the thirst of weary travelers. Gossip and politics were the entertainment. They helped fan the coals of revolution to full flame. Cape May County responded stolidly and whole-heartedly to the call to arms despite its limited population and resources.

In 1723 Cape May County was divided into three precincts—Upper, Middle, and Lower. Under the new government of the state of New Jersey, following the Revolution, the precincts became townships. Dennis, the fourth township, was carved out of Upper Township in 1826.

On February 13, 1798, the Board of Chosen Freeholders for Cape May County was incorporated to conduct the governmental affairs of the county. It was then formally organized and impanelled. Prior to that time, the Provincial Assembly had processed all matters relating to the county, including authorizing the construction of bridges (e.g., Dennis Creek, 1789) and river dams (e.g., Mill Creek, 1785).

Many roads were built over the ensuing decades to

serve the growing population and commerce, and settlements along these roads grew in size and importance. Although not officially incorporated, the settlements and their environs became known by the names given them either tracing the original owners or largest landholders (Swainton, Ludlam's Beach), or the waterways they adjoined (Tuckahoe, Dias Creek, Green Creek). Many of these areas have borne different names over the years creating more than a little confusion.

Inland and Delaware Bay settlements were the only populated areas until the late 1800s. The Barrier Islands remained with only scattered homes until the railroads opened them for development. The growth and decline of the early settlements shaped the economic and social life of the county for nearly three centuries.

During this extended period, Cape May County accumulated an extensive treasury of buildings, dating back as far as 1690. Unfortunately, many of these have been lost to fires, natural disasters, or demolition. Many, however, still exist and have been carefully restored. Still others have been modified in various degrees to meet contemporary needs or styles. These monuments to the craftsmanship of the early settlers and the enduring strength of home-grown lumber give a sense of a part of Cape May County's great history that is easy to overlook in the crush of daily activities or the rush to resort to the shore communities and the ocean.

*William Penn played a key role in the settlement of Cape May County. He was a trustee in bankruptcy for Edward Byllynge and was later involved with the West Jersey Society holdings in his search for a suitable site on which to establish a port facility. He is reported to have built a substantial home here, which was later conveyed to Joseph Stillwell, and still later moved to Higbee Beach. Here it served as a hotel named "The Hermitage" and "Higbee's House." Penn decided against Town Bank for his port and went further up the Delaware to found Philadelphia. The Quaker legacy in the county, which he reinforced, coupled with the opening up of the Dr. Coxe-Edward Byllynge landholdings for purchase by the settlers, stabilized the county and opened it for development. Courtesy of Cape May County Library*

*Built in 1803 by Thomas Beesley, this house sits just off Route 9 in the town that was named in his honor by the state legislature in 1848. Beesley, a ship's chandler by trade, was a member of the legislature at that time. The house has a wide central stairhall inherited from the Georgian period. The great chimney has a main-floor fireplace with a marble mantel carved in England.*
*Photograph by Vance Enck*

*The Crawford Dixon House at the intersection of Main Street and Petersburg Road in Dennisville, was built in 1830. At one time, it was cut in half and moved across the road. Then in 1962 this "salt box" house was moved back to its original site and restored. Jane Dixon, historian with the county planning board and a prime mover in Dennisville's designation as an historic district, lives here. The house has gunstock corner posts and was built of native pine, oak, and cedar by a ship's carpenter.*
*Photograph by Vance Enck*

*Rising Sun Tavern, as shown in this 1988 photo, is made up of three houses. The center section, dating to about 1760, was built on the site by the Ludlam family. It contained the spacious central room with a large fireplace and a bedroom on the second floor. Charles Ludlam signed the deed in 1826 conveying the property to John Smith. Smith apparently assembled the three sections to create the tavern which served travellers on the Old Shore Road, as well as nearby residents. The section on the left was moved from Cedar Grove below South Seaville about three miles from this site. The original location of the two-and-a-half-story house on the right is not known. When assembled, the Rising Sun Tavern had thirteen bedrooms. Currently owned as a personal residence by Somers Corson, curator of the Cape May County Historical Museum, the house still has nine bedrooms and two fireplaces. The Ludlam tract contained over three hundred acres extending from the "headline" to the bay. Verifying that "Everything that goes around, comes around," Somers Corson sold the land where the Seaville Service Area is located on the Garden State Parkway, so that the early use for serving travellers is continuing.
Photograph by Vance Enck*

# PATRIOTISM AND RUGGED INDIVIDUALISM DEFEAT ENGLAND

Cape May County was heavily involved in the two wars to establish an independent United States. New Jersey was the "Battleground of the Revolution." Major battles were fought at Trenton, Red Bank, Princeton, and Monmouth, and over one hundred skirmishes occurred in the state. The most dramatic direct encounter in Cape May County was the Battle of Turtle Gut on June 29, 1776. The American brig, *Nancy*, carrying much-needed gunpowder, rum, and sugar, heading south along the coast, was sighted by the English fleet, comprised of the *Roebuck, Liverpool, Orpheus,* and *Kingfisher,* who were seeking to close off the Delaware. Pursued by the *Orpheus, Nancy* headed for the safety of Turtle Gut Inlet but went aground. Captain Barry of the American ship, *Lexington*, with members of his crew, rowed to the *Nancy* in time to remove most of the cargo despite heavy bombardment by the British. Before leaving the ship Barry and his men laid a trail of gunpowder to the remaining 121 barrels of gunpowder. To this a rolled sail containing another fifty pounds of gunpowder was laid from the top of the hatch. Departing sailors dropped live coals on the sail. Among the crew, a sailor named John Hancock (not to be confused with the bold signature on the Declaration of Independence), ran back to retrieve the American Flag. Seeing the flag lowered, the British assumed the *Nancy* was surrendering and boarded the prize just in time for the big BANG. The British lost fifty men, while the Americans suffered one casualty and one wounded. The valuable cargo was carried inland and placed on the *Wasp* for shipment to Philadelphia.

Cape May raised two battalions of militia for the Continental Army. The first one fought at the Battle of Germantown, under officers John Mackey, Eli Eldredge, Thomas Leaming, Nicholas and Enoch Stillwell, and Henry, Nicholas, John, and Nathan Hand.

Cape May provided 156 men for the Continental forces, including sixteen officers, an impressive response for such a sparsely populated area. The 1773 census listed only 468 males whose ages were between sixteen and fifty. Of these, several were Quakers who were excused from bearing arms and sixty were slaves. Over fifty more were manning and commanding privateering vessels for the country.

Only one Tory was recorded in Cape May County. John Hatton of Cold Spring was the customs collector for the English crown. His troubles with the colonials led to confiscation of his property and his disappearance.

Beesley's Point at Egg Harbor was an important staging area where recruits assembled and were outfitted. It also served as a land base for privateers and as a storage area for supplies. In September 1777 the militia was called up for the defense of Philadelphia. All able-bodied men from the area gathered at Beesley's Point and left on September 19 at night, on a forced-march to the city. Information leaked to the British who deemed it a good time to raid this nest of privateers. Rebecca Stillwell saw the British fleet enter the bay for a landing and dispatched her sister to summon help. The women who assembled wheeled a twelve-foot loaded cannon into place. Rebecca applied the firebrand. The resulting shot passed over the heads of the landing party, but got their attention.

Twelve-year old Rem Golding sounded his grandfather's hunting horn. Thinking this a call to arms, the confused British troops rowed back to their ships and departed, leaving the precious stores intact.

Privateers and the small American Navy did a most effective job in thwarting the British attempts to blockade the vital Delaware water route. Cape May sailors were in great demand in this campaign. The crews of experienced Cape May descendants of the whalers, along with their knowledge of the dangerous shoals along the coast, although outnumbered, were a formidable force. Cape May offered a unique vantage point for monitoring British ship movements. Horseback messengers regularly carried this critical information to General Washington's headquarters.

The women and children left behind as the men marched off to war made much-needed clothing and planted and harvested the critical farm products, both essential for sustaining the Continental Army.

New Jersey pioneered resistance to British tyranny. The state was referred to as the "Cockpit of the Revolution" and the "Pathway to Freedom." Even before the outbreak of the Revolution, Aaron Leaming and Jacob Spicer, on appointment by the government of New Jersey, prepared a statement of Quaker ideals which was actually published in England in 1756. This manifesto heavily shaped the structure of the Constitution for the new country. Jesse Hand, Jacob Eldredge, and Matthew Whildin were delegates from Cape May County to the state meeting in December 1787, which led New Jersey to be the third state to ratify the Constitution.

The second war for independence, the War of 1812, was much harsher on Cape May County than the Revolution had been. With no land base in the United States, the British carried out their military operations from the sea. Raiding parties regularly came ashore in Cape May County to pillage the countryside seeking water and supplies. The raids played havoc with cattle herds and crops. Many businesses and boats were destroyed. One farm wife, reportedly, was forced to bake bread while the British raiders waited. Two young ladies, Miss Sarah Newton, who later married James Corson, and her unnamed servant, were kidnapped by a raiding party as they tended the family's fishing nets. They were carried to the British ship and forced to cook for the crew over a three-month period. They were returned unharmed to shore as the tides of war forced the withdrawal of the British man-of-war.

Reed's Beach, a frequent landing place for raiding parties, was ringed with "Quaker Cannons" by the antagonized residents to ward off the British marauders. This defense ruse was simply a series of logs shaped and painted to look like cannons, an ingenious idea of William Douglass, a ship's carpenter and a Quaker.

Farther south, at Cape May Point, the British resumed their successful practice in the Revolutionary War of replenishing their water supply from Lake Lily. Weary of the incessant raids, residents dug a one-mile-long ditch from the salt water Pond Lake to Lake Lily to contaminate the British's favorite drinking water.

In another incident at Cape May Point, Abigail

Hughes stood in front of "Long Tom," a twelve-foot cannon, to prevent its being fired at a British landing party headed for the shore. She counseled, "You shall not fire. We may not be disturbed if we don't; but we will surely suffer their vengeance if we do." The British rowed by the Cape and on up the Delaware shore to pillage hapless Town Bank.

Captain Orr of Cape Island, commanding a U.S. gunboat, interrupted a chase of an American coaster by two British ships. He sailed between the British warships with cannons blazing, alternately firing at one and then the other. Orr succeeded in forcing the surrender of both ships. It is ironic that Orr was killed by an explosion of the Long Tom cannon during an Independence Day celebration in 1828.

The fifth Humphrey Hughes was a very successful privateer during the war. At one point, while his ship was in hiding in Egg Harbor, he successfully escaped detection by tying pine trees in front of his masts to blend into the background. However, he is more famous for being forcibly rescued by his crew members from a Roman prison where he had been jailed for refusing to bow on his knees to the Pope, because he was "an American and recognized no one to be his better."

The War of 1812 finally ended in February 1815, with the Treaty of Ghent. The United States, and with it Cape May, could at last go about the business of building and developing.

*William Franklin, an illegitimate son of Benjamin Franklin, was appointed governor of New Jersey in 1763 through the influence of Lord Bute. He was a loyal British subject and remained so all his life. He steadfastly opposed all acts of resistance by the rebellious colonials. Franklin convened a special session of the New Jersey Assembly on May 15, 1775, for the express purpose of endorsing a plan of conciliation proposed by Lord North. This failed. A later special session convened on November 16, 1775, and proved to be a platform for Franklin to attack the "illegal acts" of the rival Assembly of Delegates that had been convened by the angry New Jersey colonials. In frustration, Franklin ordered adjournment of the British-sponsored assembly on December 6, 1775. It never met again. Franklin was subsequently arrested and deported to Connecticut for his own safety. He remained there until the end of the Revolution and ultimately moved to England where he remained until his death.*
*Courtesy Cape May County Library*

*The H.M.S. Martin was one of the British ships that blockaded the Delaware Bay during the War of 1812. It was attacked in 1813, driven ashore, and set afire. The burning hulk drifted along the bay shore to Cape May Point where it came to rest in a sandy grave. Quickly forgotten in the euphoria of victory, the wreck remained entombed until the raging waves, stirred up by the 1954 hurricane, resurrected the pieces (above). These were dug up and reassembled as much as possible and placed on display under a shelter (right) alongside Lake Drive in Cape May Point by Cape Island Development Co., Inc.*
*Top photograph courtesy of the Harry Merz Collection, through Dr. John Siliquini*
*Bottom photograph by Vance Enck*

## PATHS TO PROGRESS

When the door closed on the two wars for independence, another door opened for the United States and for Cape May County. The country went about the business of becoming a viable nation. A few skirmishes with the Tripoli pirates and the Mexican War produced small glitches along the way. Progress was steady until the major wrench of the Civil War.

For Cape May County, this was an era of consolidation and steady, solid growth. A firm economic foundation was built with the development of major industries—farming, shipping, shipbuilding, and lumbering of shingles and cordwood. The first steps were taken to build a recreation industry that really began to flourish, until the Civil War dampened that growth. However, with the development of the Barrier Islands in the late 1800s, tourism quickly became the county's foremost industry.

A network of roads sprang up after the Revolution and continued to increasingly lace the county through the nineteenth century. While travel on these roads was slow and crude, by today's standards, it provided a link to commerce and business that made development of the county possible and inevitable. The first stagecoach service ran once a week from Cooper's Ferry in Camden to Cape May as early as 1801. In 1802, the first boat started regular runs to Cape May. Arrival of the first railroad service was in 1863. Ironically, this tied Cape May County more tightly into the rest of the country at a time when the Civil War had cut off the Southerners, who were so fond of the area.

Permanent resident population figures provide a clear picture of the county's growth. The first census, in 1726, showed only 668 residents. However, sixty-four years later, in 1790, the number had increased to 2,571. By 1832, one-eighth of the county, 20,244 acres of land, was improved cleared land.

Steady, but not spectacular growth, characterized the nineteenth century census numbers:
- 1830- 4,936
- 1850- 6,432
- 1869- 7,130
- 1880- 9,765
- 1900-13,201

Slavery, which tore the nation asunder and led to the bloody Civil War, played a short but interesting role in the county's history. This controversial institution gradually crept into the area's economy. The largest slave population of 141 was reported in the 1790 census. By 1800, the number of slaves had diminished to 98 and in 1810 there were only 81 listed in the county. Quakers raised serious questions about the morality of owning other human beings, even though some were themselves slave-holders. Sentiment was strong enough to bring the state legislature to abolish slavery in 1820, more than forty years before Lincoln's Emancipation Proclamation. Slaves were not freed overnight, however. Children of slaves gained their freedom upon reaching the age of twenty-one. Older slaves had to be cared for by their masters until they died. By 1830, there were only three slaves remaining in the county. There is a slave cemetery between Route 9 and the Garden State Parkway in Swainton. Vandals and time have left few of the headstones.

There is evidence that sporadic Underground Railroad activities throughout the county did aid runaway slaves in their quest for freedom, but apparently no major or established stations existed here.

Education did not become a public responsibility in Cape May County until after the Civil War. Prior to this, local schools were established by subscription and occasionally by an individual gift. They appear in the history of the individual settlements, and not as a unified

*The early 1800s cholera epidemic originated in India. It spread along trade and pilgrimage routes. The pandemic appeared in New York on January 28, 1832. From there it spread rapidly, reaching Cape May County shortly thereafter. The exact toll in the county is not known but hundreds died. Once stricken, a victim had only one chance in two of surviving. Most of the dead were buried at night in unmarked graves in family plots or various cemeteries. This marker in the Old Brick Church cemetery in Cold Springs is a grim monument to the terrible plague that decimated Cape May in 1832.*
*Photograph by Vance Enck*

county or state program. Such schools were not free, but they were inexpensive. Subscribers would take turns boarding the teachers. Each school had its own board of directors that acted autonomously. There were no state standards until much later.

Early schools specialized in the 3-R's and discipline. Educational training, then, would seem totally inadequate by today's standards. But, it should be noted that there were only 258 county residents over twenty years old were illiterate in 1850 (personal writings from that period reveal that spelling was another matter).

Various entrepreneurial ventures over the years thrived for varying periods of time. Most disappeared for the usual economic reasons—lack of markets, technological advances, and dwindling sources of supplies. The county's historical landscape is littered with the relics and memories of these ventures. Cape May County has always been willing to try a new venture. There are references to several of these activities in the local history accounts throughout this writing.

Cape May County voted overwhelmingly for Lincoln in 1860, and responded quickly after the first shot was fired on Fort Sumter. Many in the county had friends in the South. Cape May City had long been a favorite spa for wealthy southerners. Gen. Robert E. Lee vacationed in Cape May City and introduced the white corn that the county still grows for summer feasting. After some initial foot-dragging by the Freeholders, the response from the county was universal. Hundreds of volunteers came forward during the course of the war. Many were killed or wounded. Several were captured and suffered the inhumane prison conditions of the Confederacy.

The grim casualty reports from this bloody war affected nearly every family in the county. The daily life and the economy of the county generally suffered little. Arrival of the first railroad in 1863 was to revolutionize the county's life and economy.

The nation moved to heal its wounds after Lee's surrender and Lincoln's assassination. The county continued its steady growth.

The great Industrial Revolution that radically changed the country from an agrarian society to an industrial giant, changed the county as well. The change, however, did not come from huge smoke-belching plants with thousands of laborers. It came from the increasing affluence of all Americans that spawned a recreation industry on a huge scale. Cape May County's natural assets, including the ocean, bay, equable climate, and beautiful woods, marshes, lakes, and streams, had been recognized by a select few before. Now the ease of travel by rail and the county's close proximity to rapidly developing industrial centers made the county a natural destination.

The well-heeled and euphoric gentility of the Victorian Era pulled Cape May County out of its days of back-breaking struggle for existence into a period of great productivity with a relative increase in wealth, comfort, and ease.

*Civil War volunteers from the county in pictures taken in 1864 are Charles M. Preston (right) of Company F, New Jersey Veteran Volunteers, who was promoted to sergeant in 1865. The regiment saw action in twenty-seven engagements in Virginia and North Carolina and Daniel Wheaton (left) was promoted to corporal in 1865. He was attached to the 1st Regiment, U.S. Hussars, Company A of Sheridan's Cavalry, which fought in twenty-four actions, including the final battle at Appomattox.*
*Courtesy of Cape May County Historical Museum*

*Cape May volunteers fought in many Civil War battles. New Jersey provided sixteen regiments of three-year volunteers by 1862, and added 10,470 more in 1862. In one company of the 25th Regiment, formed in 1862, from Dennis and Lower Townships, were men with varied background skills: eight carpenters, two clerks, thirty-three laborers, nine seamen, two printers, one miller, two artists, and forty farmers. Pictured here are "volunteers" from a Civil War encampment, recreated at Cold Springs Village in 1987.*
*Courtesy of Historic Cold Springs Village*

*Summer Sunday afternoons were reserved for a ride in a buggy-built-for-two (complete with parasol) with your best beau...even after you got married. This picture was taken in the late 1890s on the Goshen Road from Cape May Court House.*
*Courtesy of Cape May County Historical Museum*

*A natty Joseph Eldridge presents a touch of sophistication in a changing Cape May County. Although a date cannot be verified, this portrait was probably taken in the mid-1880s.*
*Courtesy of Cape May County Historical Museum*

*Bill Champion of South Seaville pioneered home insurance selling in the area. Mr. Champion was a traveling agent for Prudential Insurance Company. Note the tools of his trade in the handlebar basket and his coat pockets. This snapshot was probably taken around the turn of the century.*
*Courtesy of Estella Pierson*

*With increased time off, as the county prospered, young swains could don their best outfits and gather along the streets for Saturday flirtations with promenading belles. None of these gentlemen are identified, but they have the good honest faces of Cape May residents.*
*Courtesy of Cape May County Historical Museum*

*Penny Farthings were very much in vogue in the late 1800s. The nimble gentlemen perched on these high-wheelers are not identified but give all the evidence of being experts, even though these are photo studio props. The picture was probably taken in the 1890s.*
*Courtesy of Cape May County Historical Museum*

*One problem with having roads is that traveling salesmen use them. Mr. Giddings, however, was a welcome visitor, since, as his wagon proclaims, he offered a variety of fashionable items for the ladies. Based in Cape May City, he pleased the ladies in the surrounding area.*
*Courtesy of Virginia Walsh*

## UPPER TOWNSHIP

From the completion of the main roads in 1707, and the running of stagecoaches to the county, settlements sprung up along the roads, often including houses moved there for access to the transportation. Although none of the towns in Upper Township, with the exception of Ocean City, have ever incorporated, the clusters of houses and businesses acquired their own names and have played an important part in the rich history of the county.

*Daniel Boone (1734-1820) is reported to have helped a relative, William Boon, build a fireplace in his home in Upper Township during a visit to the county sometime during the mid-1700s. Fact or mythology is still a question that is often debated two centuries later. William Boon and his wife Martha are buried in the Asbury Church Cemetery in Swainton. Courtesy of Cape May County Library*

## LESTER C. MCNAMARA WILDLIFE MANAGEMENT AREA

The Lester C. McNamara Wildlife Management Area is a reincarnation of the swampy, heavily forested wilderness areas that once covered much of the region. Oddly enough, this tract, which includes a large acreage in Atlantic County and an area of Cape May County nearly as large as the Belleplain State Forest, was put together by Bethlehem Steel Corporation as a munitions testing and staging area just prior to World War I.

During the Depression, CCC project workers, with picks and shovels, started building dams and impoundments as part of a program to restore the wildlife area. Ducks Unlimited finished much of the work after the CCC program closed down. The barracks used to house CCC workers have been reclaimed by the wilderness.

The Wildlife Management Area is a favorite duck hunting preserve today.

Middletown, located on Tuckahoe Road at the edge of the wildlife area, is distinguished today by a few dwellings and its being indicated on New Jersey road maps. The former Baptist Church and several dwellings have simply disappeared.

*John James Audubon (1785-1851), the great artist-naturalist, visited Upper Township in the early 1800s. He drew several portraits of Cape May County birds which were incorporated in his immortal books.*
*Courtesy of Cape May County Library*

## BEESLEY'S POINT

The first settler of what is now Beesley's Point was probably William Goldin (also spelled Golden and Golding), an Irishman, who came to the area in 1691. He was one of the first Catholics to settle in the county. His most prized possessions were his sword and uniform, worn as an officer for King James in the war against William and Mary in 1690, and his hunting horn. This was the hunting horn that Rem Garretson later used to help turn the British away from Beesley's Point in 1777.

The name, Goldin's Point, lasted until 1750. Goldin sold his land to Nicholas Stillwell in 1736 to cover the costs of defending himself against charges stemming from the killing of a drunken Indian on Foxborough Hill (where the Atlantic Electric plant now stands). Goldin was ultimately acquitted but he sold his holdings and left the area.

Stillwell obtained a public house license in 1750 for his Ferry House at the Beesley's Point-Somers Point ferry terminus. Rebecca Stillwell, his wife, directed the maneuver that turned the British away from landing at the Point in 1777.

The first ferry in Cape May County was authorized by the legislature in 1693 and was operated by Nicholas Stillwell. It used an open boat relying on sails and oars to navigate the distance from Job's Point (Somers Point) to Beesley's Point.

For a time the point was called Willett's Point after Hope Willetts, a dedicated Quaker with substantial holdings in the area. Isaiah Stites, son of Henry Stites, an early whaler in the county, accumulated considerable lands in the area and Stite's Point replaced the Willett's name until the mid-1800s. Rhoda Stites married Thomas Beesley on June 26, 1799.

The public house and hotel operated by Stillwell passed through the hands of Nicholas Stillwell, Jr. (1792-1794), to Thomas Borden (1794-1795), to Thomas Beesley who operated it in the early 1800s. In 1806 Beesley sold the property to Capt. John Chattin who renamed it the Chattin House. The building stood on the old Seashore Road which ran near Foxborough Hill. This road was moved eastward to its present route in 1801. In 1848-1849 Richard Stites built a larger hotel across the road on the site of the present Tuckahoe Inn.

Thomas Beesley built a home in 1803 on Shore Road. He operated a chandler's shop in the old Clay House which stood where Stites later built his hotel. To the holdings acquired through his wife, Beesley added in 1803 157 acres of the original Goldin properties. Thomas, as a member of the New Jersey Legislature, was successful in getting his land's name changed to Beesley's Point in 1848. He secured a post office in 1851, and Joseph D. Chattin served as the first postmaster.

The Chattin heirs sold the Chattin House to a group known as the "Beesley's Point Fishing Club," noted for its socializing and riotous good times. The club was operated by Henry Clay, a prominent Philadelphia politician. In 1906 the club was dissolved, and the title to the property was conveyed to Savilla Clay, Henry's wife. The Clays used the building until 1915 as a private residence. After that it was operated by the Bay Front Training School which was owned by Clyde Van Hook, mayor of Sea Isle City.

Henry Clay acquired the Stite's Hotel in 1906 and passed title to his wife, Savilla, in 1909. Mabel Clay, daughter of Henry and Savilla, operated the hotel as a Red Cross headquarters during World War I. The hotel was closed during the Depression and remained closed except for brief periods of operation as a church school. It was partially destroyed by fire in 1961. In 1963 it was completely restored by Charles Harp and opened as the Tuckahoe Inn. His son, Peter Harp, continues the operation currently.

In 1927 a toll bridge was built across Egg Harbor Bay from Beesley's Point to Somers Point bringing a flow of traffic through the town. The Garden State Parkway, completed in 1953, included a bridge over the bay just a few hundred yards east of the toll bridge. This has siphoned off much of the traffic. Beesley's Point is again a quiet town with a mixture of residential architecture reflecting its three hundred-year history.

*Best known as the Chattin House, the original section of this building was erected by Nicholas Stillwell. One of the first public house licenses in the county was granted Stillwell for his Ferry House. It was from this site that Rebecca Stillwell, during the Revolution, rushed to fire the cannon that turned away a British landing attempt.*

*In 1806 Captain John Chattin bought the inn and changed the name to Chattin House. It continued to operate under that name until the early 1900s.*
*Courtesy of James Jack*

*This hotel was built in 1848 by Richard Stites on Shore Road at the edge of Egg Harbor Bay. It was a popular resort spa for many years. In its early days tourists had to travel by stagecoach or the Somers Point ferry to reach the hotel. It became accessible by rail with the opening of the Millville-Cape May Railroad in 1863. Resorters could take a short coach ride from the Seaville station to the hotel.*

*Henry Clay, a Philadelphia attorney, bought the hotel in 1906. He refurbished it and staged a number of fashionable social events to revive its popularity. Title passed to his wife, Savilla, in 1909. After being partially destroyed by fire in 1960, it was rebuilt as today's Tuckahoe Inn.*
*Courtesy of James Jack*

*The first bridge across Egg Harbor Bay from Somers Point to Beesley's Point was completed in 1927. The opening, pictured here, was greeted with great enthusiasm. For the first time, autos traveling from the north could continue on Route 9 all the way to Cape May, or from the south, all the way to New York. Before this bridge was built, travelers had to ferry across Egg Harbor Bay or detour west to bridges over the Tuckahoe River before continuing their journey.*

*The bridge, a toll bridge, was privately built and privately owned—it remains so today. Before the Garden State Parkway, with its bridge just a short distance away, opened, this bridge was very heavily traveled and was the scene of many massive traffic jams during the summer season.*

*Pictured here is the 1927 opening day procession from Somers Point to Beesley's Point.*
*Courtesy of Jane Dixon*

*The Beesley's Point school, built in 1889, was a classic one-room schoolhouse. It replaced the township's third school, built across the road in 1816. The "three R's" were taught here until 1954. Many people who attended classes here are still living in the area. Mrs. Cornelia Corson Brown attended the school with twenty-six classmates in 1916. The school was closed when the township schools were consolidated. The building has been carefully restored and is now a private residence. It is located at Ocean Avenue on Route 9.*
*Photograph by Vance Enck*

# MARMORA

Marmora is located just south of Beesley's Point. Some of the area was orginally part of Thomas Beesley's holdings. It was for a while referred to as "Beesley's." The Corson family holdings also covered part of the area.

The Trinity United Methodist Church at the corner of Roosevelt and Seashore roads was built in 1869. The rear portion is the original church, built in 1836. The ceiling of the interior is pressed metal and the pews date from 1869. The church today houses a Seventh-Day Adventist congregation. The Trinity United Methodist congregation meets in its newer building, erected in 1980, adjoining the original site. The Methodist Cemetery surrounds the older building.

There were always shops and stores located in Marmora to serve the surrounding area. The Marmora exit on the Garden State Parkway just south of the Egg Harbor bridge has created a fast-growing residential and business community because of the easy access from Atlantic City and other nearby developing areas.

*The Stratton store (above) was a familiar Marmora landmark to travelers along Route 9 (Shore Road) when it was the main route to shore points. An earlier general store, operated by Joe Henry Corson, was in the building on the left in this photo. The adjoining building was formerly Minnie Corson's store. Enterprising E. A. Stratton, the owner in the mid-1930s when this picture was taken, moved the two buildings to this site and joined them for his general store. The post office at that time was in the former Minnie Corson portion of the building. Standing at the gasoline pumps are Raymond Snead and Mrs. Zorah Corson.*

*The buildings were remodeled to become Cody's, a later familiar landmark (below) which stood at this site until it was replaced by the present WAWA store—today's landmark. Cody's building was moved to another site locally to become a private residence.*
*Courtesy of Cornelia Corson Brown*

(above) This is a memory jogger for those who lament the disappearance of "the good old days"—notice the hand-operated washing machine, a top-loader. Water had to be heated in a washboiler on washday. The top for the washboiler is resting in the fork of the tree in the background. Sharing in the joyous occasion were Helen Corson (left), Viola Kohr (center), Mary Corson (right), and, too young to join in the grown-ups good times, was Cornelia Corson (owner of this snapshot) who is eating grapes instead.

This September 1913 picture was taken just before the women joined the menfolks for the watermelon party pictured left.
Courtesy of Cornelia Corson Brown

After a hard day doing the laundry and working in the fields, everyone gathered at "the bottom of the place" on Ezekiel Corson's farm. Picnicking, from left to right, are Elmer Corson, Ezekiel Corson, Viola Kohr (visiting from Buffalo, New York), Mary Corson, and Cornelia Corson is the child in front.

This picnic spot is now part of the Garden State Parkway.
Courtesy of Cornelia Corson Brown

## PALERMO

John and Peter Corson arrived in Cape May County on a whaling boat at what is now Corson's Inlet. After coming to the mainland, they used an Indian cave in the Palermo area as living quarters until they could build a home. The cave became known as Corson's Cellar and the adjoining creek as Cellar Creek. The area where they settled was part of the Stephen Young plantation which originally extended to Petersburg and the Great Cedar Swamp. Corson's Cellar was rediscovered by Curtis Corson who owned the farm where it was located. However, that spot is now part of the median strip of the Garden State Parkway.

Palermo had its own railroad station during the time when the trains were operating. The unused train tracks still cross Route 9. Always a residential town, Palermo is enjoying the most rapid growth in its long history through several attractive new housing developments that are being located there.

*The Palermo Friendship School, built in 1830, was one of the county's earliest schools. After serving as the "reading, writing, and 'rithmetic" center for the community, the building became a private residence, then a shed, and ultimately a neglected derelict, as shown in this 1940s photograph. Through the efforts of the Historic Preservation Society of Upper Township, the building was restored to a school museum in 1980.*
*Courtesy Cape May County Museum*

*The second Baptist church in Cape May County was built at Palermo about 1825. Note that automobiles have replaced horses in the stalls of the horse sheds at the rear in this 1930s picture.*
*Courtesy of Cornelia Corson Brown*

*The Enos Corson House, built in 1790, is still surrounded by four acres of cedar, pine, and fruit trees that were part of the original plantation. The wooden-peg-constructed house still boasts the original floorboards.*
*Courtesy of Jane Dixon*

## SEAVILLE

The area that is now Seaville was originally settled by Quakers—the Townsends, the Corsons, and the Garretsons. In the early years Quaker meetings were held at members' homes. In 1700 a Friends' Meetinghouse was built at Beesley's Point on a lot donated by the Garretsons. This building was moved to Seaville in 1716. The Meetinghouse has been restored and stands alongside Route 9 in Seaville. Regular meetings are still held there.

Seaville residents Jacob Swain and his two sons invented the sailboat "centerboard." This device which raised and lowered the keel to provide swift, safe movement for even the smallest sailboat revolutionized the boat-building industry. Although the Swains received a patent for their invention in 1811, they realized very little financial gain from it. Other builders evaded the patent by placing the device at a slightly different location than the patent description.

When the Garden State Parkway was completed through the area in 1953, the southbound lanes were moved 120 feet to go around the three hundred-year-old Shoemaker Holly Tree. A picnic and rest area was built at the site. The tree stands as a stately sentinel greeting all the travelers along the Parkway. Decorated with festive lights at Christmastime, the Shoemaker Holly has become a county holiday tradition.

*The 1702 Friend's meeting house is one of Cape May County's oldest buildings. It was originally located on the Garretson plantation in Beesley's Point. Monthly meetings were aptly called "The Cedar Meeting," because the building, roof, pews, and floor were all made of local cedar. The Quakers met in various members' homes in Somers Point and Beesleys Point until this meeting house was erected. Aaron Leaming, Peter Corson, and Richard Townsend of Upper Township, and Scull and Somers from Atlantic County moved the building to its present site alongside Seashore Road in Seaville. The present building is nearly double the size of the original and brick steps have been added. A small cemetery is part of the meetinghouse grounds.*
*Interior photograph courtesy of Cape May County Historical Museum; Exterior photograph courtesy of Jane Dixon*

*Tucked among pine trees at Seaville, after years of neglect, indifference, and finally love, is the Phillip Godfrey house (above). Originally located in Swainton, it became an unwanted old eyesore that was condemned and scheduled for demolition in 1962 when Lewis and Jean Albrecht came to the rescue. On December 17 and 18, 1962, a major portion of the house was moved north on Route 9, eastward across frozen fields to the Garden State Parkway and then seven miles north (on the southbound lanes) on the parkway to its present site. Detailed research uncovered information that the original house, a one-room structure (fourteen feet by twenty feet) and a chamber above reached by ladder, was built in 1845. Growing families and increasing affluence led to several additions dated about 1780, 1800, 1830, 1840, 1880, and 1930. Over a thirteen-year period, the Albrechts authentically, meticulously, and painstakingly restored the building for their residence (below). It is today a graphic and beautiful study of the building history of Cape May County. Courtesy of Jean M. and Lewis P. Albrecht, Jr.*

## TUCKAHOE

The area was originally inhabited by the Tuckahoe tribe (or family) of Lenni-Lenape Indians. The most accepted translation of "Tuckahoe" is "where the deer are shy and hard to approach." Because of its location on the Tuckahoe River, the settlement included areas in Atlantic County—Aetna Furnace (an important source of bog iron during the two wars for independence), Head-of-the-River, and Corbin City. Once named Williamsburg, after John Williams who became the first postmaster in 1828, the town was later renamed Tuckahoe. The settlement once hummed with shipbuilding activities supplied by the sawmills and iron-making furnaces nearby. A silk mill and a canning factory were later built here. Tuckahoe once had its own lighting system which used acetylene produced by a plant located near the bridge on today's Route 50. There are very few remnants left to reflect these early businesses. The canning factory is now a warehouse. The silk factory remained until the 1920s and then disappeared.

The government offices for Upper Township are located in Tuckahoe. Most of the operations are housed in a building that served as a high school from 1908 to 1925 and after that as an elementary school until 1952.

A two hundred-acre cranberry bog was created in 1864 and remained productive until the 1950s when the owners, the April brothers, decided to close down operations.

Reading Railroad built a line from Camden to Tuckahoe in 1891. The line was extended to Sea Isle City in 1893. Reading's arch rival, the Pennsylvania Railroad, which controlled the West Jersey Line running from Millville to Cape May, sought to prevent the Reading from crossing its line at what later became known as Tuckahoe Junction. Despite a court injunction, Reading installed a crossing at night. Pennsylvania then tore it up during the day. After repeating this ritual several times, both sides amassed "troops." A riotous fight ensued between the Reading's "Irish troops" and the Pennsylvania's "Italian troops." The Irish workers were arrested for defying the injunction but were released the next morning by the justice of peace at a court session held on a flat car. A grand celebration at Tuckahoe quickly erupted. With the exception of a similar incident at Peck's Beach (Ocean City) in 1898, relative calm settled over the tumultuous rivalry between the two railroads.

*The Tuckahoe National Bank was robbed by three youths on March 13, 1925, at 9:30 a.m. Edwin L. Tomlin, a director of the bank, was fatally shot during the holdup. Edward L. Rice, the cashier, and his wife, Phoebe, who also worked at the bank, were beaten until they were unconscious. Lylburn M. Hess, president of the bank, who lived next door, on hearing the shot that killed Tomlin, grabbed his shotgun and fired at the robbers, inflicting a scalp wound on one of them as he fled from the bank to their car across the street. Hess used the same gun to commit suicide a year later.*

*The bandits wrecked their car just outside Tuckahoe on Weatherby Road. The three youths—Anderson, Laird, and Petit—were soon found and arrested and later sentenced to long prison terms. The seven thousand dollars worth of loot was recovered.*

*The people on the steps in this 1925 photograph are assumed to be Rice and Hess.*

*The bank building still stands but is unused today.*
*Courtesy of Cornelia Corson Brown*

*The "Academy," one of Tuckahoe's landmarks, currently houses a Seventh-Day Adventist school. It began as a two-story school building. However, the second floor was removed and additions were made in recent years.*
*Courtesy of Joyce Van Vorst*

*Gasoline for seventeen cents a gallon was proudly offered by John Reed at his Triangle Service Station, just south of Tuckahoe on the way to the shoppers bonanza at Woodbine. Mrs. Reed probably had just stepped out of the store for a breather after selling one-cent stamps for postcards, in this 1932 picture. In more recent days, beer, rather than gas, was pumped here after the station became the locally popular Triton Bar.*
*Courtesy of Bob Gandy*

## MARSHALLVILLE

This settlement was known as Cumberland Works in its early days. It was a part of Cumberland County until the final boundary changes in 1878. It then became part of Cape May County. The name was changed to Marshallville after Randall Marshall, Jr. who started a glass factory here in 1814. Marshall and his son-in-law, Stanger, owned interests in the Union Glass Works at Port Elizabeth, Cumberland County. They started their own works in 1814 at Marshallville exclusively for the manufacture of window glass on land purchased from John Falkenburg of South Dennis. Stanger sold his interest to Marshall in 1827. Thomas Chew Marshall, Randall's son, learned to be a glassblower and was one of the early managers of the plant. Randall Marshall died in 1841. His youngest son, Randolph, managed the glass works until it was sold to John S. Van Gilder and Thomas Van Gilder in 1847. The Van Gilders continued operation until the works quietly disappeared from sight around the start of the Civil War.

Randall Marshall built homes for each of his six children. These are still standing.

In common with most communities in the region, Marshallville housed a thriving shipbuilding industry. at one time, fourteen ships were under construction in the town.

Today there are no businesses in Marshallville. It is a quiet picturesque village stretching along the banks of the Tuckahoe River.

*Mary Reeves Marshall, wife of Marshallville's founder, Randall Marshall, died at the age of seventy. The use of silhouettes was a popular form of producing likenesses before the various kinds of photography were available. This silhouette is owned by Harry P. Folger III, a descendant of the Marshalls.*

1777 ~ MARY REEVES ~ 1847
DAUGHTER OF HENRY & HANNAH DOUGHTY (FURNESS) REEVES AND WIFE OF RANDAL MARSHALL, PARENTS OF ANN MARSHALL, WIFE OF FREDERICK STANGER.

*Thomas Chew Marshall (right) was the oldest son of Randall Marshall, the founder of the glass factory at Marshallville. He became a glassblower at his father's Union Glass Factory at Port Elizabeth. He moved to Marshallville when that factory opened in 1814, and became one of the earlier managers of the works. Thomas married Experience Steelman (left). The Thomas Marshalls produced fourteen children—six boys and eight girls. Experience died in 1867, and Thomas died the following year.
Courtesy of Harry P. Folger III*

*Marshallville Road in the heart of Marshallville on a quiet summer day in the early 1900s. The building on the right was the company store, owned by Marshall and Stille, of the glass plant when it was still operating. The store has since been demolished.
Courtesy of Harry P. Folger III*

*Randolph Marshall, grandson of the founder of the glass works, served as manager of the plant after his grandfather's death in 1841 until the business was sold in 1847 to the Van Gilders.
Courtesy of Cape May County Historical Museum*

*The "Old Covered Bridge," (right) built in 1841, stood over Mill Creek on the Marshallville Road from Tuckahoe. The bridge was replaced by the iron one (below) used today. Lew Albrecht, a former resident, and other citizens of Marshallville have led a successful struggle to have the present bridge replaced with a replica of the original covered one. The replacement has not been built but is scheduled for construction. Covered bridge photograph courtesy of Cape May County Historical Museum; Iron bridge photograph courtesy of Joyce Van Vorst*

*The "Glass Property" brick house was being built by Randall Marshall for his residence when he died in 1841 before its completion. His widow Mary and daughter Hannah lived here from 1841 to 1847. The door on the right was for the glass factory paymaster's office, while the door to the left was for the private residence.*
*Photograph by Vance Enck*

*The Stille house was built in 1836 by Samuel Stille, a shipper who at one time owned an interest in the glass works. The house was owned from 1925 to 1954 by Garet Garrett, who was editor of* The Saturday Evening Post.
*Photograph by Vance Enck*

## PETERSBURG

Abraham and John Van Gilder migrated from Long Island in the 1730s to become the first settlers in this area. With their families, they sailed down Cedar Swamp Creek to a spot near today's Upper Bridge, where they lived in an Indian cave until they could buy land. While clearing the land, Abraham remarked that "the land is of little worth." The name Littleworth lasted until it was changed to Petersburgh, after Peter Corson, the first postmaster, appointed in 1819.

By 1869 the "h" had been dropped and Petersburg had two shipyards, two sawmills, a gristmill, three stores, three shops, and about four hundred inhabitants. The schooner, *Electa Bailey*, built here by Daniel Bailey was the first three-masted ship built in Cape May County. Lumber and farm produce were carried to New York by two schooners based here. Over fifteen thousand cords of wood were shipped annually from Petersburg. At the height of the season, the fleet expanded to eight ships to carry four thousand barrels of sweet potatoes to major markets.

Thomas Van Gilder built a sawmill on Cedar Swamp Creek in 1846, using an overshot and flutter wheel power. A grist mill was added later. Both were designed and constructed by Peter Hoff who also designed many of the numerous mills that were built throughout Cape May County. Hoff, a resident of West Creek, was the county's "run-of-the-mills" genius.

A fast-moving forest fire in 1875 destroyed both Van Gilder mills and the workers' cottages. One miller's wife saved her children by putting them adrift in a boat on the pond. Although the mill ruins collapsed on the dam, emptying the pond, the boat and its precious cargo were found safely mired in a mud bar downstream.

As the forests were depleted, metal ships replaced the wooden-hulled vessels and faster methods of transportation were used to carry products to the markets. Petersburg evolved into today's agricultural village.

*The Smith Store has been moved twice. It was built by Peter Corson in 1834 across the road from its present site. Corson sold the property and then regained it in 1850. He moved the store across the road. Elmer Smith later bought the property, moved the building slightly north to its present location, enlarged it and reopened the store in 1881. The Petersburg post office was housed in the store when Corson owned it. The building is currently a private residence. Courtesy of Joyce Van Vorst*

*It is believed that this school picture was taken in the early 1900s at the Petersburg school. Several grades are apparently included, judging by the wide age range, from the front row to the back. The more solemn faces in the last two rows are apparently teachers. Some of the names were listed on the back of the photograph, but the list is incomplete. Those listed are: Pete Madera, Isaac Butler, Theodore Van Gilder, Neal Creamer, Floyd Van Gilder, James Jefferson, Gertie Madera, Leon Michle, Bessie Westcott, _____ Sharp, Rachel Young, Rebecca Creamer, Russell Eldridge, Clarence Sack, and Leroy Van Gilder.*

*The Franklin school in Petersburg, built in 1814, was the second oldest school in the county. The Franklin schoolhouse was used on alternate Sundays by the Methodists and the Baptists for their services in 1831 until the Methodists built their own church building. The school in this picture was built in 1871 and a second room was added in 1909.*
*Courtesy of Cornelia Corson Brown*

*This 1910 photo looks southeast to the intersection of the Dennisville-Petersburg Road (County Route 631) and the Seaville-Tuckahoe Road (State Route 50). The Philadelphia Store, built by Thaddeus Van Gilder, is on the right just before the intersection, Smith's Store is just beyond the intersection on the right. The Philadelphia Store was destroyed by a windstorm in 1880 and rebuilt. The large white oak tree behind the white picket fence on the corner was estimated to be over three hundred years old at that time. The circumference was over twelve feet and the height over fifty feet with a seventy-five-foot spread.*
*Courtesy of Cornelia Corson Brown*

# DENNIS TOWNSHIP

Dennis Township, covering sixty-five square miles, was created in 1826 out of territory from Upper Township. Woodbine and Sea Isle City are the only incorporated local governments, other than the township itself. All of the other towns—Dennisville, South Dennis, Ocean View, Clermont, South Seaville, North Dennis, Belleplain, and Eldora—are under the jurisdiction of the township government. Headquarters for the township government is in Dennisville.

The earliest settlers were John Townsend and his wife, Phoebe, who migrated to the township sometime between 1680 and 1685. Townsend, a staunch Quaker, had been banished from the New York colony for his beliefs. After swimming his cattle across Egg Harbor, he followed an Indian trace to a stream that was later named Mill Creek. Here he bought 640 acres from Dr. Daniel Coxe and built a home in 1690, which still stands alongside Route 47, across from his lake.

Richard Townsend, John and Phoebe's first-born, is believed to be the first Christian child born in the county. Phoebe died in 1704 at an early age. She became the first Christian woman to be buried in the county. Her gravesite is in the Asbury Cemetery in Swainton.

The seventeen-mile-long Great Cedar Swamp extends across much of Dennis Township and into Upper Township. The swamp divides the township and the county into two sections.

The large cedar forest and the swamp provided the natural resources for lumbering, shipbuilding, shinglemaking, and shipping that made Dennis Township and Cape May County an economic force in the region. The areas surrounding the swamp and the network of creeks were the first to develop substantial settlements and centers of commerce.

Before the forests were depleted by overharvesting, cedar trees over 500 years old were found. One giant was documented as 1,080 years old.

Nearly half of the township today is included in the vast expanses of natural wonderlands. Many of these are officially established and protected as natural preserves, including Beaver Swamp and Wildlife Management Area and Dennis Creek Fish and Wildlife Management Area. Both of these tracts straddle the township line between Dennis and Middle. The eleven thousand-acre Belleplain State Forest extends over much of the western part of Dennis and Upper townships. Much of the Great Cedar Swamp is protected as a nature preserve and remains in a relatively pristine state.

In addition to these natural inland treasures, large areas of marshlands lay between Ludlam's Beach (Sea Isle City) and the Parkway. These include: Gull Island, Townsend's Sound and the areas around Townsend's Channel, Mill Creek, Mill Creek Thoroughfare, Sunks Creek, the Big and Little Elder Creeks, Middle Township Creek and the areas bordering on Ludlam's Bay (north), and Townsend's Inlet (south). These provide a paradise for boaters and fishermen and magnificent vistas from the Parkway and the Barrier Islands.

Although Town Bank was the main whaling center in Cape May County, the shoreline at Peck's Beach (Ocean City), Ludlam's Beach (Sea Isle City), and Whale Beach (Strathmere) offered excellent locations for processing whale carcasses. The last recorded lease for whaling on Ludlam's Beach is dated 1777. The area attracted whalers whose family names are synonymous with Cape May's development: Godfrey, Stites, Leaming, Ludlam, Van Gilder, Young, and Corson.

*Dennis Township municipal court and some township offices are located in this building in the center of Dennisville on the Dennisville-Petersburg Road.*
*Photograph by Vance Enck*

*Ludlam's School was the first community school built on its own land in Cape May County, and the start of New Jersey's public school system. Henry Ludlam deeded the land for one dollar to the citizens of Dennis on September 3, 1801. A very community-minded man, Ludlam boarded the succession of school teachers. Originally broadside to the Main Road, the school was moved just prior to the Civil War to its present location on Route 47 in North Dennis. During the Civil War, patriotic lads came here to enlist. It was here they were sworn in and shipped off to the bloody battlefields of that war. No longer used as a school, the building is a meeting center. The Dennis Township Historical Society holds its regular meetings here. Photograph by Vance Enck*

*The Ludlam family cemetery on Jakes Landing Road (near North Dennis) contains the graves of Thomas Ludlam, Jr., (died 1825) and his wife, Zilpah Smith Ludlam (died 1829). Both graves have headstones and footstones. The fifth stone, to the right, is a footstone with the initials "R. L." and is assumed to mark the grave of one of their children. The cemetery is being restored by the Dennis Township Historical Society as a part of their Jakes Landing restoration project. Jakes Landing was owned by the Spicers before the Ludlams. The landing was used by the Ludlams (both Thomas, Sr., and Thomas, Jr.) for shipping cedar shingles made on their property. A block house was built at appropriately named Mosquito Point for the storage of shingles, but also proved a great asset for smuggling operations during the War of 1812. A number of patriotic and rummy folklore stories surround the history of the landing. Photograph by Vance Enck*

John Grace, at age twenty-one, enlisted as a soldier in the Third New Jersey Battalion to help fight the British in the war for independence. He saw action in the battles of Bennington, Brandywine, Monmouth, the Western Pennsylvania campaign, and the final battle at Yorktown. In 1779 he struck an officer who refused to release horses to him for use in retrieving supplies he had hidden from the British. On careful review of the case, General Washington sentenced Grace to imprisonment—four hours in the commander's tent. Later, Grace was sent by Washington as a scout in response to a request from General Gates. Grace carried with him a letter from General Washington, which said, "He is my trusted scout whom British gold cannot buy." Grace was discharged in 1783, and, with the help of State Representative Jeremiah Leaming, was finally pensioned in 1818 at ninety-six dollars a year. Grace died in 1835 and was buried in an unmarked grave. At the suggestion of Seaville's Reverend Jacob Price, in 1895, school children collected funds to erect a monument to this Cape May patriot. So clear was this a children's tribute that contributions from older people trying to "get into the act" were returned. The monument (above), placed in South Dennis Union Cemetery, is shown being unveiled at the dedication ceremonies on May 31, 1904 (below). The man in the center is believed to be Aaron Hand, county superintendent of schools.

*Above photograph by Vance Enck; Below photograph courtesy of Cape May County Historical Museum*

## BELLEPLAIN

"Belleplaine" was born as a stop on the first railroad that came through Cumberland County on the way to Cape May County in 1863. Around that station building grew a small settlement, first residing in Cumberland County. The town did not move, but the county boundary line did, in 1878 to bring Belleplaine into Cape May County. The final "e" was dropped in 1921.

The name was bestowed by Jeremiah Vansellar, West Jersey Railroad's first superintendent, to romantically honor Anabelle Townsend, one of the loveliest belles in the county.

The Methodist church here held its first services in the station house between trains. Enough settlers arrived by 1867 to justify its own post office with George Blinn appointed as the first postmaster.

Small industries were started in the town. An active brickworks kilned here in the early years. However, there is no trace of these activities today.

Belleplain has expanded very slowly throughout its history, but the residents here delight in their quiet sylvan setting.

## BELLEPLAIN STATE FOREST

Acquisitions of the land to form Belleplain State Forest began in 1928. Rollen B. Mason, a Dennis Township trustee for thirty-nine years, led the drive for the state to take on this major conservation project.

The federal government provided substantial support by creating the Civilian Conservation Corps program, enacted on March 31, 1933. The first CCC camp here opened on June 7, 1933, at Woodbine. Young men, ages eighteen to twenty-eight, were paid one dollar a day, plus food, clothing, and lodging as participants. Barracks were later built in the forest to house the three camps located there.

The Meisle Cranberry Bog was converted to a 26.2-acre lake, named Lake Nummy, after the last Kechemeche king whose settlements dotted the county. In excavating the bog, an Indian canoe was found buried in the mud. It was given to the state museum in Trenton where it was restored and is now displayed.

In addition to the lake, the CCC built dams, buildings, and a boat and bath house. Probably the most significant contribution came through extensive reforestation of the tract. During the Depression, young men of the CCC reforested the area by planting 525,396 seedlings on 3,001 acres of the park. Before Congress cut off funding, forcing all CCC camps to close on June 30, 1942, over 250,000 man-hours had gone into establishing the park and its facilities.

The forest was extensively used for training purposes during World War II. The U.S. Army Fourth Division (fifteen thousand soldiers) held training maneuvers here. Along with the 113th Infantry Regiment, they patrolled the beaches and bridges in defense of the vital coastal and river areas of South Jersey.

Camping opened to the public in 1955. There are now over two hundred campsites located throughout the forest. An abundance of wildlife, hiking trails, boating, and swimming facilities, as well as the campsites, have made this a very popular natural paradise.

A not-so-idyllic footnote is that the forest was also a favorite area for bootleggers during the Prohibition Era. Revenuers naturally became frequent visitors. One of the most famous raids by government agents ended in a shoot-out with the Benson Boys, which nearly wiped out the Benson clan.

The state of New Jersey originally amassed 5,464.52 acres for the forest. This has grown to over 11,000 acres. The original investment for the initial tract was $46,879.77, which nets-out to a cost of $8.42 per acre. The investments by the state and federal governments are still returning handsome dividends in public enjoyment and in preservation of a very precious ecological system.

*Lake Nummy, named after the last Kechemeche king, is a popular 26.2 acre swimming and boating area in the heart of Belleplain State Forest. It was created from the Meisle Cranberry Bog by Civilian Conservation Corp recruits in the mid-1930s. The bathing beach is the sandy stretch on the left side of the lake. Belleplain State Forest surrounds the lake.*
*Courtesy of Robert "Skip" Berry*

## OCEAN VIEW

John Townsend, one of the very earliest and the most famous of the county's settlers, built his home in 1690 in what is now called Ocean View. The dam he built on Mill Creek to provide water power for his sawmill created Lake Magnolia.

A wintergreen distillery operated near the lake using native wintergreen to make an oil used both as a flavoring and as a liniment for relief of rheumatic pain. Dr. Palmer Way operated a hop farm near the lake and farmed bogs producing several varieties of cranberries.

Ocean View was originally included in the area referred to as Seaville. When Dennis Township was created in 1824, Ocean View was placed in the new township and Seaville remained in Middle Township.

William Doolittle served as the first postmaster when the first office opened in 1872.

Ocean View's sweeping view to the Atlantic Ocean is now interrupted by the Garden State Parkway. It is today a pleasant, small residential community stretching along Shore Road with some excellent examples of restored Colonial and Federal style homes.

*John Townsend's home is the oldest house in the county. The original portion has survived very well for nearly three centuries giving support to the additions surrounding it. Contemporary contributions to this landmark are the television antennas and the telephone and electric lines. This beautiful home sits on a hillside overlooking Seashore Road, with a magnificent panoramic view of Lake Magnolia. It has been home to Townsend's descendants for most of its life.*
*Photograph by Vance Enck*

*Lake Magnolia was a natural "ol' swimmin' hole" for area kids (and grown-ups). This 1907 newspaper picture raises the question, "Are they skinny-dipping?" Chances are, they were, since not many autos were passing at that time.*
*Courtesy of Cornelia Corson Brown*

*The Ocean View school student body of 1903. Miss Minnie Way, the teacher, is probably standing in the doorway. Pupils identified on the back of the photo, but not by position, are: Oscar Stratton, Maggie Lloyd, Bertha Sutton, John Lloyd, Ethel Parsons, Laura Devaul, Myra Way, Alice Stiles, Elizabeth Jerrell, Belle Cuca, Emil Way, Tony Cannso, Leslie Howell, Jeanne Parsons, Estella Cole, Anna Lloyd, Fred Jerrell, Frank Smith, Lin Way, and Harry Muller.*
*Courtesy of Cape May County Historical Museum*

*A bustling shopping afternoon at Burt Way's store, on the right, on a 1907 summer day in Ocean View. At least three different types of vehicles are tied-up in Burt's "parking lot." The store, since torn down, sat at the intersection of Seashore Road (Route 9) and Main Street. The next building on the right, "down the road a piece," was moved about one and a half miles to Corson Tavern Road. Ocean View Trailer Sales now occupies the site.*
*Courtesy of Clair Howell*

*Volunteer fire departments have a long, proud, and vital history in Cape May County. Ocean View's department is showing off its state-of-the-art equipment in this mid-1930s picture.*
*Courtesy of Cape May County Historical Museum*

## CLERMONT

This area on the mainland along Route 9 was originally purchased by John Townsend from Dr. Coxe in 1695.

A post office was established in 1849 for Townsend's Inlet, serving areas that are now Swainton (in Middle Township) and Clermont. William Stites was the first postmaster. Clermont was given its own post office in 1886. The town name was derived from Clermont, Florida, which had captured the fancy of Sallie and Lester Todd, who moved to Florida from here and whose descriptions led the remaining residents to adopt the name.

In 1880 the population of Townsend's Inlet was 309. Growth over the years has been slow. Lester Todd established a sawmill for making cedar shingles and pine siding. He also set up a gristmill which never went into operation because the Todds moved to Florida before it was completed.

Clermont was a tourist attraction for some time. The Holly Tree Inn, operated by Sherman Todd, charged ten dollars a week for room and board in the early 1900s. The tab included daily fishing trips on a party boat from the inn's pier which was built out into Townsend's Sound. The proprietor, Sherman Todd, even though blinded by a hunting accident as a boy, was an expert bartender and fiddler. Lucy Todd, Sherman's sister, married the leader of the band that played at the inn on Saturdays. One of the first "broadcasts" in the county may have been the nine-party line system, installed in 1910, which tuned in to hear Lucy Todd Barton singing, "Somewhere A Voice is Calling." The first Holly Tree Inn burned to the ground. A new inn was built on the old foundation, but it too came to a fiery end. The second fire ended Clermont's tourist industry. Travelers on Shore Road today are hardly aware they have passed through the town.

## SOUTH SEAVILLE

Development of a settlement at South Seaville was inevitable as soon as the first roads were laid out in 1707. At one time, five trails or roads intersected at the town site, four of which still exist today. Most important of these was the old King's Highway, the only route into the county through the Great Cedar Swamp and to Dennis Landing. South Seaville is located between Beesley's Point and Dennisville. For a time it was called Gracetown, presumably to honor John Grace, General Washington's trusted scout, who settled here after the Revolution.

South Seaville played an important role as the central point for farming activity in the area. It was part of the original Townsend plantation and close to John Townsend's mill operations. Lumbering and shingle cutting industries later developed here because of its location adjacent to the Great Cedar Swamp.

The placement of roads made it a stagecoach stop in the early days. The greatest push, however, came with the inauguration of the Cape May and Millville Railroad lines. South Seaville was a major stop on the line and later a junction point with the Pennsylvania route. Stagecoaches originating here carried passengers from the station to the bustling Beesley's Point resort area.

Reflecting the nation's religious revival of the mid-1800s, the South Seaville Meeting Association was formed in 1863, the first to be established in New Jersey. An outgrowth of the three-day quarterly conferences of the Methodist-Episcopal churches, it inaugurated outdoor camp meetings at the Agricultural Fairgrounds built on the site of an Indian campground and just a few hundred feet from the railroad station. Beginning with a tent compound which was set up for the meetings, the South Seaville Campground was developed later, in which lots were sold and cottages built. A thirty-two-room boarding

*The thirty-two-room Grove House, built in 1881, housed the main dining room on the first floor. Visiting preachers, workers, and those who did not own cottages were provided room and board here. Some of the tenants assembled to provide this 1915 memento. Fire codes halted the use of the dormitory rooms, but the dining hall is still used for feasts.*
*Courtesy of Audrey Sullivan and Doris Young*

house with a central dining room was built in 1881. The large tabernacle was completed in 1883. At its zenith, over ten thousand people attended the ten-day camp meetings. Annual meetings are still held on the campgrounds.

A post office was established in 1867 when the population had reached five hundred. Remington Corson was the first postmaster.

The Garden State Parkway bypasses South Seaville. The railroad lines were closed in the 1950s. Except for the times the camp meetings erupt on the scene, South Seaville is today a pleasant, quiet, rural town.

*An eager welcoming committee is lined up in 1915 at the entrance to the campgrounds. The arch is believed to date to 1893.*
*Courtesy of Audrey Sullivan and Doris Young*

*Auditorium, South Seaville Camp Meeting, circa 1915.*
*Courtesy of Audrey Sullivan and Doris Young*

Laird's General Store (above) stood at a corner on Main Street in South Seaville. The two unidentified workmen in this 1900 photo may have just stopped on their way home to catch up on all the latest news. The store burned on January 12, 1913, apparently from arson connected to a robbery.

Payne's Cigar and Dry Goods Store (below) was first Wheaton's ice cream parlor. After Laird's burned, H. B. Payne opened a general store in the new building, as shown in this 1919 photo.
*Courtesy of Mrs. Estella Pierson*

Blemko Inn could have been the source for many traveling salesman stories. The inn was a popular base for salesmen who rented carriages in South Seaville to make their sales calls during the day and returned to rest overnight. On the meadow in front of the inn, about 1900, are owners Georgiana and John Bonham. The inn on King's Highway was bought in 1984 by the Spatolas, restored, and is now used as their home and as a gift shop.
*Courtesy of Patricia and John Spatola*

*A grove purchased by the South Seaville Meeting Association in 1875 was subdivided into tent sites. Building small elaborately decorated cottages in true Victorian style became fashionable. This is the Mary F. Godfrey cottage built in 1878-79 by Capt. Richard W. Godfrey of Tuckahoe. After twenty-five years of Godfrey family ownership, the cottage was sold to the John Tozour family of Delmont, who are arrayed on the cottage porch in this early 1900 picture.*
*Courtesy of Audrey Sullivan and Doris Young*

*All is not serious hymn-singing and sermons at the annual camp meetings. Much recreation and family fun is built into the program, as this glimpse of the 1987 egg toss reveals. Eggs are tossed back and forth until the "yolk" is on the one with the hardest hand.*
*Courtesy of Audrey Sullivan and Doris Young*

## ELDORA

Located between East Creek and West Creek on Route 47 (which generally follows the first road built to Cumberland County), the town was first named Stipson's Island, followed by West Creek and, much later, Eldora. The name Eldora was selected in 1892 through a local contest.

Eldora was once a bustling hub of business activity. Delaware shipping regularly included a stop at the docks here. Locally made cedar shingles, lumber, and farm produce were bartered for shot, shoes, and sorghum. Levi's General Store was for many years the gossip center and general newsroom for the area. According to legend, a proprietor known as "Old Skinflint," was so tight that he bit off portions of crackers to insure correct weights. The store building has been moved to the Smithville complex in Atlantic County where it has been restored and now serves as a specialty shop.

Around 1890 Isaac Dawson, a minister, built a plant exclusively devoted to canning tomatoes. The finished products were shipped via West Creek to Philadelphia and from there to loyal consumers in England. In 1892 a papermaking plant was built on Mill Pond but failed and was replaced by a pickling and canning operation.

Very few traces remain of any of these industrial ventures. Today, Eldora is a small residential community quietly spread along Route 47.

*This plant was built in 1892 to manufacture paper on the basis of samples prepared by Joe Springer, who sold the property to the paper company. Unfortunately, the water from the pond and the cedar pulp produced only a brown paper instead of the fine quality white paper samples shown by Springer. At that time, there were no supermarkets and no demand for brown paper. The paper company failed and the Philadelphia Pickle Company bought the plant and a section of the pond for fifteen hundred dollars in 1903 to cure pickles and can tomatoes and later applesauce made from local Eldora-grown produce. The plant continued operating until about 1920. It has since disappeared.*
*Courtesy of Cape May County Historical Museum*

## WOODBINE

Years before the town was created, Mrs. William Townsend of Dennisville chose the name, Woodbine, to memorialize the extensive fields of wildflowers in the area.

An early developer, John Moore, laid out a town plan in 1887 with the Millville and Cape May Railroad station at its center. Four years later, the Baron De Hirsch Fund bought a 5,300-acre tract from Moore and others for under forty thousand dollars.

This purchase was the opening of a chapter in Cape May history that is totally different from any other in the county and is indeed unique in the United States.

Baron De Hirsch was a Bavarian by birth and a very successful French industrialist and banker of the late nineteenth century. His offer of $10 million to alleviate the suffering of Jews in Russia was unceremoniously refused by that government. Undaunted, De Hirsch established, through his will, a $2.4 million fund for accomplishing his dream.

After acquiring the Woodbine tract, the trustees of the fund established a plan for developing a Jewish refugee resettlement project. An eight hundred-acre tract, laid out on both sides of the railroad line already built through the area, was dedicated as the site of the town. The rest of the land was divided into sixty-two farm plots containing thirty acres each.

*Four "company" houses, among those built as homes to house immigrant settlers on the eight hundred acre tract set aside for the development of the town of Woodbine, stand along an unpaved street in this early 1900s photo. The rear portions of these buildings were apparently additions, giving the houses saltbox style profiles. The uniformity of the original structures, as well as the additions, clearly mark them as good examples of an early Cape May County tract development. The houses were built for occupancy by the craftsmen, butchers, slaughterers, and merchants who were to serve the farming community development around the town.*
*Courtesy of Cape May County Historical Museum*

*Each refugee family settled on a farm plot provided by the De Hirsch Fund, which included thirty acres of land, a house, outbuildings, one cow, one horse, twenty-five chickens, seed, and equipment. This carefully staged picture, taken in 1892 or 1893, is a nearly complete graphic inventory of the starting endowment. The colonists were required to repay the fund the $1,200 investment over a ten-year period, beginning with the first harvest, with only interest payable for the first three years.*
*Courtesy of the archives of Eleanor Callaghan*

In 1892 650 acres were cleared and twelve miles of roads constructed. In the same year, the first sixty families, mostly from Odessa, Russia, and parts of Roumania, were resettled here. The remainder of the land was cleared and filled with families. As the town developed, industry was encouraged by grants of free land to locate in Woodbine. Most of the resettled families had come from cities in Europe and were not experienced in farming. The rugged nature of the land, plus the language and custom barriers, made the first years of the project's development very difficult.

The first winter was especially hard for the settlers. What resources they had were quickly depleted. Their only income came from cutting cordwood and what little factory work was available. De Hirsch trustees adamantly refused to subsidize the colonists, insisting they must be self-supporting. A farmers' revolt developed with angry meetings, fiery telegrams, and work strikes. No crops were planted for two years and most other work halted. The trustees finally realized that farming alone would not be successful, so they moved to encourage industry in order to produce an economic base that was half farming and half industry.

In 1895 the Woodbine Agricultural School was established to teach the latest and best farming techniques as an aid in overcoming these problems. As the first secondary school in the United States to undertake such a program, it attracted much state and national attention. The school was successful in providing many leading agricultural experts in the early part of the twentieth century. In 1912 there were 660 applicants for the sixty-nine available student openings.

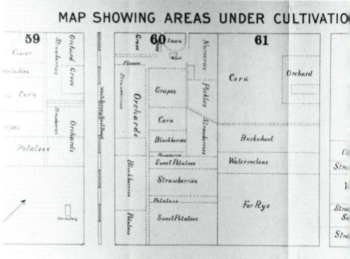

*The agricultural school, founded in 1895, became world renown. Built on two thirty-acre farming plots, it was the first secondary school in the country to specialize in farming studies. The greenhouse and the students are shown in this 1896 photograph (left). The map of the garden areas shows the variety of crops studied and the extent of the training provided (right above).*

*The 1897 photograph of the Woodbine exhibit at the Cape May County Fair provides still further evidence of the diversity of the training school's program (bottom left). Exhibits by the agricultural school won a silver medal at the 1900 Paris Exposition, and the Grand Prix for secondary education, as well as several medals, at the 1904 St. Louis World's Fair. The school numbered many leading agricultural experts and leaders of the early 1900s among its graduates. The school's superintendent lived in this house on the grounds of the school complex (bottom right).*
*Courtesy of the archives of Eleanor Callaghan*

Partly due to criticism that the program was too expensive to operate and partly due to a gift of land in Peekskill, New York, for relocating the school, the Woodbine Agricultural School was closed in 1917. World War I disrupted the planned move and the school was never reopened. Instead, a scholarship fund was established to aid students attending other agricultural schools.

Relationships between the settlers at Woodbine and the rest of Dennis Township were generally strained because of the ethnic differences. On March 3, 1903, the New Jersey legislature incorporated Woodbine as a borough. The first mayor was Hersh L. Sobsovitch, who had been responsible for establishing the agricultural school and was a colony supervisor.

Woodbine developed rapidly. By 1910 there were nearly forty industrial operations. Schools were built. The Cape May County Art League, currently headquartered in Cape May City, was founded here in 1929, as the first county art league in the United States.

The De Hirsch Fund Trustees gradually withdrew from the affairs of the community, and, in 1930, severed all connections. In the ensuing decades, Woodbine continued to grow and flourish until the end of World War II. At one time, there were eleven major employers providing 950 jobs, and fifty poultry and produce farms in the area. These farms served the major markets of the region—New York, Philadelphia, Wilmington, Baltimore, and Washington. Many World War II uniform items were manufactured here. In its heyday, Woodbine was the economic hub of Cape May County. It was the shopping mecca for the whole region in the 1920s and 1930s.

*To serve its rapidly growing population, Woodbine had built four public schools and a four-year high school by 1914. The second school, pictured here, was built in 1900. The first school was the agricultural school, established in 1895. Cape May County's first kindergarten was included in this school system.*
*Courtesy of the archives of Eleanor Callaghan*

A naval air station, with three 3,500-foot runways, was constructed here during World War II. The former CCC barracks, located on the site, were filled with sailors on coastal defense duty. After the war, the Navy gave the facility to Woodbine. Today, only private airplanes use the landing strips. The city and the Chamber of Commerce are currently seeking to develop the facilities as an industrial park.

The end of World War II caused the industries to close and Woodbine started on a decline. There are very few small industries left, and no major ones. Only a few of the second and third generations of the original refugee settlers' descendants remain.

After closing the Agricultural School in 1917, the trustees offered the facilities as a gift to the state of New Jersey. The state gladly accepted and set about renovating the school. Only four of the original buildings remain. This transformed complex was reopened, in 1921, as the Woodbine State Colony for Feebleminded Males with thirteen retarded boys in residence. Today, known as the Woodbine Development Center, with over seven hundred male clients, it is the area's largest employer.

In its relatively brief history, the Woodbine experiment produced many alumni whose names read like a "Who's Who" of the Jewish community. The farming industry that grew up around the town did much to further New Jersey's nickname, "The Garden State." The influence of Woodbine in stabilizing the county's economy was quite substantial. There are only deteriorating reminders of the vital community that once flourished here.

*The Brotherhood Synagogue was completed in 1896, and consecrated on November 29 of that year, four years after the first Jewish refugees arrived. They planned, developed, built the synagogue, and fabricated every piece of the fifty-foot long, two story edifice. The total cost was six thousand dollars, spent for raw materials. Bricks were made on one of the community farms which had a large quantity of usable clay. Later, a frame synagogue was also built but it has since been demolished. The brotherhood, over the years, has been vandalized and firebombed. The last resident rabbi left just after World War II. The brotherhood is currently open for high holy day ceremonies for which a rabbi is imported. It has been designated a national landmark.
Photograph by Vance Enck*

## DENNISVILLE

Dennisville is located on land originally owned by Jacob Spicer from the 1690s to 1726. He sold a large parcel of this land to Joseph Ludlam in 1726. In that same year, two of Ludlam's sons, Anthony and Joseph, settled on opposite sides of Dennis Creek.

The areas that are known today as Dennisville, North Dennis, and South Dennis were originally named Dennis Creek. Located at the junction of the first roads in the county and on the heavily traveled Dennis Creek shipping route, the area developed naturally into an important settlement. Dennisville officially acquired its name in 1854 and South Dennis in 1874.

Dennis Creek was the first town in the county to have its own post office, which opened in 1802. Dennis Creek itself was the main avenue for coastal shipping, serving the county for several decades. Two-masted ships of the 50-ton to 250-ton class regularly plied the then navigable creek, where men and mules were used to move the ships on the trip between the Delaware River and the town.

A shipbuilding industry quickly developed and

*For many years the Dennisville boat-landing was the shipping hub of Cape May County. Departing ships carried lumber, shingles, produce, and local products. Arriving ships brought food items, shoes, clothing, spices, liquor, and other staples not produced in the county. These late 1890s pictures provide views of the landing area. The top picture shows the iron bridge over Dennis Creek, which replaced the longstanding covered bridge demolished in 1893. Shipping through Dennisville relied on smaller one and two masted coastal schooners and sloops, shown below, that could easily navigate the narrow Dennis Creek for the seven mile stretch to Delaware Bay.*
*Courtesy of Jane Dixon*

continued as a major industry for most of the nineteenth century. Interior areas of the county were preferred shipbuilding locales because of the protection from the high tides and raging storms along the Atlantic Ocean coast. The natural supply of good lumber for the ships made the area especially desirable. From 1848 to 1901 at least fifty-six ships were built at Dennisville. The leading shipbuilders were the Leaming Yards, and, later, the Isaac Gandy and Jesse Diverty shipbuilding operations. Ships were built lengthwise along the creek and launched sideways into the water.

*Shipbuilding was one of Dennisville's major industries for over seven decades. Shown here is the* Gertrude Abbot, *one of the last built on the Dennisville stocks. Pictures 1 and 2 show the early stages of laying the keel and placing the ribs. Note in picture 1 the stacks of timber that had been picked "on the stump" and, after being cut, was brought to the shipyard to age. In picture 3 the ship's sides are being completed. Picture 4 shows the launching in 1876. Only the hulls, decks, and bowsprits were finished at the shipyards. The completed hull was towed seven miles to the Delaware Bay and then to Philadelphia or Camden to be sparred and rigged with sails made in Philadelphia. Sizes of ships built in Dennisville grew from one mast to three and tonnage from an average of 100 in the 1840s to over 400 in the 1880s and 1890s. The largest built in Dennisville was the* Thomas L. Pollard, *built in 1890. The Pollard's length of 157.6 feet, beam of 34 feet, and 17-foot draft made towing her 707 tons down Dennis Creek to the bay a most difficult project.*
*Courtesy of Jane Dixon*

1.

2.

3.

4.

Lumbering in the area also produced timber for construction of buildings. The most valuable product was cedar shingles. Early shingles were cut and shaped from standing trees. Later, forests of partially petrified trees buried in the swamps were discovered during searches for peat moss fuel. Shingles cut from living trees were noted for their durability and easy maintenance. "Mined" shingles were reported to have even longer useful lives (up to one hundred years) and were in great demand. For over a century, they were the preferred siding and roofing materials. Shingle making was a foremost county industry. Cedar shingles are reported to have provided the first roof for Independence Hall. Charles Pitman Roberts and James Annely of Dennis Creek supplied over twenty-five thousand mined shingles for the mid-1800 replacement roof for that national landmark.

Dennis Creek's shipping industry produced several captains who built many of the elegant homes that still line the streets of Dennisville. Several of these homes are opened to the public during the town's annual Christmas House Tour.

In 1848 proud residents promoted a referendum to relocate the county seat from Middletown (Cape May Court House) to Dennisville. In addition to its shipping and shipbuilding center Dennisville then had seventy homes, five stores, two taverns, an academy, and a Methodist Church. Goshen, another shipbuilding center to the south in Middle Township, joined the race for the county seat. Middletown handily won the selection by 524 votes to Dennisville's 435 and Goshen's 44.

Iron ships, faster transportation, and cheaper materials combined to erode Dennisville's industrial base. Today, Dennisville, South Dennis, and North Dennis are charming, picturesque, small residential towns. Intensive restoration of many of the fine old homes and buildings is doing much to revive interest in the area's rich history. On November 24, 1987, Dennisville was placed on The National Register of Historic Places due to the untiring efforts of Jane Dixon, owner of the Nathaniel Holmes house, and historian with the County Planning Commission, with the assistance of Elwood Jarmer, county planner. The designated area covers sixty acres and includes sixty-nine buildings.

*Dennisville's blacksmith shop on Main Street was a gathering place for local men to trade news and information. Blacksmiths were important tradesmen. They shod horses, replaced carriage wheel rims, and made household pots and kettles. Note the wheels waiting to be finished and the style of carriages in this 1880s picture. This shop also made some of the iron fittings used on ships built at the local shipyards. The sign just behind the horses reads "H. Cobb."*
*Courtesy of Jane Dixon*

*Mill Pond, on the right, was formed by the dam under the road where the wagon is crossing. The dam is still in existence under Route 47. The building on the left is what remained of the original mill on the site. Note the lady with a parasol on the right (suntans were not stylish in those days). The pond was a naturally popular "swimmin' hole" as evidenced by the swimmers in the pond. Mill Pond is a picturesque part of Dennisville. A lighted Christmas tree floating on the pond is an annual treat for travelers and a beacon for visitors taking the annual candlelight house tour during the holiday season. Courtesy of Jane Dixon*

*Students were assigned the duties of bringing in firewood and tending the stoves in this Dennisville school. Younger pupils in the lower grades met on the first floor and classes for the upper grades were held on the second floor. Note the four girls in matching dresses, obviously made from the same bolt of cloth. The teacher and twenty-eight students were memorialized in front of the Dennisville school in this early 1900s picture. A fire in 1905 destroyed the first floor. The building was cut down to one floor and is now used as the Dennis Township Municipal Court building.
Courtesy of Jane Dixon*

*Reported to be the smallest post office building in the United States, the South Dennis unit was scheduled for destruction until friends intervened to save it. Moved three times, it is now located on Delsea Drive. Restored by the Dennis Township Historical Society, it was dedicated July 1988 as the society's first museum and library.
Photograph by Vance Enck*

*Joseph Falkenburge, who built this South Dennis house in 1801, was something of a man of mystery. He apparently came to the area in the latter 1790s from Tuckerton in Ocean County where his family owned substantial land and several businesses, including a tavern that was a favorite hangout for pirates and privateers. Joseph married Abigail Ludlam, a daughter of Henry, who later died in childbirth. Falkenburge was a tailor by trade, but more importantly he was a merchant and one of Cape May County's first real land barons. He was a very wealthy man and was involved in many financial ventures in the area. He died on April 30, 1846, and is buried in South Dennis' Union Cemetery.*

*His estate, including over one thousand acres of land, building, and town lots, was divided among his grandchildren: Joseph S. Leaming, Coleman F. Leaming, Abigail L. Leaming, Ellen H. Leaming, Charlotte Leaming, Richard S. Leaming, Jeremiah Leaming, and Susan Leaming. His lovely home, along Route 47, was one of the very few brick houses built in the county. The bricks were reportedly brought to this country as ships' ballast. The home contains several secret passages which may have been connected with his reported involvement with slave traffic. The small building to the rear contained slave quarters and the kitchen.*
*Photograph by Vance Enck*

# MIDDLE TOWNSHIP

As incorporated in 1798, Middle Township encompassed an area approximately ten miles long by ten miles wide. Although the incorporation of Avalon, Stone Harbor, North Wildwood, and Wildwood reduced the size to seventy square miles, Middle is still the largest township in the county.

In contrast to Upper and Dennis townships, there was more than one major landowner among the early settlers. Shamgar Hand purchased one thousand acres from Dr. Coxe, which included the Cape May Court House and Dias Creek areas and southeast to the ocean. Christopher Leaming, Aaron Leaming, and Arthur Cresse owned the land where Rio Grande is located. Burleigh and Whitesboro were once a part of the Cresse plantation. Richard and Jonathan Swain came to Cape May Court House in 1706. Their father, Ebenezer, joined them later and they farmed all of what is now Swainton. Samuel Matthews bought the land where the county park and zoo are located from the West Jersey Society in 1700. All of these settlers first came to the area as whalers and later moved inland as permanent residents.

## CREST HAVEN

For most of two centuries, the Crest Haven area has been devoted to use for public services.

The area developed around the almshouse. The first almshouse was built on the site in 1833. Designed as shelter for the elderly and indigent, it grew over the years in size and function. Today, it is the Cape May County Rest Home. Currently, the Crest Haven complex is shared by several county agencies.

Cape May County Prison is located here on a 14.5-acre tract. This latest prison was opened in June 1977. The main prison houses 124 inmates and the adjacent workhouse, another 20. Included in the prison site is a 5-acre farm, tilled by the inmates, that produces much of the vegetables consumed in the prison. Surplus crops are given to the rest home.

As a part of the sheriff's office area, are kennels for the county's "K-9" corps, consisting of six trained dogs; two each are specifically trained for bomb detection, drug detection, and trailing.

The twelve-acre Cape May County Veterans' Cemetery is adjacent to the prison grounds. Burial in this site is open to Cape May County veterans. The cemetery was opened in 1980.

Several activity centers of the County Board of Education are scattered throughout the complex. There are special education and counseling centers. The largest facility is the "vo-tech" school. First authorized in April 1915, Cape May County Vocational School classes were conducted in several areas of career training. The present building opened with an eighteen-shop program in 1969. Four more shops were added in 1973, and the Robert N. Toft Career Center began operation in 1979.

Student enrollment is about two thousand a semester. Training courses in culinary arts, auto repair, nursing, and dental assisting, computer operations and technology are offered in the day programs. Evening classes in the same subjects are offered, as well as special courses in the various arts and crafts. Adult high school equivalency courses are also offered.

*Cape May County Veterans' Cemetery contains over 6400 gravesites, of which 750 are currently filled. Memorial trees, donated by families of veterans, are planted throughout the cemetery. Special services are conducted here on Memorial Day and Veterans' Day each year.*
*Photograph by Vance Enck*

*Minutes of the Freeholders' meeting, on February 20, 1821, authorizing a commission to administer the alms house and records of the first meeting of that new commission are part of the Crest Haven archives. A portion of those records is shown in the photograph. The first actual alms house building was not erected until 1833. The original building was small, probably containing four rooms. Several additions were made, greatly enlarging the capacity, as shown in the center picture, circa 1870. Today's complex (below) now serves as a county rest home and sanitarium. Photographs courtesy of: above—Crest Haven, center—Jane Dixon, below—Vance Enck*

## BURDETTE TOMLIN HOSPITAL

Plans for building a hospital near the county seat were conceived in 1941 when Burdette Tomlin, a local businessman, contributed $25,000 to be matched by other funding. Original costs were projected at $100,000, but World War II put the plans on hold. A gestation period of nine years elapsed before the hospital was delivered. Federal funding of one-third of the cost eventually completed the necessary amount for paying the final bill of $700,000.

Additions in 1960, 1971, 1980, 1984, and 1986 have increased the size from sixty-five to over two hundred beds and have included extensive specialized clinics and a CAT scanner. The staff now numbers over six hundred, with 150 medical specialists and a volunteer corps of over one thousand.

*When Burdette Tomlin Hospital doors opened on October 8, 1950, the sixty-five bed facility had fifty-six employees, including twenty-eight doctors. Only emergency, maternity, and surgical services were offered. The one-patient emergency room operated from a converted utility room. The non-air conditioned operating room, located over the laundry room, sometimes reached the temperature of 115 degrees F. Architecturally, the two-story building was designed to be compatible with the newest courthouse built in 1927 in nearby Cape May Court House.*
*Courtesy of Burdette Tomlin Hospital*

## CAPE MAY COUNTY HISTORICAL MUSEUM

The first county museum was opened in the basement of the Cape May County Court House in 1930. It was developed by the Cape May County Historical and Genealogical Society, founded on March 12, 1927, which still operates the museum. Over the years, space became a problem as important and valuable acquisitions were made.

In 1970 the society purchased the Jonathan Holmes house and relocated the museum. With the added space and appropriate quarters, the museum has grown to become one of the finest in the state.

The parlor from the Matthews House in Fishing Creek was reconstructed, after being moved piece by piece, as part of the main museum.

To the rear of the museum is a barn building, dating to 1800, which was moved from the Fendall Smith property in Marmora. An addition to the barn was built to house the original French-made Fresnel lens from the third Cape May Point lighthouse.

Also located on the property are the traffic control house, originally at the intersection of Mechanic and Main streets in Cape May Court House and a children's playhouse, presently used for presenting slide lectures. A new office and library building was added to the property in 1988. Housed here are extensive collections of genealogical references, photographs, and documents, as well as the entire collection of the Cape May *Star and Wave* (the county's first newspaper), which is now stored on microfilm.

The museum offers guided tours on a regularly scheduled basis.

*Opening day ceremonies for the Cape May County Historical Society Museum, November 8, 1930. Representatives of several historical groups were present, including the D.A.R.; the Atlantic County, Bridgeton, and Cumberland County historical societies; as well as the Board of Freeholders and American Legion. Lewis T. Stevens (fifth from right, first row) was president of the Cape May Historical and Genealogical Society at the time. Stevens wrote* History of Cape May County *published in 1897. This is still the most often used reference for historical information about the county prior to 1897. Stevens was also a state senator.*
Courtesy of Cape May County Historical Museum

*The Cape May County Museum is currently housed in the Johathan Holmes house on Seashore Road (Route 9) two miles north of Cape May Court House. Located on the Cresse plantation, this house began with two rooms built by the Cresse family. In 1755 Holmes bought the house and made additions between 1778 and 1800. The Cape May County Historical and Genealogical Society acquired the property in 1970 and moved the museum here from the county courthouse. The new building on the left houses the office and library of the society. Note the mile marker in the foreground, indicating fourteen miles to Cape Island.*
Photograph by Vance Enck

## CAPE MAY COUNTY PARK AND ZOO

Located two miles north of Cape May Court House is the 120-acre County Park. Originally part of the Matthews' plantation, the park began with a forty-acre tract donated to the county in 1942. The tract contained small lakes, creeks, and the Matthews' family cemetery. Matthews placed the cemetery in the dead center of his extensive peach orchard. The plot was also used as a burial ground for the poor and for slaves. Part of this cemetery still exists in the park.

A small mound in the center of the park's lake, visible from Route 9, is a portion of the first road built in the county. This section of the original corduroy log road was purposely left as a landmark. A footbridge crosses the lake to this monument.

Subsequent acquisitions brought the park to its present size. Improvements have been made by adding playgrounds, a bandstand, picnic areas and, more recently, a large zoo. The zoo was started in the mid-1970s as a petting zoo for children. The first "exotic" animal, a lion, was later added. The zoo population has grown to 150 animals, including bison, a panther, a giraffe, a valuable Grevy zebra, and monkeys, as well as a number of birds. The surrounding park has walking trails through wilderness areas.

The park has become a popular attraction for family visits to enjoy the zoo, attend summer concerts, and picnic in the park.

*"Oh, Give me a home where the buffalo roam," and they did in Cape May County, a few centuries ago—along with panthers, bears and bobcats. These buffalo and one panther, in the Cape May County Zoo, are the only descendants still around as reminders of those wild and woolly days in the county.*
*Photograph by Herb Beitel*

*One of the most interesting residents of the county zoo is the reticulated giraffe, with an overwhelming love for children. The minute a small tyke appears, the long neck goes into all sorts of contortions to get near the little one. As soon as there are only adults, the neck unbends to assume its maximum regal, aloof height and the giraffe trots around its yard, looking for another child to adore.*
*Photograph by Herb Beitel*

*The county park is much enjoyed by tourists and residents alike. The playground's new equipment is a child's dream-come-true, with all sorts of climbing bars, ladders, slides, and teeter-totters on which to exhibit their derring-do. Picnic areas and trails attract families for a whole day's outing. The pagoda in the lake is the site of numerous weddings each spring, summer, and fall.*
*Photograph by Herb Beitel*

## SWAINTON

Richard Swain and his son, Jonathon, came to Cape May County around 1706. The Swains acquired several hundred acres of land, including part of Five Mile Beach, which came to be known as Swain's Plantation. Swain's Channel and Reuben Swain's Thorofare (a son of Richard, who died in the epidemic of 1713) still carry the family name. Originally lumped with Clermont and Ocean View under the post office title of Townsend's Inlet, the areas were separated by post office names and divided by the line of the newly created township.

One of the earliest Methodist churches was built in 1812 alongside Shore Road. When the original church became too small for the congregation, it was sold to an ex-slave John West, who moved it to East Goshen as the first church in Cape May County for the colored population.

The second Asbury Methodist Church was named after Bishop Asbury, a student of John Wesley, who traveled the Cape May County circuit.

Much of the original land of what was Swainton is today devoted to the Cape May County Park and areas considered part of Cape May Court House, including the Crest Haven Nursing Home, the National Guard Armory, and Cape May County Community College.

*Asbury Methodist Church was built in 1852. The church was organized in 1812. The first building, erected in 1838, was later sold to a colored congregation formed by John West, an escaped slave. This first building was moved by oxen over the log and oyster shell road to East Goshen, where it still serves. The cemetery located around the Asbury church contains several old tombstones, including that of William Boon, who was related to Daniel Boone. Photograph by Vance Enck*

## CAPE MAY COURT HOUSE

Shamgar Hand, the first owner of the Cape May Court House area, in addition to being one of the area's first settlers, was one of the county's leading citizens. He was on the commission that planned and built the first roads in the county. Some of the earliest court sessions were held in his home, beginning in 1704. He also was a judge at that time.

His lands were first surveyed in 1703 by Jeremiah Hand. The area was first named Romney Marsh after a section of Kent County in England. This name was replaced by the apt Middletown in the mid-1700s because the town was at the geographical center of the county. When the county's second post office was opened here in 1803, the confusion with the other New Jersey Middletown led to the present prosaic official name of Cape May Court House.

The first jail house was built in 1705 on the Queen's Highway, east of Gravelly Run (Burleigh). The first Baptist church building in the county, erected in 1715, became the first county government courthouse in 1744 when the Baptists built a new church and sold their previous building to the county. This building continued in use for the government offices until a new courthouse was built in 1774 on an acre of land donated for that purpose by Daniel Hand, son of Shamgar Hand.

Mechanic Street started as a dirt road called Mechanic's Row because it was lined with shops and homes of craftsmen. On the street was master builder, Daniel Hand, Jr. His neighbors were blacksmiths, cobblers, tinsmiths, cabinet makers, tailors, and coffin makers.

Court House was challenged in 1848 as the county seat by Dennisville and Goshen, and a referendum was held on the issue. When the votes were counted, Cape May Court House had won by forty-five votes more than the combined total of its rivals.

The first train arrived at Court House in 1863.

Activities to celebrate the event included firing Long Tom, the twelve-foot cannon that had seen service protecting Cape May County in the Revolution and the War of 1812, as the train arrived. The cannon exploded on firing. Operating the ramrod were Clint Hewitt, who was severely wounded, and Charlie Crawford, who lost an eye. They survived, but Long Tom did not. The legendary cannon disappeared soon thereafter and has not been recovered.

Two burglars, in the course of their night's occupation at Yourison's store on Mechanic Street early on Washington's birthday in 1903, started a fire that reduced twenty-two buildings to ashes in the heart of the business district. Lost were The Gazette Building, Yourison's Hardware Store, Douglass' Brothers Law Office, the 1774 Courthouse Building that had been moved from its original site, Foster's Grocery, Mrs. R. R. Sharp's Dry Goods Store, and two hotels, as well as other buildings. Court House quickly rebuilt after the disaster.

The current courthouse on Main Street was built in 1927. Before acquiring the John Holmes house on Shore Road to house its collection, the Cape May County Historical Society's museum occupied the basement of the building. The Cape May County Art League presented regular exhibits in the courthouse before moving to the Physick estate in Cape May. The county offices have expanded into a complex of buildings on Main Street and Mechanic Street. The excellent county library is a part of this complex.

Cape May Court House has grown gradually over the years, never having decreased in size as have many other older settlements in the county. The old courthouse, the Surrogate's Building, and many picturesque homes flank the tree-lined streets. Shopping centers and businesses have grown up on the fringes of the town and added just a tinge of hustle to the quiet town.

*The Bellevue Hotel, built on the Main Street site of the old Union Hotel that burned in the 1905 fire. This is the same location where Daniel Hand first opened his publick house in 1764.*
*Courtesy of Harry N. Merz collection through Dr. John Siliquini*

Cape May County has had several jails throughout its history. The first was built in 1764 and burned down ten years later; it was immediately rebuilt according to one account of that time. There is no clear record of the jailhouse history until the one built in 1868, shown above. Obviously, there weren't too many criminal types around then. Some time in 1894, a newer jail and sheriff's office was built facing on Main Street (below). The first hanging in the county took place in the adjacent courthouse yard, when Richard Pierce was executed on February 19, 1894, for killing his wife. The jail was moved back from Main Street to make room for the new county office building in 1927, and was finally torn down. The current and modern jail, built in 1976, is located in the Crest Haven complex, east of the Garden State Parkway. Courtesy of: above—Jane Dixon, below—Maria C. Bechtold

*The county building complex shown here in this late 1880s photo includes the jail (left); the sheriff's office (center left); the surrogate's office, built in 1885 (center right); and the stately courthouse (far right). The fledgling politicians posing in front of the jail are unidentified.*
*Courtesy of Cape May County Historical Museum*

*Samuel Buck house (right) on Mechanic Street dates to 1790. John Paul Jones, "Father of the American Navy," is reputed to have lived here for nearly two years, beginning in 1773, when he fled to America to escape a murder charge in England. There is no verifiable record of his whereabouts for over twenty months, and it is suspected that he may have been in Cape May Court House. His name was actually John Paul to which he apparently added the common "Jones" to escape detection. The Buck house originally had a dirt floor, and access to the second floor was by ladder. There is a wealth of handcrafted woodwork which has been painstakingly restored. The Jonathon Fifield house (left), was built in 1820. With the exception of entirely different treatments in the windows, the architectural style of the two houses is almost identical.*
*Photograph by Vance Enck*

*Jonathan Hand's law office, on Main Street just north of Mechanics Street, was built in 1801, when Hand was twenty-one years old. Jonathan, in addition to being a lawyer, was captain in the Cape May Militia during the War of 1812 and county clerk from 1831-1834. Perhaps his greatest achievement was convincing the beautiful Sarah Moore Wilson to become his bride. Sarah, at the age of twelve, was one of the thirteen girls who spread flowers along the path of George Washington as he passed through Trenton in 1789, on his way to taking office as the new republic's first president. The flower event was memorialized in a painting which is widely copied. Jonathan and Sarah's home can be seen through the porch posts of the office. The house, built in 1803 after their marriage, includes cedar floors, unusual "9 over 6 windows" and an elegant staircase.
Photograph by Vance Enck*

*The stately courthouse (center) was built during the summer of 1848 through early 1849 by Daniel Hand for a total cost of $6,284.33. Hand's father had given the one-acre plot of land to the county in 1764 and the county administration buildings were erected here. Dedicated on March 1, 1849, this new building served as the center of county government until 1927 when the current offices were built. This "Christopher Wren" style building is still used for special functions, including theatre productions in recent years. To the right is the First Methodist Episcopal Church built in 1854-55, also by Daniel Hand, for a cost of $2,700. The brick building to the left, built in 1885, housed both the surrogate's office and the clerk's office with separate adjacent doorways. The building is still used for county offices.
Photographed by Vance Enck*

*The courtroom (below) in the interior of the 1848 courthouse. A local theatre group recently presented "Witness for the Prosecution" here. A staging of the signing of the U. S. Constitution was staged here during the bicentennial of that event in 1987. Gabriel Holmes, pictured here, (above) was the last "court crier" for the county court. His chair is on display in the Cape May County Historical Museum. Courtesy of Cape May County Historical Museum*

*Springer's Union Hotel stood at the corner of Main and Mechanic streets. Its dining room, extending the entire length of the hotel, was a favorite of local residents. Hidden by the Bennett's Livery hack is the office of the Court House Light, Heat and Power Company, which occupied part of that end of the hotel. The building was moved to the Ludlam farm on Stone Harbor Road, apparently to make room for the First National Bank building. The local office of the Title Company of Jersey is currently housed in the building.
Courtesy of Jane Dixon*

*The* Cape May County Gazette *staff posed for this family portrait in the 1880s (right). The* Gazette *was founded by Alfred Cooper in 1880. Burton J. Smith and Dexter D. Burns acquired the paper from Cooper in 1927. The* Gazette *merged with the* Wildwood Leader *in 1976 to become today's* Gazette Leader. *The building shown here burned in a disastrous fire on Washington's birthday in 1905. The* Gazette's *records and files were saved, but the printing equipment was lost. The new Gazette Building is shown at the left in the 1910 photo below. It currently houses the Cape May County bureau of Atlantic City's* The Press. *The* Gazette *offices have moved to North Wildwood.
Courtesy of above—Cape May County Historical Museum, below—Jane Dixon*

*Even though it is not painted yellow and has no flashing lights, this is a school bus—circa 1911—pictured in front of the Court House High School. The side flaps, even though heavy duty canvas, do not generate much confidence for protection on rainy or snowy days. We wonder if this was a clever class photo for the senior "annual," or did the seniors pose before embarking on their class trip?*
*Courtesy of Cornelia Corson Brown*

*Glass-making was, at one time, a flourishing industry in Court House. The Cape May Glass Works plant (top) was built on 4th Avenue at the railroad in 1901 by Leander Taylor and Harry Stites. A more modern plant, the Hereford Glass Company (center), was built just a block away at Hereford and the railroad in 1908. The two companies had merged prior to the outbreak of World War I. The plants produced standard milk bottles and specialty bottles, as well as numerous other unique glass items. Illustrating some very practical uses in the company's products in this 1919 photo (bottom) are Paul Ambrose, far left, and Claude Long, left foreground. The other Market researchers apparently chose to remain anonymous. In 1968 the remains of the plant were totally destroyed by arson.*
*Courtesy of Museum of American Glass at Wheaton Village*

*Woodrow Wilson, then governor of New Jersey, came to Cape May County to open the Stone Harbor Ocean Parkway on July 4, 1911. Wilson went on to visit Green Creek and Cape May City. He proved his political savvy by telling complaining petitioners they needed better representation in the state legislature, which resulted in Democratic victories, for one term at least, breaking the Republican stranglehold on Cape May County's delegation in Trenton. Note the banner over Mechanic Street: "Court House-Stone Harbor." Promoters of Stone Harbor development shrewdly tied their whole pitch very closely to Court House for prestige and political clout. It worked.*
*Courtesy of Jane Dixon*

## BURLEIGH

Gravelly Run, as Burleigh was originally called, was located on a much-used Indian trace. It was here the reputed gathering of the Lenni-Lenapes was held in 1735 that ended in the decision to leave the area. King Nummy, the last king, decided not to lead the migration. He stayed behind to care for the children of his sister, Snowflower.

Shamgar Hand and the Cresse family owned large plantations in the area.

Deborah Corsey was named postmistress when Burleigh's post office opened in 1886.

*Downtown Burleigh on March 2, 1908. In the foreground is the Methodist church which is today the Good Faith Fellowship Chapel that can be seen from the Garden State Parkway. The store in the distance on the right side of the road was the general store and post office. The sand road is Seashore Road, today's Route 9. Note the hand-hewn rail fence and the telephone lines, a recent addition to the landscape at the time of this picture. Obviously, automobiles were still pretty rare, judging from the narrow wagon tracks in the road. Courtesy of H. Gerald MacDonald*

*Burleigh's business district in 1908 was the general store and the post office. The proud owners and postmaster are standing in the center of their enticing display of local produce, a washboard, lantern, and what may have been wash boilers still in the crate. The overhead sign on the left touts "Butterworth's White Liniment," a popular nostrum of the day.*
*Courtesy of H. Gerald MacDonald*

*Burleigh's public school, shown here around 1900, has since been demolished. The grass has been cut, as the site pictured here is now part of the Wildwood golf course, which sits across the Garden State Parkway, opposite the rest of Burleigh today.*
*Courtesy of Cape May County Historical Museum*

## RIO GRANDE

The earliest roads, King's Highway (Shore Road) from Tuckahoe to Cold Spring and the road south from Dennisville and Goshen (Delsea Drive), intersected at what is now Rio Grande. The Aaron, Leaming, Hildreth, and Cresse plantations covered the area. Early names for the settlement were Leaming's, for their land holdings at the site, and Hildreth's for their enterprises in the area. The name Rio Grande (often pronounced "Rye-o Grande," locally) was chosen because a name was needed for the post office opened in 1849. The seventh Aaron Leaming especially liked the name of the Texas river, and it was adopted.

As a major stop on the stagecoach routes, Rio Grande developed naturally. The town's greatest growth, however, started with the coming of the railroads in 1863. Rio Station was the last stop in the 1880s for passengers bound for the new resorts developing in Five Mile Beach (Holly Beach and the Wildwoods). Arrivals were taken by the Hildreth's stagecoach from Rio Grande across the meadows and then by sailboat to the Five Mile Beach Island.

Mill Pond, along Delsea Drive where the Wildwood Pumping Station is now located, was the site of one of the three covered bridges in Cape May County. This bridge crossed the dam which held the pond created for Joseph Hand's sawmill. There were also cranberry bogs adjacent to the pond.

The pumping station, on the site of the old sawmill, was built in 1912 and serves Wildwood's water needs via two pipelines across the meadows. The second water line runs under the Village Shoppes of Rio Grande on Route 47, formerly the old sugar company property.

"Penuel," the first church in Cape May County, was built by the Baptists on the Leaming plantation in 1714. It served as the Baptist church until replaced by a new building constructed in Cape May Court House in 1743. The original church was purchased by the county freeholders for use as a court house.

Rio Grande is one of the few inland areas that has steadily grown. Today, shopping malls, businesses, and residential developments are prevalent in the area.

*The corner of Wildwood Road and Seashore roads (above) looking east towards Wildwood, circa 1925. The brick pillars, topped by white globe lights, were signals to alert drivers of the turn-off for Wildwood. These landmarks have since disappeared. The area on the left was the site of the Rio Grande Sugar Company plant. It was developed as Marlyn Manor in the late 1940s and is now Village Shoppes shopping center. Looking west on Green Creek road (below), now Route 47, circa 1920. The road is now four lanes in this area. Rio Mall has replaced the buildings on the left. A filling station and the Rio Grande fire station are in the area of the vacant field to the right. Grange Hall, with the small tower, on the right was torn down to make way for businesses that have been built along the road. Farther west, Joseph Hand's cranberry bog was on the site now occupied by Menz's famous and sprawling restaurant. The car, four pedestrians, and a walkway on only one side of the road certainly provide the flavor of the times. Courtesy of H. Gerald MacDonald*

*Sweet plans for an industrial base in the county prompted the state legislature to offer a bounty of one cent a pound for cane sugar and one dollar a ton for the cane. John Hilgerth's and Sons of Philadelphia built the sixty-thousand dollar building (a princely sum in those days) for processing cane grown on the surrounding one thousand, five hundred acre farm. Operations began at the sugar mill on September 21, 1881. In the first year, the plant processed 319,000 pounds of sugar but the yield of only five tons per acre was economically disappointing. Rio Grand Sugar Company replaced the Hilgerth's and Henry Hughes became manager. Sugar was not harvested from the cane by the usual method of pressing with heavy rollers. Rather, it was removed by steaming the cane and slaked lime in the large vats. The smelly, sticky juice was then distilled to produce cane sugar. A narrow gauge railroad was built covering all areas of the property for horse and mule drawn cars to bring in cane from the field and return the processed cane to*

*the fields for fertilizer. Parts of the roadbed can still be seen in the area. Seeds from the cane were hauled to "pig island" on the farm to feed the one thousand hogs. Proving not to be too smart an enterprise, the legislature dropped the bounty in 1890, and the mill closed.*
*Courtesy of Cape May County Historical Museum*

*"Ye Old Mill," a logging mill on Mill Pond, operated for several years processing logs from nearby forests. This same site is now occupied by the Wildwood Pumping Station.*
*Courtesy of Wildwood Historical Museum*

## DIAS CREEK, REEDS BEACH, PIERCES POINT, KIMBLES BEACH, HIGH BEACH, AND DEL HAVEN

This area along the Delaware River bank was traveled by the Indians and there is evidence of several traces and campgrounds in the area. Route 47 follows one of the main Lenape paths.

Dias Creek was on one of the main stagecoach routes from Philadelphia, and was designated as one of the major settlements in Cape May in an 1828 article in Bridgeton's *West Jersey Observer*. The name Dias Creek was established when the post office was opened in 1824. The name "Dyers Creek" appears on maps as late as 1878. The origin of Dyer and Dias is unknown. There is some speculation that dye colors dumped in the creek by one of the fulling mills, used by early settlers to prepare cloth for making their clothing, gave rise to the name.

Reed's Beach was a favorite landing place for British raiding parties during the Revolution and the War of 1812 as they sought water and slaughtered cattle roaming the area. "Quaker guns" placed along the shoreline finally dissuaded the British from further forays later in the War of 1812.

During World War I, Bethlehem Steel located a shell testing plant near the beach. A miniature railroad was built for railcars carrying cannon to test-fire shells. After the war, the plant's frame buildings became the first houses on the beach.

The road to Reed's Beach was built by Grand Reed, who also built the first houses in the area. His oldest daughter, Belle, married Harry Erricson, who operated a bait shop and grocery store. Belle also taught piano and provided music for silent films at the Cape May Court House movie house. In the 1920s and 1930s, charter fishing boats operated from a temporary pier at Reed's Beach each spring. The boats were filled with eager anglers bused from the Court House train station. There were over one hundred homes at one time. Hurricane Gloria destroyed many of them.

Local residents, for many years, gathered horseshoe crabs off the beaches during the spring egg-laying season as grist for a crab factory just south of Pierces Point.

Today, the area is sparsely populated. Reed's Beach, Pierces Point, Kimbles Bach, and High Beach are small summer cottage colonies. Del Haven, the southernmost part of the township, is a recently developed town of year-round homes and summer cottages.

## GOSHEN

The first Aaron Leaming (there were at least nine) was Goshen's first settler. He began raising cattle in the area in 1693. By 1710 there was a settlement with a cluster of houses. Located on Delsea Drive, it was an early stagecoach stop on the Philadelphia-Cape May route.

Goshen's first industry was a king crab mill that ground those strange creatures into fertilizer. Workers relaxed at the end of the day by congregating at Smith's General Store to play their accordians and snack on cheese and crackers. Goshen's "Boardwalk," across the street

*Smith's General Store in Goshen was apparently a favorite "posing place" for snapshots during the summer of 1917. The store was always a busy place; not just because it was the general store, but also because it was the post office from 1909 until the winter of 1922 when it burned. A new store, on the same site, continued to serve as the post office until 1949. The all-male picture (left) is a Smith family portrait. The large man in the white shirt on the porch is Nelson Smith, postmaster from 1909 to 1949. Harry Smith, Nelson's son, is seated on the steps to the left. The dignified gentleman with the skimmer (which assures us that the photograph was snapped between Memorial Day and Labor Day) is Griffin Smith, the patriarch of the Smith family, who served as Goshen's postmaster from 1865 to 1870. In the picture above right, Everett Smith is on the bicycle. There was chauvinism even then, no doubt. Note the absence of adult males in the female portrait and no females in the male photograph. And what about the sharp contrast in vehicles?
Courtesy of Rebecca Smith Vallelay*

from *the* store, extended fifty feet along a ditch and offered added people-watching diversions.

William L. Stevens built a can house for canning tomatoes that employed thirty-five to forty workers. Tomato skinning alone involved eighteen to twenty workers. That plant operated until about 1908-1910 and closed.

Goshen's greatest fame came from the shipbuilding and lumbering industries that flourished there for most of the nineteenth century. One of the first ships built there, a fifty-seven-foot, 130-ton sloop, was advertised for sale in an 1815 Philadelphia newspaper. The first continuously operating shipyard was started by William F. Garrison, Jr., in the later 1850s. The *John F. Wainwright*, the first ship constructed at the Goshen shipyards, was launched sideways into Goshen Creek in 1859. Sideways launching was a standard practice due to the narrowness of the creek. Between 1859 and 1898, twenty-six ships were built on the "two stocks" at Garrison shipyard. The ships built there were fashioned from the plentiful local stocks of oak and cedar timbers. Lumber used for the ships was chosen "on the stump," meaning that standing trees were selected while still growing, cut and placed in the shipyard to season before becoming part of the vessel.

The advent of steam-driven iron ships finally closed-down Cape May County's shipbuilding industry around 1900. The Goshen Landing shipyards launched their last ship, the *Diamond*, in 1898.

The fifth post office in the county was opened here in 1818, with Richard Thompson, Jr., named as postmaster.

Goshen was in the running to become the county seat for Cape May County on a referendum in 1848, but lost out to Cape May Court House which already held the title.

Goshen has been "graced" from its earliest days. John Grace enlisted in the Continental Army on June 17, 1777, and was discharged June 5, 1783, after fighting at Brandywine, Monmouth, Bennington, and Yorktown. He was a highly trusted scout of General Washington and General Gates. A monument to him stands in the Union Cemetery in South Dennis.

Eugene Clifford Grace, son of another Grace—John W. and his wife, Rebecca—was born on August 27, 1876. The proud parents operated Grace's General Store. Eugene Grace, in true Horatio Alger fashion, went on to be elected president of Bethlehem Steel on April 1, 1913. He held this post until 1946 and continued as chairman of the board until his death on July 25, 1960. The family homestead was given to the Methodist church as a parsonage and still stands.

The once bustling shipbuilding and lumbering activities have vanished almost without a trace. Goshen is today a very pleasant rural community on Delsea Drive. The gracious old homes and rich history are seldom acknowledged in today's rush to the shore.

*Goshen's future, its teenagers, about 1910-1915, in their Sunday Best. Posing for a casual photo are: (standing) Leander Corson, Wesley Grace, Jr., and Eugene Hays; (seated) Bessie Grace, Jame A. Smith, and Rene Schull. This souvenir photo offers a capsule study of dress during the early years of the century.*
*Courtesy of Rebecca Smith Vallelay*

*A younger version of Goshen's future, taken about the same time as the above photo, include: (standing) Hettie Townsend, Ethel Grace, Julia Champion, Grace Wyott, and Allie Hays; (on the ground—chivalry was still alive) Charles Stillwell, Samuel Warthman, Monroe Townsend, and Eugene Grace (who later became president and chairman of Bethlehem Steel).*
*Courtesy of Rebecca Smith Vallelay*

*Cord wood for shipment on the way to Goshen Landing, via Delsea Drive, about one mile from Goshen. The three wagons in this picture are being driven by William High on the first wagon, Billy Garrison on the second, and Billy's sons, Jake and Jay, on the third.*
*Courtesy of Rebecca Smith Vallelay*

*Shipping was a major Goshen industry. The December 19, 1885,* Gazette *reported twenty vessels tied-up at Goshen docks, including twelve schooners and eight sloops. Pictured here in the late 1800s are* Hattie *and* Uncle Dan. *The latter was owned by John Grace. These boats carried as much as forty cords of wood—all of which was loaded from little wheelbarrows.*
*Courtesy of Rebecca Smith Vallelay*

*A major Cape May County highway was Delsea Drive, as pictured here going through the heart of Goshen. However, the dog lying in the middle of the road does cause some doubt about the amount of traffic. This photograph captures the flavor of the early 1900's mainstream of the county. Especially, note the picket fences and dirt walkways along the dirt roadway.*
*Courtesy of Robert E. Clarke*

*St. Elizabeth's Catholic Church is the oldest Catholic church building in the county, but not the oldest parish (Cape Island holds that honor). The structure was erected before 1810 as the Port Elizabeth Academy in Cumberland County. The building was sold on February 25, 1843 to Thomas Marshall for $111.00 to become a Catholic church, basically for the glass plant workers. When the workers left the area, the church stood empty for some time. In 1878 Father Dwyer determined to move the church to Goshen where it was needed. The peg construction permitted disassembling the building. The parts were loaded onto Capt. Augustus J. Meerwald's ship,* Liffy, *and floated down the Maurice River and Delaware Bay and then up the Dennis Creek to South Dennis where wagons accepted the load and completed the trip to Goshen. The first mass was held on September 10, 1879. Additions and changes over the years have not altered the basic structure.*
*1988 photograph by Vance Enck*

*Goshen public school "upstairs class," October 1913. The two-story school divided the pupils into two groups, with the "lower pupils," grades one through four, on the first floor, and the "big kids," grades five through eight, were the "upper pupils" on the second floor. Neatly dressed for their annual photo (and more recently numbered), are: 1-Perry Christian, 2-Bertram James, 3-Sarah Peterson, 4-William Goslin, 5-Lester Davis, 6-Mable Bright, 7-F. W. James (teacher), 8-Rita Shaw, 9-Marrie Batt, 10-William Fozer, 11-Everett Smith, 12-Pearl Kirdhide, 13-Florence Erickson, 14-Albert Massy, 15-Jane Smith, 16-Stanley Watson, 17-Radcliff Massy. The unnumbered young man to the far right is unknown.*
*Courtesy of Rebecca Smith Vallelay*

## WHITESBORO

Two towns have been established in Cape May County to attract and provide a settlement for specific groups of people. Whitesboro for "colored people" is one, and Woodbine for Jewish refugees is the other.

George White, a black congressman from North Carolina, served two terms in the House of Representatives, 1897-1901. He settled in Washington, D.C., but he developed White's (as the town was originally called), a settlement in the North where more opportunities were available for his former neighbors from Whiteville, North Carolina. The land was originally part of the Cresse plantation.

Congressman White acquired seventeen hundred acres for his community. Attracting black settlers was a slow process, complicated by the failure to attract businesses that would provide job opportunities.

The first settlers were the Henry Spauldings. Noah Cherry and "General" Askew were early settlers. Both Cherry and Askew were Civil War veterans and friends of Congressman White. Cherry saw duty in Sherman's March to the Sea. They cleared lots for settlers and sold the wood for use in Philadelphia. Both were buried in the Whitesboro Cemetery which had to be relocated for the Garden State Parkway. Their graves, however, were not disturbed and may be seen from the southbound lanes of the Parkway.

*George Henry White (1852-1918) was a native North Carolinian and the last of the black leaders who emerged during the Reconstruction Era after the Civil War. After holding several state posts, he was elected to Congress in 1896 and served two terms. He was defeated in 1900 in his bid for a third term. White was the last black to serve as a member of Congress until 1928. It was during his tenure in the nation's capitol that he became interested in establishing a black community to capitalize on the economic advantages available in the North. He chose Cape May County's Middle Township to seek fulfillment of his dreams. The town he founded was first called Whites, and later named Whitesboro. He convinced some settlers to move to the area and a number of wealthy colored people to resort to Cape May. Unable to persuade enterprises to utilize the many advantages of the area, George White's dream community failed to fully materialize. It has, however, continued as a functioning community with a great sense of pride in its heritage.*
*Courtesy of Ernestine Ross Brown*

*Henry Spaulding, his wife, Hattie, and son, Theodore, were the first family to settle in Whitesboro. Henry was appointed in 1900 by George White to be the administrator and charged him with the responsibility of developing the new community. Theodore went on to become the first black judge on the Pennsylvania Superior Court bench.*
*Courtesy of Ernestine Ross Brown*

*Participants in a 1960s Free Ancient and Accepted Masons Lodge Installation Ceremony gathered for their formal portrait on the steps of the First Christ Church in Whitesboro.*
*Courtesy of Ernestine Ross Brown*

# LOWER TOWNSHIP

Lower Township is the smallest of the four townships in the county, with just under thirty square miles of area. It encompasses only about five percent of the total area in the county. However, it has the highest population and therefore, the greatest density of residents of any incorporated area of the county. With Upper Township, it ranks among the top of the fastest growing areas of the state.

Town Bank, the county's first settlement, was located here. Dr. Coxe, the first owner of the county, and his successors, the West Jersey Company, were headquartered here.

In addition to whaling, a number of industries, mostly homespun, flourished here. Capt. Richard Downs operated a fulling mill on the appropriately named Fulling Mill Creek. For nearly a century the mill prepared and dyed the cloth used by residents for making their clothing and household items. Downs died in 1747 and the mill gradually disintegrated. Pens used to hide cattle from hungry British marauders during the War of 1812 were also located near this site. That area is now partly paved over by the runways of the county airport at Erma. WPA workers found parts of the fulling mill foundation while creating a firebreak.

Salt was manufactured by boiling water from the Delaware Bay in large iron vats near the area on the bay where the Cape May Canal is now located. These manufacturing plants were favorite targets of the British in the two wars of independence.

Angry at the tolls exacted for using the county's first highway, King's Road, settlers built a parallel free road from Cape Island to Cape May Court House and named it "Shunpike." It is now in two sections because the canal cuts aross it. Both sections are still in active use.

*Running from Cape May Court House to Cape May City, Shunpike was built by John Tomlin of Goshen and neighbors in Middle Township, who had much hay, wood, and produce to sell in Cape May and did not want to add tolls to their marketing costs. There were despised tollhouses on Kings's Highway at Burleigh and Cold Spring at the location of the Old Brick Church. A tale is told of a drover who disclaimed any ownership of six mules that seemed to be following him and his horse. Once through the gate, a whinny from the horse prompted the "orphan" mules to leap the gate and continue their quest for a home.
Photograph by Vance Enck*

Higbee Beach played a prominent role in the early history of the county. One branch of New England Creek emptied into the bay where the canal is now located. A deep "hole" in the bay offered an excellent mooring site, at first for whaling fleets and later for sloops that carried wood, cut by farmers eager to clear their land, to Philadelphians desirous of warming their homes. Still later the first passenger ships from Philadelphia used a dock operated by Joseph S. Higbee, who also operated the Hermitage, an inn at the site. Higbee acquired the land in 1823.

The steamboat landing was later moved south to the end of Sunset Boulevard, where the concrete ship now stands vigil.

The Cresse plantation stretched along much of the bay side of the township. The landholdings were split up over the years. The Newtons acquired part of the land in the Town Bank area. The first blacksmith shop in the area, operated by Edward Price, stood on the Newton property from the 1780s until Price's death in 1825. His son continued the business for several years. One of the last tracts of the Cresse plantation was sold by the heirs of Eliza Stites Cresse in 1868 to Dr. Emlen Physick of Cape May and to the operators of Rio Grande Sugar Cane Company.

Farther to the east of this tract, a 250-acre tract of land, located at the present starting point of the Garden State Parkway was acquired by Caleb Carman, Jr. Built on this land was the county's first gristmill, powered by the tidal water flow. The land came into the hands of the Schellenger family who operated the mill for many years. Ultimately, Henry Ford assembled a twelve-hundred-acre farm tract in the area, which included the Carman tract and, with it, the mill site. Camp Wissahickon, a World War I naval training station, was located on this land. Today a housing development, Tranquility Park, occupies much of this land north of the canal which cuts through the original tract.

*Higbee's Hotel, as depicted by local artist Johanna Ridpath, before it was demolished in the 1940s. The hotel contained forty-four rooms and served the early steamboat landing when it was located at Higbee's Beach. One of the sections is reported to have been William Penn's home, built during his two-year stay in the area, and later moved here by George Stillwell. The hotel was originally operated by Joseph S. Higbee, who first named it the Hermitage. The building was last used as a private home during the Depression.*
*Painting by Johanna Ridpath courtesy of Burnice Wilson Palmer*

*The serious business of learning how "to tie the knot" was not a bachelors' party for prospective bridegrooms, but an essential part of the training for future crews of sub-tenders, mine-sweepers and destroyers. Approximately five hundred sailors a month were inducted here and over three thousand were trained in basic naval skills. Camp Wissahickon, located on the old (Henry L.) Ford farm, was built in 1917 as a naval training station during World War I. The training center was located where Route 109 today joins with the Garden State Parkway at mile post "0." After the war, the base was closed and much of the lumber from the barracks and other buildings was recycled for the local building boom that followed the war.*
*Courtesy of Virginia Walsh*

Still farther east, adjacent to the Ford tract, now on the ocean side of the Parkway, was situated the large holdings of Christopher Leaming, a cooper for the whaling industry. His land included all of the areas of the present Coast Guard base and East Cape May and the Diamond Beach area. The first Cape May "diamond," a very large stone, found, polished, and revered by the Kechemeches, was given to Lenni-Lenape King Nummy as a symbol of fealty; he, in turn, gave it as a gift to Christopher Leaming. It was diamond-cut in Antwerp and remains a prized heirloom of the Leaming descendants.

In 1942 the federal government dug the Cape May Canal to connect the Inland Waterway, extending along the New Jersey Atlantic shore, with the Delaware Bay. Work on the canal was pushed "emergency full-speed ahead" shortly after World War II started. The completed canal provided a quick route to the Delaware Bay for Coast Guard and Navy anti-submarine surface vessels required because of the intense U-boat activity at the Delaware Bay entrance. A vital added plus is that this route avoids the very dangerous "rips" at Cape May Point where the Delaware Bay and the Atlantic Ocean currents collide.

The Inland Waterway along the Jersey Shore now traverses the canal to the Delaware Bay then north fifty-five miles to connect with the Chesapeake, Delaware, and on to the Chesapeake Bay.

The Cape May Canal cuts a swath across the Cape that truly keeps Cape May City an island community. The canal was originally nicknamed "Scotty's Ditch" after Senator Scott who strongly campaigned for its creation.

The emergence of Cape Island and Cold Springs as tourist attractions in the early 1800s brought about the rapid and solid development of Lower Township. With the opening of the barrier island Wildwood communities by the arrival of the railroads, Lower Township's future was assured.

Numerous housing developments, shopping centers, and business areas permeate the township. However, much of the township is still devoted to wildlife areas; among these are the Higbee Beach Conservation Area and the Cape May Point State Park, as well as the wetland areas along the ocean side.

The incorporated area of Lower Township includes the settlements of Villas, Rio Grande, North Cape May, Fishing Creek, Diamond Beach, and Erma. Incorporated areas of Cape May Point, West Cape May, Cape May, Wildwood Crest, Wildwood, North Wildwood, and West Wildwood have been carved out of Lower Township, but are so much of the same economic, geographic, and social fabric that it is difficult to treat them separately. However, there are important differences that distinguish each area.

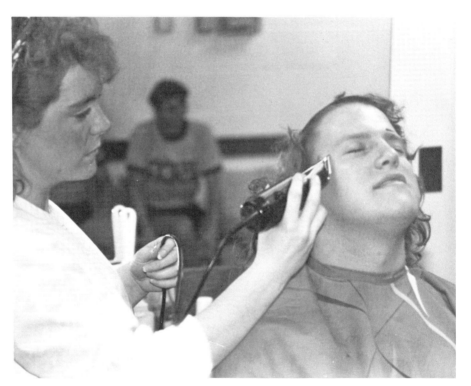

*He will certainly remember Cape May. One of the first steps, on his way to being a Coast Guard Sampson, is becoming lightheaded at the hands of this present-day Delilah. The only Coast Guard recruit training center in the country is located at Cold Spring Harbor, just outside Cape May. The base is also home for the Coast Guard cutter fleet and an airborne search and rescue fleet, whose helicopters provide constant reassurance to bathers on cape beaches and boaters along the coast. Courtesy of the United States Coast Guard*

*Proposals for a canal route across Cape May County were considered as early as 1808. Work finally started in 1942, after the sinking of a destroyer, the* USS Jacob Jones, *and two tankers,* Indian Arrow *and* Evening Star, *off the coast of Cape May by German U-boats. Work on the four-mile long, one hundred-foot wide and twelve-foot deep canal was completed by March 1943. The new waterway, in addition to giving new meaning to the old name "Cape Island," opened a faster route between the ocean and the bay that avoided the very dangerous "rips" at the entrance of the bay and added an important link to the Inland Waterway. The canal is busy with commercial and pleasure craft and is regularly patrolled by Coast Guard cutters.*
*Photograph by Vance Enck*

*A sign of the explosive growth in Lower Township is this condominium and apartment complex going up in the Diamond Beach area, between Wildwood Crest and the Coast Guard Electronic Center. The pace of growth has placed the township as the third fastest growing area in New Jersey.*
*Photograph by Vance Enck*

*Cold Spring Chapel, built in 1884, was originally built near the intersection of Old Shore Road and Jonathon Hoffman Road. The Cape May Canal, built in 1942, ran through the old site, so the chapel was moved to a lot on Jonathon Hoffman Road. The Mormon Church purchased the building in June 1979 and still hold services here.*
*Photograph by Vance Enck*

*Diamond Beach Racetrack, at Town Bank, opened in the summer of 1867. Trotting races were featured on the mile-long track. Although not quite as elegant as England's Ascot, Diamond Beach was a fashionable gathering place for visitors for several decades. This photo was taken circa 1912. Note the latest dress styles and parasols. Even though they were resorting at a beach area, suntans were not in vogue. The dejected horse in the lower left obviously would rather have been on the track and not in work harness.*
*Courtesy of Cape May County Historical Museum*

*An 1894 picture of the Free Masons Hall in Cold Spring. The Patriotic Order of the Sons of America also met here. The building became part of the Lower Township Municipal Building. In 1986 it was moved to Historic Cold Spring Village to become the county's maritime museum.*
*Courtesy of Eleanor Callaghan*

*Volunteer fire departments from the county battle for the championship in the annual waterball contest. The object is to get the ball across the opposing teams' goal line, using high-pressure hoses—no hands are allowed. There isn't a dry eye in the lot at the awards ceremony.*
*Photograph by Herb Beitel*

*Grave visiting was a revered tradition in Victorian times. On occasion, chairs would be brought to make extended stays more comfortable. This picture, circa 1890, shows (left to right) Isabel Miller Matthews, Ellen Cresse Hand, Clinton Hand, and Ocie B. Eldredge at the Jacob Spicer family cemetery on the Spicer homestead grounds. Sandman Boulevard (Ferry Road) now covers the ground of this family plot. The headstones were reproduced and stand in Cold Spring Old Brick church cemetery.*
*Courtesy of Cape May County Historical Museum*

*For a half century, Gus Yearick's topiary garden, on Fishing Creek Road, cut a unique niche in Cape May County attractions. The clipper ship (center), featured in a 1930s* National Geographic *magazine, started the garden. The Statue of Liberty, behind the ship, was the next step in creating a miniature New York Harbor. Gus expanded the garden to include a little league team, a major league team, with Babe Ruth at bat and a ball in the air, a peacock with a tree for its tail, animals, and Santa Claus, among numerous other sculptures. An example of pure topiary art, all parts were fashioned from bushes and hedges without the use of chicken wire or artificial forms. The garden, unfortunately, lost its form in 1987, shortly before Mr. Yearick's death.*
*Courtesy of Barbara Petrucelli*

## ERMA

The first settlement to develop away from Town Bank, as the whaling industry declined, was the nearby Erma. Richard Swain founded the enclave in the early 1700s. The Swains were prolific and their numbers prompted the cluster of homes to be called Swainton. This is not to be confused with the present Swainton, located in Middle Township. Richard built the first house in the area, and it remained in use until it was torn down in 1931.

Erma became the official name when a post office opened in 1893. Reuben Johson chose the name Erma to honor Erma Bennett who married Swain Ludlam. Whether unrequited love or just good friends, we do not know.

The first school classes in 1802 were held in a building on Tabernacle Road, moved from Cape May Point. The site was purchased by Matthew Whilden. Tuition was three dollars per quarter.

Cape May-Millville Railroad tracks were laid through Erma. John Bennett's store, on Seashore Road, stood near the rail crossing and the station was named after him. The name Bennett's Station still appears on maps.

Also bearing the name is Bennett's Bog, today a wildlife sanctuary owned by the New Jersey Audubon Society. The preserve consists of three bogs on either side of Shunpike, connected by an artificial ditch. Endemic to the preserve are a number of southern plants which are not extant anywhere else in New Jersey.

Reuben's Thorofare, running through the nearby meadows, was named after young Reuben Swain, who died in the 1813 epidemic. In earlier days, it was a shipping point for local lumber cut to clear farmlands and much in demand for fuel in Philadelphia and other cities.

The first telephone company in Lower Township was located in Erma. It was formed by Luther Ingersoll, a returning Spanish-American War veteran, who, with local businessmen, organized the Citizens Local Telephone Company using Stromberg-Carlson equipment and wires strung from Cold Spring to Woodbine, with tie-ins to Keystone Telephone Company and Delaware and Atlantic Company to carry long distance calls. The company flourished for ten years until a disastrous nor'easter of near hurricane force "blew them into the water," crippling the system. Keystone Telephone Company took over Citizens and refloated the telephone system's operations.

Today, Erma is a quiet area, interrupted only by the sound of airplanes landing and taking-off at the Cape May County Airport, with a number of new homes dotting the landscape, reflecting the general growth of the township.

*Reuben Johnson's store at Bennett's Crossing. The dapper gentleman, fourth from the left, is Reuben Johnson himself. Next to him is Edna Weeks, niece of Augustus Swain, and to her right in the center of the three men is Augustus H. Swain, son-in-law of Reuben Johnson. The horse is unidentified, as are the other members of the group. The picture is believed to be in 1898 or 1899, after the 1898 opening of the Erma post office. Courtesy of Cape May County Historical Museum*

## COLD SPRING

Cold Spring—and it is singular, not plural—appears by name in county records as early as 1688. The spring itself bubbled clear, fresh water up through the salt marsh.

First discovered by the Indians who camped in the area, the delights of the refreshing waters were passed on to the early settlers. The spring became a mecca for visitors as early as 1700. As more and more people resorted to Cape Island, an excursion by horse and buggy over the "good road" to savor the therapeutic waters was a fashionable ritual. Cool spring water was retrieved by lowering a corked bottle into the spring, then pulling the cork out allowing the bottle to fill with the fresh water. A shed with a bar was soon constructed nearby. The bar did, indeed, dispense "fire water" to contaminate or enhance, depending on the point of view, the natural libation. A gazebo was built over the spring in the 1800s to replace the previous barrel that marked the fountain.

Cold Spring Hotel was built in 1828 about halfway between Cold Spring and Cape Island. A tenpin alley stood nearby, where Thomas B. Schellenger, Francis S. Eldridge, and Alexander Marcy, in their youth, set pins for $2.50 a week.

When the trains came to Cape May, the tracks passed within a few feet of the spring. A cinder from one of the engines started a fire that destroyed the gazebo on August 24, 1878, and it was never replaced. Parts of a rock wall around the spring still remain but are difficult to locate along busy Route 9. The spring is unused and unnoticed today. Most people are unaware of the role this spot played in Cape May County's history.

The first road built in the county ran from Tuckahoe to Cold Spring and later to Cape Island. Cold Spring was a major stagecoach stop. An important settlement grew up around the spring and Carman's Mill.

Caleb Carman, one of the earliest settlers, built a tidewater gristmill at the head of Cold Spring Creek, now called "Mill Creek," after Carman's Mill.

Jacob Spicer acquired large tracts of land in the area when the land was finally offered for sale. He built a home in 1702 on his plantation. Spicer was an influential member and leader in the community. His son, Jacob, Jr., was a very successful merchant and one of the county's representatives at various Revolutionary councils.

Cold Spring has, in addition to being an early tourist attraction, given life to other famous institutions: Cold Spring Academy, Cold Spring Presbyterian Church, and, most recently, Historic Cold Spring Village.

*Views of the famous Cold Spring. The gazebo, at the top, was built in the early 1800s and was destroyed by fire in 1880. The lower pictures show the stone wall built around the spring after the gazebo burned. Parts of the wall can still be seen, with careful searching, near the Route 9 entrance to Historic Cold Spring Village. The location is not marked. Water is no longer drawn from the spring. And there is no memorial, other than the name for the area, to memorialize the important role it played in the county's history. The Pennsylvania Seashore right-of-way on the left, did not exist in the spring's heyday. Route 9, to the right, was the main road from Cape May. The area, which sported a bar and picnic area, was more like a park than the peculiar interruption to high-speed travel arteries pictured here.*
*Courtesy of Cape May County Historical Museum*

## COLD SPRING ACADEMY

Reverend Moses Williamson founded the Cold Spring Academy in 1857. This was the first school in the county to provide classes at the high school level. At first, classes were held in the Cold Spring Presbyterian parsonage kitchen. So popular was the school, that the Academy building was erected near the church. Students came from all areas of the county. Those who could not return home at night were boarded in the parsonage. Classes and discipline were quite rigid. Punishments are reported, in addition to the standard whipping, to have included locking the offender in a closet and pouring cold water down the back. Many graduates from the school went on to college and entered various professions. Numerous academy scholars became church ministers. When Reverend Williamson died on October 30, 1880, the school began its decline. The building was eventually sold to the Lower Township Committee which used it for meetings. It was also used as a polling place. Later, the building was torn down and the land included as part of the Cold Spring Church burial grounds.

Cold Spring Academy, the first secondary school in the county, was a mecca for scholars and a source of stern discipline. The building was torn down and the site is now part of the Old Brick church cemetery.
Courtesy of Cape May County Historical Museum

## COLD SPRING PRESBYTERIAN CHURCH

"The Old Brick Church" on Seashore Road is the third building to house the congregation. First services were held in Coxe Hall and the church was founded in 1714. The first actual church building, a small log structure, was erected near the site of the present building in 1718. Rev. John Bradner was the church's first minister, and the small stream east of the church still bears his name. The second house of worship for the congregation, a frame building, was used from its dedication in 1762 until 1824. The present meeting house of brick was erected in 1823.

Words for the famous hymn, "Beulah Land," were written by Edgar Page, a member of the church. "Beulah Land" was first published in 1878.

The adjoining cemetery is a panorama of the county's history. The oldest grave is that of Sarah Spicer, buried here in 1742. Tombstones, but not the graves, from the Town Bank cemetery were moved here when that area started sliding into the Delaware Bay. Several Whildins, direct *Mayflower* descendants, are buried here along with many other renowned family names. It is claimed that there are more *Mayflower* descendants buried here than any other burial yard outside Massachusetts.

Dr. Emlen Physick is buried here, with other members of his Cape May family. A mass grave for many victims of the 1823 cholera epidemic is located here, as are graves for several shipwreck victims for whom there were no records.

Old Brick church attendance was an important part of the excursions to the Cold Spring spa. It is still one of the most important churches in the county.

Old Brick church and cemetery, as they appeared in the later 1800s. The two doors to the church depict a vanished era—one door was for the men and the other for women. There is now a single entrance in the center.
Courtesy of Cape May County Historical Museum

*Interior view of the original Old Brick church. The stove was used to heat bricks as foot warmers for worshippers. The church was not heated nor lighted. These luxuries were not considered proper for worship services. Note the height of the pulpit, which was purposely designed to provide the minister with instant authority. At the rear of the balcony on the right was the slave stall, without benches, where slaves stood during the marathon services, which often lasted four or five hours.*
*Courtesy of Cape May County Historical Museum*

*The oldest grave in the Old Brick church cemetery is that of Sarah Spicer, wife of Col. Jacob Spicer, a founder of the church.*
*Photograph by Vance Enck*

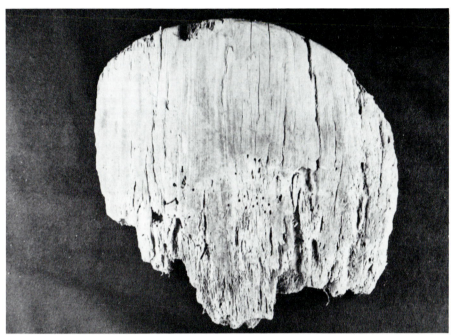

*Many early tombstones were made of native cedar because it was durable, and imported granite and marble were very expensive. The remnant pictured above is owned by local historian, John Merrill, and is probably over two hundred years old. The only other known cedar headstone in the area, shown on the left, is on display in the office of George Carpenter, the Closer for the cemetery of Cold Spring Church. While the cedar markers lasted a long time, the old practice of burning off old grass in the fall destroyed many of these grave markers over the years.*
*Photographs by Herb Beitel*

## HISTORIC COLD SPRING VILLAGE

Cold Spring Village started when Dr. Joseph Salvatore and his wife, Anne, acquired, in 1978, the 1897 Cold Spring Grange Hall next to the Hildreth house, their summer home. Learning of other historic structures in danger of destruction, they began acquiring and moving them to the twenty-one-acre site of present Historic Cold Spring Village. The collection includes homes, stores, railroad stations, a tavern, and an octagon-shaped chicken brooder, all dating from 1740 through the 1800s. The Salvatores opened the village to the public in 1982. Determining that their dream of a living history museum complex could only be accomplished with public assistance, in 1985 they deeded the entire complex to Cape May County. It was the largest gift ever made to the county. With aid from the National Trust for Historic Preservation, the New Jersey Council on the Arts, the county, and an advisory board required under the conditions of the gift, Historic Cold Spring Village has been developed as a celebration of the Federal Period of American and local history. Activities over several months of the year focus on various aspects of life and events in the county's history. Also included are antiques, crafts, and other special shows for the enjoyment and experience of residents and visitors alike.

One of the most recent acquisitions has been the late nineteenth-century Lower Township Hall, which was moved here and developed as the Cape May County Maritime Museum. The first exhibit effectively detailed the whaling chapter of the county's history. Other events scheduled at the village will continue recognition of the Constitution through the two hundredth anniversary of the Bill of Rights in 1991, and the three hundredth anniversary of the creation of Cape May County in 1992.

*Old Grange Hall, built in 1897, was the seed from which Historic Cold Spring Village grew. Dr. Joseph Salvatore and his wife, Anne, who owned the adjacent property, purchased it. The hall is now a restaurant at the Seashore Road entrance to the village.*
*Photograph by Vance Enck*

*The Capt. George Hildreth house, also known as the "Lilac House" was built in 1840 on Seashore Road, adjacent to Historic Cold Spring Village, is owned by the Dr. Joseph Salvatores. After marrying a southern belle, Captain Hildreth built this house with strong antebellum architectural features to keep his bride from getting homesick.*
*Courtesy of Jane Dixon*

*Making apple butter the old-fashioned way is Donald Pettifer, Historic Cold Spring Village executive director. He is an avid hands-on training advocate. This demonstration was one of the many activities regularly scheduled at this living museum.*
*Courtesy of Historic Cold Spring Village*

*"Chow time" at a reenactment of a Civil War army encampment, staged at Historic Cold Spring Village. The food was cooked on site. The soldiers were local "volunteers." The encampment was complete with camp followers.*
*Courtesy of Historic Cold Spring Village*

## VILLAS AND FISHING CREEK

Villas and Fishing Creek are separate communities today, but their histories are so closely intertwined that it is difficult to treat them separately without being repetitious.

Fishing Creek was one of the very early settlements in the county. As whalers moved inland to escape the ravages of the bay waters and to seek another livelihood as whaling died out, the Fishing Creek area, adjacent to Town Bank, was a natural first stop. Here farms were established and lumbering became a major industry. A dock owned by Jesse Hughes was the main shipping point. Thomas Hughes' home in the vicinity of the dock was the site of a big rally for Gen. William Henry Harrison when he ran for president. Hughes was an active politician. Thomas's home burned in 1931. The first post office at Fishing Creek (the sixth in the county) opened on June 20, 1818, with Robert Edmunds serving as the first postmaster.

The War of 1812 saw many skirmishes along the Fishing Creek beaches. The British frequently blockaded the Delaware Bay and raided the area, foraging for food. At the first sight of a British raiding party, a musket shot sounded the alarm. Settlers hurriedly hid their cattle and other valuables (in that order), then ran to the beach to fight off the intruders. There were many casualties and the William and Silas Matthews homestead was used as a hospital. A room from that house was carefully disassembled and reconstructed as part of the Cape May County Historical Museum.

Fishing Creek was the center of a very successful farming community. In the 1920s, Joseph Millman bought a farm in Fishing Creek which he sub-divided and promoted as a modest bungalow development. He named it Wildwood Villas to shirttail on the success and fame of the Wildwoods. Millman often set up a table on the Wildwood boardwalk to sell his lots. The wildwood part of the name was dropped by the postal department when the Villas post office was opened in 1931. Millman was an effective and generous developer. He provided the land and much of the funding to build a fire station and a recreation building. His home still stands on Millman Lane, across the intersection from the Lighthouse Restaurant (formerly Layre's Dutch Kitchen). That area of the Villas Beach was the center of Cape May's caviar industry. From 1899 to 1914, fishing fleets of John Bates and Ellsworth Hughes, among others, set large nets to catch the sturgeon as they swam up the Delaware to spawn. Each barrel of eggs sold for $140, which was much more lucrative than other commercial fishing. Cape May's caviar finally joined the whaling industry in extinction because of overkill.

Villas and Town Bank became largely retirement communities because of the modest cost of the houses and the easy financing terms. Many of the original bungalows have been weatherized for year-round living. Nearly all of the homes being built today are all-season residences. The growing population contributes heavily to Lower Township's ranking as one of the fastest growing areas of New Jersey.

*Fishing Creek's second school was built on Bayshore Road in 1888. The deed recited a cost of sixty dollars. Expenses for the school year were just under five hundred dollars. Youngsters started attending school here when they were four years old. The building has been remodeled and is now a private residence in Villas.*
*Photograph by Vance Enck*

*Roxanna Corson was "the" teacher at the Fishing Creek School for many years. She retired in 1886 and died the following year at the age of ninety. Her grave is in the Cold Spring Cemetery.*
*Courtesy of Cape May County Historical Museum*

## NORTH CAPE MAY

Ebenezer and John Newton were whalers who shrewdly bought large parcels of land. Their plantations included the bay shore from New England Creek south and much of the land east of the original Town Bank. Ebenezer's plantation located just east of Town Bank encompassed all of the land that is now North Cape May and the current Town Bank. Cape May's Dr. Emlen Physick owned the plantation for some time during the late nineteenth and early twentieth century.

A very old white oak tree standing on Bayshore Road just north of Town Bank Road was a famous landmark used frequently as a reference point for land descriptions in the area. The tree was saved from destruction by Dr. Physick who paid for having the road moved to spare the tree.

New England Creek, an area of the present Ferry Terminal, served as a harbor for small and medium-sized vessels carrying wood and produce from township farms to metropolitan markets.

The land of the Newton-Physick farm was subdivided in the 1930s for a planned residential development. This project did not succeed. A revival after World War II produced a whole new community that is now North Cape May. The Cape May Ferry Terminal with its connecting road from the Parkway and the Cape May Canal gave added impetus to continuing development. A large shopping center located at the corner of Bayshore Road and Lincoln Boulevard (Ferry Road) includes businesses that serve most of Lower Township. A large medical complex is being built just to the east of this shopping center.

*Joseph Millman, developer of Villas, gave the land for the volunteer fire company headquarters and the lumber for the building in 1932. Residents raised the money to complete the building and buy the fire-fighting equipment. This picture was taken shortly after the completion of the project. The fire company retained the Wildwood Villas name until the 1950s. This fire station was located on Bayshore Road between Delaware and Atlantic avenues.*
*Courtesy of Dorothy Bowman*

## SEMPER PARATUS

The Coast Guard has had a long and important connection with Cape May County and particularly Cape May City. Most publicized of the early steps were the lifesaving stations, established along the coastline. At first, there were only three, but eventually there were sixteen, spaced at three mile intervals from Cape May Point to Beesley's Point. The Life Saving Service was initiated in a crude fashion in 1848, after 338 shipwrecks occurred in the previous decade along the New Jersey and Long Island coasts.

The Coast Guard officially came into being in 1915 when the Revenue Cutter Service, founded by Alexander Hamilton when he was U. S. secretary of the treasury, and the Life Saving Service merged. The Coast Guard was created as a part of the military services and was quickly put on active duty during World War I, fighting the battle against German submarine marauders along the coastal shipping lanes. Life-saving stations played an important part in this surveillance. A naval base was established at Sewell's Point at the east end of Cape May. An amusement park, "The Fun Factory," built in 1913, was the kernel around which the base grew. The park had not been used since 1915. The buildings were quickly converted for military use only to be lost in a fire on July 4, 1917, while the naval personnel were participating in an Independence Day Parade in Cape May City.

A dirigible hanger was built as a part of the Navy's fascination with lighter-than-air craft, to house a dirigible built in England. The craft crashed in the English Channel on its trial run. Dirigible and blimp interest was only sporadic after that. The hanger was later used as an airplane hanger, and was finally torn down in 1943.

The Coast Guard and Navy used the base jointly during the 1920s. Extensive activity centered at the base during Prohibition as the Coast Guard valiantly attempted to stop the invasion of "demon rum."

Pioneering airplane activity continued on the base as the clouds of World War II gathered on the horizon. Naval operations resumed in full force as the U-boat menace became a reality with several sinkings along the coast during the early part of World War II. Cape May, as a result, was actually closer to active battle zones than many areas of Europe.

After the war, the Coast Guard assumed full possession of the base at Sewell's Point. It was used as a cutter and airborne search and rescue base, and as a recruit training center. When the San Diego training center closed, Cape May became the only Coast Guard recruit training center in the country.

Erosion has been a constant problem for the base. Federal programs are currently being pushed to prevent the base from joining Town Bank and South Cape May under the coastal waters.

The base graduation ceremonies and drills of recruit classes attract many spectators. Jogging companies of Coast Guard recruits are colorful attractions on the local Cape May streets, and they are regular participants of foot races in the area. The base band is a star feature in many area parades.

*Over five hundred shipwrecks along the Jersey Coast in a few decades prompted the formation and intensification of the Life Saving Service stations along the entire East Coast. This picture was taken in 1918 from a Coast Guard cutter of a burning and sinking four-masted schooner off Cape May. The Coast Guard was formed, in part, to rescue survivors of such calamities. Courtesy of Cape May County Historical Museum*

*The Fun Factory at Sewell's Point was quickly turned into a naval facility at the start of World War I. The skating rink was converted to a mess hall and dormitory. So urgent was the need that most of the work on the building was done by hand, with local workers using their own tools. On July 4, 1917, the main building was destroyed by fire while the sailors were marching on parade in Cape May. This picture was taken at the height of the inferno. The site where this building stood is now the rifle range for the Coast Guard base. Tokens from the amusement pier are still being discovered in the area.*
*Courtesy of H. Gerald MacDonald*

*The brig, in 1918, for the naval base at Sewell's Point. The guard, a yeoman first class, is really not doing yeoman's duty, since that is a clerical rating. We also wonder if hand fans were furnished in hot weather—the ventilation system seems to leave much to be desired.*
*Courtesy of H. Gerald MacDonald*

*U.S. Navy blimp, the C-3, is readying for takeoff on February 7, 1919. The special hangar at the Cape May base was completed in 1918. This picture was apparently taken at Camp Wissahickon, about two miles from the hangar, during a landing exercise. The suspended gondola was typical of the early design of the lighter-than-air craft popularized in World War I.*
*Courtesy of H. Gerald MacDonald*

*This 1948 aerial shot of the Coast Guard base shows various size cutters at the docks. The larger ship at the left is probably a buoy tender. The runways of the airfield extend across the top of the photo. Beyond the airstrips can be seen the Atlantic Ocean's waves breaking on the beach.*
*Courtesy of H. Gerald MacDonald*

*The base at Cape May is the Coast Guard's only training center in the country. Care and handling of rifles is still a must for any service person. Any veteran can recount how much fun these drills were.
Courtesy of the United States Coast Guard*

*Recruit training at the Cape May Center includes firefighting and damage control under shipboard conditions. Note the bulkhead and ship doorway with the fire burning in a ship's compartment.
Courtesy of the United States Coast Guard*

# TRAILS TO DESTINY

Three basic influences have combined to shape the history, economy, and development of Cape May County: natural resources, character of the residents, and means of transportation.

Of these, changing modes of transportation have had the most pervasive and dramatic effects on the country's development. Some, like the railroad and the automobile, had an immediate impact on the life and the economy of the county. Other changes seeped into history more slowly, but all of them directed the course of the county's growth.

Foot traffic provided the first transportation as the Indians, by trial and error, blazed traces across the swamps and throughout the county.

Boats using the Atlantic Ocean and Delaware Bay brought the first explorers and settlers to the county's shores. Early settlers followed Indian traces inland to spread throughout the county. Roads built later generally followed these paths. Horsedrawn stagecoaches and individual horseman traveling the roads established regular routes of commerce with other parts of the world and, at the same time, encouraged settlements along the routes.

The first road built in the county, in 1707 and extending from Beesley's Point to Cold Spring, was built of logs. Another, from the Cumberland County border to connect with the first road at Seaville, was built immediately thereafter.

Stagecoach runs from Copper's Ferry in Camden to Tuckahoe and then on down to Cold Springs started as early as 1770. In 1801 after completion of a road into Cape Island, there were weekly runs from Cooper's Ferry to Cape Island via Bridgeton. Service was expanded to include runs leaving Camden on Tuesdays and Thursdays. In 1827 the Tuckahoe-Shore Points route to Cape Island advertised two weekly trips leaving from Wessell's Ferry in Camden for Cape Island on Wednesdays and Saturdays.

Early stagecoach runs took two days to cover the route. Roads were generally rough corduroy canyons through forest banks for many miles of the trip. Occasionally, vistas of cleared farmland, marshland, and small settlements would pop into view. The settlements generally offered the welcome break of a public house and a general store of some kind. There were inns to accommodate overnight guests before continuing the rough, sometimes arduous journey. Road conditions underwent vast improvement through the ingenious and effective practice of permitting farmers to work off their taxes by improving and maintaining the roads. Journeys to the cape could then be accomplished in one long day, leaving at 3:00 to 5:00 a.m. and arriving at 9:00 p.m. No description of the stagecoaches was found; therefore a few notes on the rigors of the trip itself, but nothing about the coaches nor the number of passengers carried. An 1824 account indicates the coaches were drawn by four horses.

The one-way fare, in 1827, was $4.50. "Feeder" lines were also operating in 1827, from Tuckahoe Bridge to the Beesley's Point resort, and from Cape May Court House to Tuckahoe Bridge.

Stages also carried the mail and freight to most of the county. Even mail and passengers arriving by boat at Cape Island and later, after the 1860s, at stops along the railroads were "coached" to their final destination.

Passenger boats from outside New Jersey provided service only to the Cape Island. There were no suitable harbors elsewhere in the county to accommodate them. Ferry service to other areas has existed at various times and special small boat trips between cities along the barrier island also operated from time to time.

First ship service began in 1815, during the summer months, with regular once-a-week trips from Philadelphia to Cape Island by the fast sailing sloop, *Morning Star*. It also offered the gentlemen fishing trips after arrival at the Cape. The packet schooner, *General Jackson*, started regular summer service in 1816.

---

Republic, *the most famous of the steamships cruising from Philadelphia to Cape May, was launched on March 12, 1878. She was 280 feet long and licensed to carry 2500 passengers. The regular trip started at the Race Street wharf in Philadelphia (1) at 7:30 a.m. (although this picture was taken at 8:15, note clock tower) and took five to six hours to reach the Cape May landing near Cape May Point. While cruising down the Delaware, passengers might rent one of the sixteen staterooms with two berths or one of the two private parlors. They could enjoy the passing scenery from one of the one thousand chairs on the 480-foot circumference of the promenade deck (2). If hungry, the dining salon on the lower deck served breakfast, lunch, or dinner. For the thirsty, a wide variety of refreshments were served at convenient kiosks throughout the ship. For a diversion, thirty-nine-inch-tall "commodore" Doyle (3) performed comedy acts and exchanged repartee with passengers on the deck. Arriving at Cape May, the* Republic *would churn to the dock with flags flying and whistle blowing (4). Curious onlookers lined the shore (5) to witness the drama of the docking process and the excitement of debarking passengers. Some arriving passengers tarried at the Delaware House at the end of the dock (6) to imbibe (left) or bathe (right). The more impatient, eager to savor Cape May City's many delights, would rush to the Delaware, Cape May Sewell's Point train line's open coaches pulled by a "dummy" engine (7) for the three miles to the bustling hotel center in Cape May. The* Republic *left at 3:00 p.m. for the return trip to Philadelphia, arriving about sunset. Round trip fare at one time was one dollar and fifty cents; one way was seventy-five cents. Steamship runs were made only in the summer. The dock shown in 5 and 6 was assembled in the spring and dismantled in the fall to avoid destruction by ice floes. Steamships made the last trip in 1916.*
*Courtesy of, 1—Harry N. Merz collection through Dr. John Siliquini, 2, 3, 4, 5, 6—Cape May County Historical Museum, 7—Dr. Irving Tenenbaum*

1.

2.

3.

COMMODORE DOYLE
Smallest Sailor Afloat
of the Palace Steamer Republic

4.

5.

6.

7.

Direct steamboat service from Philadelphia began in July 1819 by Captain J. J. Burns with the *Vesta*. Capt. Wilmon Whildin, a *Mayflower* descendent, initiated steamboat service to New Castle, Delaware, in 1816, where Cape Island bound passengers transferred to the *Morning Star* for the final leg of the voyage. Whildin provided direct service to the cape in 1820. The larger, more luxurious *Superior* replaced *Vesta* on the Cape Island run in 1821.

These early steamboats were woodburning sidewheelers, subject to all the perils of winds and tides and, of course, the mechanical eccentricities of those crude steam pioneers.

Boat passengers were brought ashore on the bay side of the cape at first by whaleboats from the ship anchored about a mile offshore to Higbee's Landing, now Higbee's Beach. A tavern, operated by Thomas and Rhoda Forrest, welcomed the arriving frolickers. Joseph Higbee, a river pilot, purchased the tavern in 1823 and built a large hotel on the site. The landing site was later moved closer to Cape May Point near the end of Sunset Boulevard where the remains of the concrete ship can now be seen. The dock was set up in the spring and taken down in the fall because of the ice and storm hazards.

Steamboats replaced the diminutive *boats* as passenger vessels increased in size, elegance, and services. Probably the most famous were the *Cape May* and the *Republic*, which also had the dubious distinction of presiding over the end of the steamboat era.

Steamships continued service until the early twentieth century, when the convenience of trains and the American passion for automobiles overwhelmed them and ended that important chapter. Steamship service to Cape May County ended in 1916.

From the beginning of the passenger ship era, in 1801, Cape May's fame and growth as a premier seashore resort grew steadily, and from the 1840s through the 1870s, explosively! Development of Cape May to the south and Beesley's Point to the north planted seeds for the recreation industry that has survived over two centuries to become the county's major industry.

*Iron Horses* started replacing the four-legged variety in the 1860s. Arrival of these smoke-belching iron marvels triggered a revolution in the county that reshaped just about every aspect of the county's life before reaching a crescendo in the early 1900s, and then deteriorating until the last train, south of Tuckahoe, departed from Cape May Court House on October 10, 1983.

*The arrival of the trains was an event for local delivery men as well as for the passengers. While waiting for the train in 1910, these horse-drawn passenger wagons lined up at the Wildwood freight station for a "formal" photo. The official looking gentleman in the dark suit, to the left, is the station agent. The station building shown here still exists.*
*Courtesy of H. Gerald MacDonald*

It all began when the Cape May-Millville Railroad incorporated in 1853, with grand plans for a railroad from Camden to Cape May. Money problems restricted the first operations to runs terminating at Woodbury. The road was extended to Glassboro and a further extension to Millville was completed in 1859. In 1863, the first train arrived at Cape May Court House. In the summer of that same year, the first train puffed into Cape May City. For this momentous occasion, a fifteen ton locomotive was brought by boat to Cold Spring Landing where, under its own power, it carefully crept into Cape May over temporary tracks that had been laid just a few hours before the event.

Also in 1863 C. M. & M. R. R. opened its line to South Seaville Junction which became the terminus for passenger, mail, and freight service to the upper portions of the county.

In 1879 the C. M. & M. R. R. was taken over by the West Jersey and Seashore Railroad. An extension to Sea Isle City and Ocean City was in the planning stages by W. J. & S. R. R., using the South Seaville terminus. Under the pressure from Seaville residents, who feared the effects on their town, Sea Isle Junction was established one mile north of the town. The final route of this extension was maneuvered by Charles K. Landis, Sr., to touch his development, Sea Isle City, and then continue to Ocean City. Operations to Sea Isle City began in 1882. The year 1884 saw completion of the route through Whale Beach (Strathmere) over Corson's Inlet to Ocean City.

In 1880 the Pleasantville and Ocean City Railroad built tracks from Pleasantville to Somers Point, with a ferry connection to Ocean City.

West Jersey & Seashore started moving south along the shoreline, taking its tracks over Townsend's Inlet via a bridge built by the Seven Mile Beach Development Company and given to the railroad. They also received the right-of-way for the entire length of the island and station sites in Avalon, Peermont, and Stone Harbor.

W. J. & S. R. R. and its affiliated routes were under the direct or indirect control of the Pennsylvania Railroad.

Beginning in 1893, the Pennsy lines faced stiff competition from what finally emerged as the Philadelphia-Reading Railroad. The first step of the Reading Line, as it became known, was to form the Philadelphia and Seashore Railroad through the direct leadership and efforts of Philadelphian Logan M. Bullitt and Cape May businessman James E. Taylor on January 4, 1893. P. & S. R. R.'s first train ran over new tracks to Sea Isle City on July 27, 1893. The system completed building tracks from Tuckahoe to Cape May in 1894. Independently built spurs were constructed by real estate developers to connect their railways with the mainline. The Risley Brothers built a railroad in 1914 from their Stone Harbor project to Cape May Court House, connecting with the Reading Line. Wildwood and Delaware Bay Short Line Railroad was formed to build a connection from Wildwood to Wildwood Junction, below Whitesboro, to connect with the Reading Line.

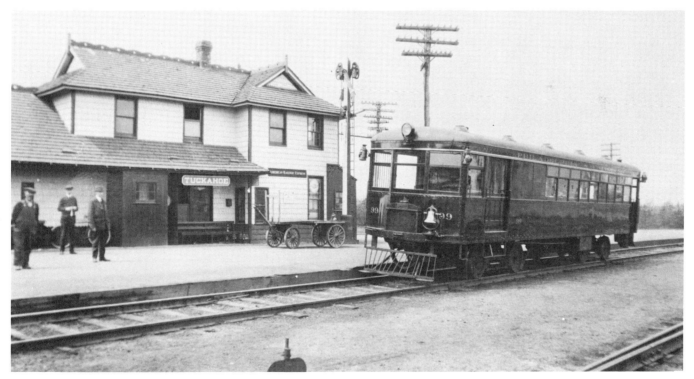

*"If you can't beat 'em...join 'em." Responding to revenue losses because of the public's preference for cars and trucks, the Reading Railroad switched to self-propelled gasoline engine cars between Atlantic City and Tuckahoe. These cars, almost immediately nicknamed "The Meadow Mouse," only required a two-man crew and provided a substantial reduction in operating costs as well. The picture was taken at the Tuckahoe station at the end of the first run on April 14, 1923. Thus began the gradual extinction of the dirty, noisy, but romantic steam locomotive.*
*Courtesy of H. Gerald MacDonald*

*Feeder railway lines cropped up in most of the barrier islands, using steam, electric, or gasoline engines to carry frolicking vacationers from one fun spot to another. Tracks often were laid along the beaches (above). Sometimes, these offered exciting, but perilous, excursions, during stormy high tides, as in this 1921 photo on the route from Cape May to Cape May Point (below). That 1921 storm destroyed most of the tracks along the beach and sounded the death knell for the line.
Courtesy of: above—
Cape May County Historical Museum, below—H. Gerald MacDonald*

From its inception, rail service from Philadelphia used railroad-owned ferries to cross the Delaware River. The first all-rail route without a ferry crossing came with the opening of the Belair Bridge to Belair, New Jersey, in 1896. Although a few miles longer, the convenience of this new route made it immediately popular. With the 1926 opening of second bridge, the Benjamin Franklin, ferry service headed for extinction. Likewise, train service followed suit as automobile travel became easier and preferable.

The battles between the arch rivals, the Pennsylvania and the Reading lines, were legion. Their tracks had to cross at some points. At Tuckahoe, Reading would install a crossing at night; *Pennsy* would tear it out the next day. At one point, Pennsy ran a locomotive back and forth across an illegally placed crossing to prevent its use by Reading. Open conflicts took place in Tuckahoe and Ocean City, with skirmishes in other locales.

The violent rivalry ultimately died out. In its place, a string of wasteful and poor business competitive practices followed. Trains on both lines scheduled departures at the same time. One of the local entertainments involved watching the trains racing each other, at full throttle on parallel tracks, across the flat meadows. Competition was heavily based on speed and beating the other's time by one or two minutes. Fortunately, no accidents resulted from this high-speed rivalry. However, there were a few accidents, some fatal, from other causes.

*Horseless carriages* ultimately closed-in on the Iron Horse. Competitive inefficiencies could no longer be tolerated. Finally, on June 25, 1933, the Pennsylvania and the Reading consolidated under the name Pennsylvania Reading Seashore Lines (providing salve for everyone's ego).

Rail service steadily deteriorated. The number of scheduled runs was reduced. Service on some sections was discontinued and replaced by bus connections. A 1948 rail strike tied up mail service which had been mostly a railroad monopoly and forced the post office to contract with independent truckers for mail transport. The railroads never fully recovered and the last mail train to Cape May County chugged into history on February 26, 1949.

Train No. 401, running from Camden to Cape May on Saturday morning, just one week before Christmas in 1926, was traveling fifty-five miles an hour when an open switch at Bennett Station (Erma) sent it careening down a dead-end siding. Even with emergency brakes, the three-car train cleared the 400 feet of siding track and demolished the station. The engine and tender rolled over, killing Engineer William Saumenig, who was riding in the locomotive to qualify as an engineer on this run, and a crew member, Jules Blake. Fortunately, the two passenger cars and combination baggage and passenger car with six passengers on board remained upright. David Smith, the operating engineer, also managed to escape. The passengers and the rest of the crew were unhurt. The subsequent investigation of the accident blamed the track-walker, August Burneski, for leaving the switch open and the Reading Railroad for poorly placed signals. Ill-fated engine No. 300 was repaired and remained in service until the late 1940s.
Courtesy of H. Gerald MacDonald

*The "Fishermen's Special" standing in front of Cape May's Lobster House in 1940 is patiently waiting for the happy, perhaps seasick, anglers to return from the day's sport. Tracks on the pier were first used for shipping fish hauled in by the Cape May fishing fleet. One-day excursions from Philadelphia were added later. Similar excursions ran to Wildwood's fishing piers. The arriving trains, one writer noted, "with fishing poles sticking out through the windows looked more like a huge porcupine than a sleek modern train." Departing trains looked the same but also carried the heavy perfume from the fruits of the sea and the coach interiors bore a resemblance to hospital emergency wards.*
*Courtesy of H. Gerald MacDonald*

*An excursion group waiting to board their train in the 1920s. Neither the purpose nor the destination of the excursion is known. The dapper attire rules out a fishing excursion. The coats indicate winter. The best conjecture is a professional group on an inspection tour.*
*Courtesy of Dr. Daniel R. F. Schwenk*

*Budd Cars, named after the Philadelphia manufacturer, were introduced into Cape May County by Pennsylvania Reading Seashore railroad in 1950. To the first six cars purchased in October, six more were added in May 1951. By 1955, all steam locomotives had disappeared, replaced by more flexible, more economical "Budd" light cars. In this August 1975 picture on the Cape May Canal drawbridge is train No. 361, with engineer William Ewan and conductor Bill Lehman in charge.*
*Courtesy of H. Gerald MacDonald*

Pennsylvania Reading Seashore Railroad Company systematically and repetitiously petitioned the state and federal agencies for authority to abandon what rail service remained. Against a background of public apathy, the repeated arguments of declining demand and revenues became self-fulfilling prophecies. The company finally succeed in gaining approval to close down all rail service south of Tuckahoe. Passenger service ended in 1983 and freight soon after that.

At the height of their glory, railroads were the lifeblood of Cape May County. They were solely responsible for the emergence of tourism as the county's prime industry. The Jersey Shore, with all its natural attractions, became easily accessible in terms of time, cost and comfort to a wide region. Real estate promoters routinely used excursion trains to lure prospective buyers to their developments.

Trainloads of excursionists fled the hot, steamy cities to enjoy the cool, fresh breezes, and refreshing waters of the shore resorts. *Shoobies* were a railroad-produced phenomena as the *day-trippers* flocked to the shore for an affordable outing, carrying their lunches in a shoe box.

*Finally overrun by the tide of autos and trucks, rail service in Cape May County, south of Tuckahoe, rumbled into extinction with this last train, pictured leaving Cape May Court House on Saturday morning, October 10, 1983. A drive to restore freight service surfaced in early 1988. Some dream of returning passenger service as well.
Courtesy of H. Gerald MacDonald*

*The first train puffed its way into Cape May County's history in 1863, and the last, south of Tuckahoe, dieseled out in 1983. During that 120-year epoch, the United States ended the Civil War, fought three wars, including two world-wide conflicts and went through money panics and one depression. Cape May County progressed from a farm economy, through attempts at industry into a major center for recreation activity. Along the way the population grew tenfold.
Courtesy of H. Gerald MacDonald*

*Train and streetcar runs along rights-of-way down the center of main streets of all the barrier island cities were gradually eliminated. After extinction of the runs, cities moved to widen their streets. This September 30, 1980, picture shows rails being torn up along New Jersey Avenue in Wildwood. All the rail ribbons that once seemed to disappear in the perspective of distance, in the cities, now permanently disappeared in the pavement. Passenger cars became derelicts. These two (below) tarried behind the Admiral Hotel in Cape May before going to that great roundhouse in the sky.*
*Courtesy of: above—H. Gerald MacDonald, below—Harry H. Merz collection, through Dr. John J. Siliquini*

*The proposal for an automobile ferry connection across Delaware Bay from Cape May, New Jersey, and Lewes, Delaware, called for using ship hulks sunk into the sandy bottom to form docking spaces. The plans, unfortunately, had to be put on ice when the first ship scheduled to be sacrificed, the World War I experimental concrete ship,* Atlantus, *broke its moorings during a storm in 1921 and sank of its own accord in the wrong place. It quickly became a favorite lands-end tourist attraction, however.*
*Courtesy of the Harry N. Merz collection through Dr. John Siliquini*

Rusty and overgrown ribbons of rails still lace the county. Some stations still stand. Many have been adapted as homes, some as sheds. In 1988 groups of dedicated railroad fans moved to restore rail freight service, with the ultimate dream of bringing back passenger trains loaded with *shoobies* rolling smooth over meadows and marshes on their way to a shore vacation.

Aside from the nostalgia and the fact that barrier island cities owe their existence to the railroads, one of the greatest legacies from the Iron Horse Era is a monument enjoyed exclusively by the automobiles that did the donors in. These are the wide main streets, running the length of every barrier island city, that mark where the railroad rights-of-way once existed. The tracks have long since been removed for scrap or simply paved over. These wide boulevards are important relief for the self-inflicted horseless carriage congestion.

Ferry service to the county has existed for much of the county's history. The first ferry operated between Somers Point and Beesley's Point in 1693. It continued in service until 1762 when a toll bridge was built over the Great Egg Harbor River.

The first steamboat service from Philadelphia transferred passengers to sailing sloops at New Castle for ferrying to Cape May.

Car ferry service from Lewes, Delaware, to Cape May was the grand plan of Baltimorean Colonel Desse Rosenfeld, in the early 1900s. He obtained several backers among Cape May County residents for his scheme which called for using grounded ship hulks as a loading dock and pier. To accomplish this, he bought the surplus World War I concrete ship *Atlantus*. Four of these low-cost ships had been built toward the end of World War I. The *Atlantus* was launched at Brunswick, Georgia, on December 4, 1918, too late for war service. After a few runs, it proved too expensive to operate and was scheduled for scrapping, when Colonel Rosenfeld acquired it and had it towed to Cape May Point. Before being properly placed it broke its moorings in a storm and sank in 1921. This ended the project. Pounding by the ocean tides and storms are slowly breaking up this monument to a failed dream. The remnant of the *Atlantus* is still a tourist attraction off the end of Sunset Boulevard.

Car ferry service did become a reality under the aegis of the bi-state Delaware River and Bay Authority. The first trip across the bay, on July 1, 1964, featured dedication ceremonies at Lewes and Cape May attended by Delaware Gov. Elbert N. Carvel and New Jersey Gov. Richard J. Hughes. The maiden voyage was hardly auspicious, beginning with the authority chairman fracturing his thumb while assisting the Delaware governor's wife in breaking the traditional, but, in this case, stubborn, bottle of champagne. This was followed with several delays that completely upset the schedule of events, and concluded with a very hard affirmative docking at Cape May that damaged the dock. However, during the first six months of operation, which included a seventeen day shutdown because of a strike, the authority's four vessels carried 78,030 vehicles and 984,308 passengers during that twelve-month period, continuing the constant annual increase in use. The five millionth vehicle made the crossing in the spring of 1988. The fleet of five new bay liners acquired over the last few years provides year-round service except during severe weather or ice conditions.

*Before ferry service could be implemented, Route 9 had to be rerouted and extended to the planned terminal facilities at the bay end of the Cape May Canal. This 1962 aerial view shows construction underway. The tall tower in the upper center is the Cape May Point lighthouse and in the distant upper right is North Cape May. The intersection in the center is Shunpike and the new Route 9. Lower Township Consolidated School is to the right of the pictured end of Route 9. The "Y" intersection in the foreground is the connection to Route 109, leading to the Garden State Parkway just a mile distant. Courtesy of Delaware River and Bay Authority*

For many drivers, this ferry service provided a popular alternative route, avoiding the teeming traffic of the interstate routes over the Delaware River Bridge and through large cities. The seventy minute cruise across the sixteen mile expanse of Delaware Bay is a pleasant excursion enjoyed by many county residents and visitors.

Trains made development of the barrier island resorts possible. Automobiles assured their success. From crude, eccentric, and erratic roots, the automobile, with the aid of many dedicated pioneers, revolutionized the American dream and ultimately assumed control of much of it. With it came opportunities, needs, and, naturally, problems.

Paved roads, or at least passable ones, were one of the very first requirements to be met. Cape May county roads had steadily improved from the rough corduroy, log, and paths of Colonial times to smoother dirt thoroughfares. Paved roads, however, became necessary to replace wagon-wheel-rutted and dusty dirty roads. The number of miles of paved roads rapidly increased. With this progress came consolidation of the road system. The number of roads in the country was actually 100 less in 1960 than the count of 450 in 1860.

Auto races were held on the broad expanses of Seven Mile Beach, Five Mile Beach, and, the most famous, the Strand of Cape May. In the summer of 1905, two racing meets, sponsored by the recently formed Cape May Automobile Club, were held on the beach in front of the Cape May Hotel (now the Christian Admiral). Henry Ford, Walter Christie, and Louis Chevrolet competed in the event that drew world-wide interest. One woman driver won two different events on consecutive days. These races occurred and world records were set long before Daytona Beach and the Utah Sand Flats became significant to the world of auto racing.

*Auto ferry service between New Jersey's Cape May and Delaware's Cape Henlopen became a reality on July 1, 1964, when the first crossings were made with pomp and fanfare—and a few perils. Terminal facilities were not completed at either terminus and the first year was something of a pioneer venture. Shown in this July 1965 photo is the first fleet of four ships pressed into service:* S.S. Delaware, S.S. New Jersey, S.S. Cape May, *and* M.V. Cape Henlopen. *Terminal and support facilities have been completed at both ports. Service now operates year around. The five millionth vehicle made the crossing in 1988.*
*Courtesy of Delaware River and Bay Authority*

*Growing fascination with the speed of autos produced several races along the county's wide beaches. Most famous were the "speed trial" contests in 1905, run from Sewell's Point to the Cape May Hotel. Shown here are the racers driven by Henry Ford, Louis Chevrolet, Alexander Winton, and Walter Christie in that race meet. In those days pictures were converted to postcards, almost overnight, for souvenir hunters. The contests were held in July and August. Note "Sparrow's" mailing date of August 26, 1905.*
*Postcard courtesy of Virginia Walsh*

Improved roads encouraged more and more private autos to throng the highways carrying their occupants away from the sweltering cities to the shore's cool, invigorating breezes and surf. Monumental traffic jams inevitably followed. It is hard to believe today that the eighty mile trip from Philadelphia to Cape May could require six to eight hours on a busy weekend as late as the 1950s.

Public pressure for a better way ultimately brought about today's network of parkways, expressways, and connecting routes. The first step was the Beesley's Point Bridge in 1927, finally linking Cape May and Atlantic counties via the heavily traveled Route 9.

The next major step was the *Route of the Gull*, providing a ribbon of pavement extending from Cape May to Atlantic City, across the Barrier Island resort settlements. The same trip could be made as early as the 1890s by a complicated combination of train, trolley, and ferry routes. It provided an enjoyable, scenic, all-day excursion for visitors and residents alike, but frustrated impatient travelers.

The WPA (Works Progress Administration), established by the federal government as a Depression-busting measure, opened the door to the first dramatic county-wide road improvement programs. On February 21, 1934, the Cape May County Bridge Commission was formed by the Board of Freeholders, with Luther G. Ogden of Cape May and G. W. Bergner of Avalon as Republican members, and George N. Smith of Wildwood Crest as the Democratic member. The commission was created for the purpose of tapping into available funds in order to build bridges and connecting roads with the county. It quickly set about planning and building bridge links to connect the existing wide main streets in a continuous route from Cape May City through Ocean City—interrupted by toll booths, of course.

*Traffic line-up for opening day ceremonies of the Beesley's Point Bridge in 1927. Privately built and owned, this bridge is still privately operated. The toll is now forty cents. Opening of the bridge was a momentous event for several reasons. It closed a gap in Route 9 that had previously added miles to the trip into Cape May County by creating a jog west to reach other bridges across the Egg Harbor River. By providing direct access from the north to Cape May County areas, this bridge tied all of the county into the burgeoning travel market spawned by America's love affair with the automobile. The once thriving Beesley's Point resort complex, detached from the transportation mainstream by the new network of roads and railroad routes in the area, was once again brought into the main road system. Every silver cloud has a dark lining, however. This line-up foreshadowed the monumental jams that soon resulted, especially on weekends, from the increased traffic.*

*Note the spread of the handlebars on the vintage motorcycles on the left.
Courtesy of Jane Dixon*

*Bridge links to the forty-mile course of Ocean Drive from Cape May to Atlantic City were completed posthaste during 1939 and 1940. Many were built simultaneously. Construction costs were financed with federal funds through an extension of the WPA programs. The Cape May County Bridge Commission, formed by the county for the project, built the bridges and owns them. Federal laws required that projected funding under the program be self-liquidating and self-sustaining. Toll booths were a must. Shown below is the toll booth on the Great Channel Bridge, connecting Nummy Island and Stone Harbor, shortly after opening in 1940. A drawbridge was required on this span. Note the crossing gates and warning lights used when the bridge is opened.*
*Courtesy of Cape May County Bridge Commission*

Bridges were built: over Cold Spring Inlet connecting Cape May City with Wildwoods; over Grassy Sound Channel from North Wildwood to Nummy Island; from Nummy Island over Great Channel to Stone Harbor; over Townsends Inlet from Avalon to Sea Isle City, and across Corson's Inlet from Strathmere to Ocean City. The final connection, from Ocean City to Longport, had been built in 1928. The bridges and connecting roads were built rapidly, so that the forty mile Ocean Highway was completed by the end of 1940, tying all the Cape May County coastal resorts together.

Although each of these resort cities continued to attract different types of visitors, the bonding achieved by this new highway gave a unity and a new meaning to the *Jersey Shore*.

*As early as 1915, parking at beach areas was beginning to be a problem. The lucky touring car, with two spare tires on the back, is about to find a space on Cape May's Beach Avenue. Note the cloth tops on all the autos. In the background is "Pavillion No. 1" Pier. This picture was taken from the Stockton Bath House area, revealing a full spectrum of summer afternoon seaside attire.*
*Courtesy Harry N. Merz collection through Dr. John Siliquini*

*Gerry Church at the wheel of his 1909 Maxwell poses in front of Cape May's Stockton Bath Houses. Note the brass radiator, carriage lamps, headlights, and fittings. Be sure to inspect the brake lever just below Mr. Church's hand and the "pneumatic horn" system with the pump bulb and long tube, just back of the brake lever.*
*Courtesy of Harry N. Merz collection through Dr. John Siliquini*

*A gangland execution? The end of a wild highspeed chase down Beach Avenue with Thompson machine guns blazing? There is no way to know. Harry Merz, who owned the picture, only noted, "A 1923 Willys Knight Touring Car being pulled from the drink."*
*Courtesy of Harry N. Merz collection through Dr. John Siliquini*

*Two unidentified Cape May men stopped their cruise along the boardwalk long enough to proudly pose in their sporty 1907 Buick. Note the exposed springs at the front, jump seats in the rear, tool box on the running-board, and the latest in head covering styles, on the dapper "dudes."*
*Courtesy of Harry N. Merz collection through Dr. John Siliquini*

*Undertaker Thompson's brand new 1923 Buick hearse in this christening photograph on Beach Avenue at Ocean Street, with the Morning Star Villa in the distant background.*
*Courtesy of Harry N. Merz collection through Dr. John Siliquini*

The outbreak of World War II, in 1941, put a damper on the growth of the Jersey Shore's recreation industry. Many young men and women were away in the armed forces, and everyone else was deeply involved in the war effort on the home front. Military bases were established in several strategic locations in the county.

Heavy German submarine activity along the coastal shipping lanes, especially at the entrance to the Delaware Bay, resulted in strict blackout regulations that virtually halted nightlife activities and restricted beach use. Gasoline rationing and reduced automobile production severely reduced shore excursions and vacations. Building material shortages halted all but the most necessary new construction. The Jersey Shore essentially went on hold until VJ Day in August 1945.

With the end of the war, pent-up demand for new homes, new cars, and creation of new families swept over the nation like a flood tide. The shore areas emerged from limbo as armies of vacationers, arriving in their new cars, hit the beaches. Many built second homes in shore communities and commuted on weekends in their sleek post-war cars. Traffic in pre-war had already caused congestion problems and with the post-war boom these problems quickly reached critical proportions.

Plans for a toll highway, extending the entire length of the state near the coast was revived. The Garden State Parkway Authority was created and the 170-mile limited access highway was built. The Cape May County section was completed in 1954, opening easy access to the county resorts from northern New Jersey and New York. Only a four mile stretch of this new road, running parallel to Route 9 from the county park to the southern end of Cape May Court House, was toll free and plagued with stoplights and cross streets.

Traveling from Philadelphia to the shore continued to be an arduous and frustrating journey. The Black Horse and White Horse pikes, even though expanded to four lane highways and connected to the new Garden State Parkway, experienced massive traffic jams and delays. Opening of the Atlantic City Expressway did much to alleviate the worst of these problems.

Completion of the Delaware Memorial Bridge and the later twinspan connecting the Delaware and New Jersey turnpikes in 1967, opened the door for convenient access to shore areas for all sections of the region, most notably Washington, D. C., Baltimore, and Wilmington. Vacationers and second home buyers from these areas quickly capitalized on the new opportunities to resort to the Jersey Shore.

Increased auto traffic from the south has cried out for better, faster routes from the Delaware Memorial Bridge entry for a long time. Route 55 within the city limits of Vineland in Cumberland County has been a four lane, limited access highway for some time, but the feeder roads from the bridge and to the shore remain tortuous, dangerous, slow two lane arterial highway. Completion of a high-speed network to the shore is the stuff of which biennial political campaign promises are made and subsequent fiscal performance rejects. Mounting pressures from the growing economy of the South Jersey area are again raising hopes that this political football will be forced over the goal line.

A similar problem with the two-lane Garden State Parkway bridge over Great Egg Harbor Bay at Beesley's Point was relieved when the parallel twin span was completed in 1976 after years of summer season delays of up to forty-five minutes finally forced action.

The toll-free stretch of the Garden State Parkway alongside Cape May Court House has recently closed off or provided less dangerous and more usable access to and from the twelve cross streets. The two traffic lights still create long traffic lines and delays at busy times. Plans for extending the limited access lanes across this section with cloverleafs or jug-handle exits and entrances call for completion within a few years.

Even with all of the completed and planned traffic improvements, the pressures and problems still seem to outpace the solutions. Garden State Parkway lanes will soon be increased from four to six lanes all the way from Atlantic City north. A need for further extension all the way to Cape May seems likely.

Mankind's eternal dream of flying through the air like

*A rough landing for this plane in 1922. It came down near Benny's Landing Road in Cape May Court House, and just a short distance away from the schools. Hannah Swain of the Cape May County Historical Museum recalls coming out of the school and seeing pieces of the fuselage fabric fluttering in the trees around the wreckage. Not much is known about the plane, but the pilot apparently walked away from this one. Courtesy of Cape May County Historical Museum*

the birds, going back as far as Icarus's ill-fated overexposure to the sun, became a reality with Orville and Wilbur Wright's short flight at Kitty Hawk, North Carolina, in December 1903. The explosive growth of air travel has not yet had a major impact on Cape May County. To be sure, there has been heavy military air traffic from time to time, especially during wartime, but commercial and private flying has never been extensive.

Sewell's Point on Cold Spring Harbor at Cape May became a naval air station during both world wars. A blimp hanger was built here in early 1917 to house lighter-than-air craft, and runways were built for airplanes as part of the anti-submarine campaign protecting Delaware Bay and coastal shipping routes. The first squadron of seaplanes arrived here on October 14, 1917.

Between wars, the base was used by the Marine Corps and the Navy at various times for air, as well as water and land, operations. The base was turned over to the Coast Guard in 1926, and rum-runner hunting crafts were based there during the Prohibition Era. Coast Guard aviation pioneers, operating from the base, established world speed records for amphibious planes in the 1920s and 1930s. One, Chief Warrant Officer Thrun, was killed in 1935 when the Gruman seaplane he was testing crashed in Cape May Harbor on take off.

Before and during the World War II, the threat of German U-Boat activity brought the return of extensive air activities. An airfield and base were built at Woodbine, complete with arresting gear and catapults, to train pilots in aircraft carrier launchings and landings. Work on what is now the Cape May County Airport, at Erma, was begun in October 1942 and the base was commissioned on April 1, 1943. This base was largely used for assembling squadrons and support groups before assignment to aircraft carriers.

At the end of the war, the base at Cold Spring was turned over to the Coast Guard and soon was referred to as the Cape May base and the base at Erma became a county facility. Coast Guard air operations from the Cape May base now concentrate on patrol and search and rescue missions.

The first commercial flights to Cape May County Airport were inaugurated by Allegheny Airlines, later to become U.S. Air. In 1988 U.S. Air was replaced by Eastern in serving Cape May County.

Although long distance direct jet flights are currently scheduled to Atlantic City, no such service has been extended to Cape May. Nor is it likely in the foreseeable future. Existing facilities are not adequate for such service and weather can pose serious problems. Commercial air traffic, even air mail service, to the county has never been in heavy demand. Other methods of reaching the county destinations are fast enough and frequent enough to meet most existing needs.

Cape May County's history and economic development have been heavily influenced by the available transportation to and from county destinations. Unquestionably, steamships opened the doors to Cape May City. Arrival of the rail lines gave birth to the barrier island resorts. Automobiles insured the Jersey Shore's future success as tourism emerged as the county's major industry. The future may yet "take wing" with air travel.

*Allegheny commuter flights to Philadelphia and, at one time, Newark, were operating regular daily schedules from the Cape May County Airport in the 1960s, when this picture was taken. Allegheny changed its name to U. S. Air in the 1970s and inaugurated the use of smaller jet-prop planes. Eastern Airlines took over servicing the county in 1988.
Courtesy of Jim McGill*

*Arrival of the first "Sun Tan and RA" Special from Philadelphia to Cape May via a Delaware River Bridge was a cause for celebration on June 28, 1930. The all-rail route, although slightly longer than the ferry route from Philadelphia, was a welcome service. Greeting the train at Cape May were Queen May Sea, II, Sally Lou Ludlam (now Mrs. Jaggard of Cape May Court House). Honored at the coronation ceremonies were engineer Charles Perkins of West Cape May and conductor Harry Steer of Rio Grande.
Courtesy of H. Gerald MacDonald*

*Taken in May 1926 by Ira Goldinger, who was the block operator, this photo gives a rare view of the interior of the B. D. Tower (Woodbine Junction), which controlled the switches and train movements. Note that in addition to the telephone for communication, the box to the right houses a telegraph key. The phone was used by the Pennsylvania line and the telegraph by the Reading line.*
*Photograph by Ira Goldinger, courtesy of H. Gerald MacDonald*

*This 1923 "Demolition Derby" took place in West Cape May at 5th and Broadway. The partially demolished store in the background was repaired and still stands. Mr. Kane, who was driving the Maxwell (no, it is not a Model-T), was not injured. Don't let anyone say, "They don't make 'em like they used to." Note the tire without a trace of the wheel itself and the exposed gas tank.*
*Courtesy of Charlotte Daly*

Garden State Parkway construction in 1953 and 1954 unearthed much history that had long been buried, but it also forced demolition or removal of much history as well. The Amos Corson House, reportedly built in 1790, sat in the path of the median strip between the north and southbound lanes in the vicinity of Seaville. The house was also called "The Bachelor House" either because it was used by Amos Corson as a bunkhouse for woodcutters, or because it was owned at one time by William Bacheler—"or all of the above." This structure had to be moved or demolished. Not until the Parkway lanes had been built around it was action taken. It was first moved to a location across the road from the county park. Later, it was moved to Historic Smithville in Atlantic County, where it was to have been restored and is still awaiting that restoration. The man at the handpump is believed to be Marvin Jones. The others, including the toddler propped against the tree, are not identified.
Courtesy of Jane Dixon

*A dirigible hanger was built at the Cape May Naval Base in 1917. Two hundred and fifty feet long, one hundred and thirty-three feet wide and sixty-six feet high, it was originally intended as the home base for the ZRZ dirigible which crashed in the English Channel on its maiden flight. The hangar was used to house smaller blimps during World War I (top) and for planes later (center). Neglected and little-used, the structure had deteriorated so badly that it was demolished in 1941-42. The hangar floor was used as an operations area for land based navy bombers during World War II (bottom).*
*Courtesy of: top and bottom—H. Gerald MacDonald, center—Cape May County Historical Museum*

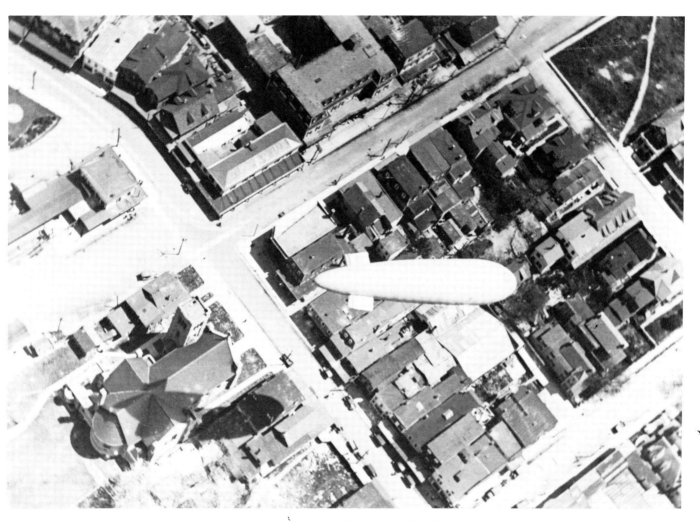

*An unusual picture, circa 1920, taken of a blimp from another blimp. The lighter than air ship has just passed over the intersection of Washington and Ocean streets in center city Cape May. Our Lady Star of the Sea church and parsonage are at the lower left. The Reading Railroad depot is just across the street, next to the vacant lot in the upper left. Mecray's Market is the large building at the corner, across from the Reading terminal.
Courtesy of Harry N. Merz Collection through Dr. John Siliquini*

# THE JERSEY SHORE AND THE BARRIER ISLANDS

For the first two centuries, following the arrival of the first settlers, Cape May County's history centered around life in the inland communities and the settlements along the Delaware Bay. Industries were started, developed, and many slipped into oblivion, leaving few traces of their existence. Among these were whaling, caviar processing, lumbering, shipping, shipbuilding, trapping, and the manufacturing of salt, shingles, glass, clothing, paper, and leather. Farming and fishing have endured.

A clearer picture of the results of two centuries of development emerges from an inventory taken in 1870, just before the "shore-syndrome" entered the county's life. In that year the county's territory consisted of 170,171 acres. Of that, 4,424 acres were beaches; 58,224 acres were marshland on which the tides rose and fell; 10,443 were underwater acres in bays, sounds, and creeks. Of the dry land, consisting of 96,480 acres, only about one-fifth or 21,402 acres was under cultivation; this was about 11 percent of the entire county. The living population consisted of 8,529 people and 3,512 domestic animals. There were 8,094 whites and 435 "colored" living in the county's incorporated areas (the four townships and Cape May City). The largest was Middle Township, with a total of 2,195. Cape May City was third with a total of 1,393.

Domestic animals included 816 horses, 4 mules and asses (the county was never very politically oriented), 1,545 milk cows (apparently there was no bull in the county then), 13 oxen, 382 sheep, and 1,751 swine.

Indian corn (86,218 bushels), butter (68,319 pounds), Irish potatoes (22,360 bushels), and sweet potatoes (21,193 bushels) were the major farm products.

The value of real and personal estate equaled $5,599,383. Total tax revenues were $36,637, with $22,870 extrapolated by cities and towns, $11,529 by the county, and $2,278 by the state. The local public debt was $0.

In the thirty years following this bucolic period, "The Shore" exploded on the county scene with a force that radically changed the character of Cape May County. Cape May City and West Cape May already existed. The Barrier Islands which wrecked ships and were only used only to graze cattle, became the base for the bustling famous cities and resorts of Cape May Point, Wildwood, Wildwood Crest, West Wildwood, North Wildwood, Avalon, Stone Harbor, Sea Isle City, Strathmere, and Ocean City. The population and economic centers of the county moved to the sandy beaches along the Atlantic Ocean. Cape May County would never be the same again.

Such growth in such a short period of time is a miracle made up of many tales of daring, adventure, wealth, and dedication that are critical parts of the county's history. Each of the shore communities has its own separate story; each has its own distinctive constituency.

*Railroads made development of The Shore possible. Americans' innate wanderlust was only intensified by the faster, safer, cheaper mobility offered by trains. Rail lines laced the county, providing access to the wonderful ocean beaches, breezes, and bathing. Shore communities sprang up almost overnight. Pictured here, circa 1913, is the Stone Harbor Terminal Railway trestle across the Great Channel. The train is on its way to Cape May Court House. The roadway and rail right-of-way are now part of Stone Harbor Boulevard. Courtesy of H. Gerald MacDonald*

*Automobiles gave Americans added mobility, still further fortifying their urge to travel. The horseless carriage insured the success of The Shore in by-passing crowded, dirty, hot, rail carriages with their own private capsule that ignored confining schedules and went anywhere the owners wanted—Fast! Pictured here, on Beach Drive in Cape May, circa 1910, is a rare panorama of the change from horse-and- to horseless-obviously going in opposite directions.*
*Courtesy of Harry N. Merz collection through Dr. John Siliquini*

*Once the travel barrier was broken, The Shore communities developed miraculously fast. Five-Mile Island, pictured here, was inhabited almost entirely by grazing cattle until the 1880s. This aerial photo shows part of Wildwood in the late 1920s. Hunt's Pier is the large complex jutting out over the beach.*

*The Shore offered a readily and constantly available escape from the sweltering cities. And escape they did—by the hundreds of thousands. Whether one ventured out in the latest daring swimsuit or remained modestly encased in city street attire, the breezes and smell of the ocean were exotic and refreshing. This early 1900s picture of the Cape May City beach and one of its piers tells the whole story.*
*Courtesy of Harry N. Merz collection through Dr. John Siliquini*

## CAPE MAY POINT

Cape May Point is *land's end* for New Jersey, where the Delaware Bay and the Atlantic Ocean meet.

Jonathan Payne, the first landowner, sold the *Point* to John Stites in 1710. For many years the Point was known as Stites Beach. Captain Alexander Whildin acquired the land through marriage to Jane Stites. They built a house here in the early 1800s. Captain Whildin later went down with his ship. His son, Alexander, who inherited the land, left the Point for Philadelphia where his success as a wool merchant brought him into contact with the great retailer, John Wanamaker. The two sponsored development of the Point as a religious community in the late 1800s.

During the two centuries prior to the Point getting religion, the area was a haven for pirates and grazing cattle. Captain Kidd was reported to have frequented the

*Alexander Whildin, with John Wanamaker, formed an association with Dr. V. M. D. Marcy, Downs Edmunds, and others, all active Presbyterians, in 1875, to found a religious community on 265 acres of land purchased from Mr. Whildin. The charter of that association prohibited the sale of liquor. The Point is still dry. Two hundred and seventy-five lots were quickly sold and Sea Grove, as they named their settlement, was a flourishing community.*
Courtesy of Cape May County Library

area. This folk tale has prompted many a treasure seeker to get sore muscles excavating sand, especially in the area of a gnarled tree that stood until 1893, near the site of the old lighthouse, that was called "Captain Kidd's tree." There is no record of any treasure being found.

During the two wars for independence, British raiding parties were frequent visitors, helping themselves to the fresh water from Lake Lily in the center of the Point and to any cattle they found. Finally, during the War of 1812, exasperated colonials dug a mile-long canal from the salt water Pond Lake to Lake Lilly, making the water undrinkable. The British got the message and did not return. The ditch was filled in after the war and Lake Lilly once again filled with fresh water.

The steamboat landing for Cape May City, located at the end of Sunset Beach at the Point, handled thousands of visitors. Horsedrawn rail cars ran from the dock area through the Point to Cape May transporting arriving and departing visitors. These cars were later replaced by electric streetcars. No settlement, except for a bar at the dock, grew at the Point until Whildin, Wanamaker, and other avid Presbyterians founded Sea Grove in 1875.

The carefully laid out town's streets emanated from a large circle at the center. One of the first buildings erected was a 100-foot diameter open octagonal pavilion on the center circle. Hotels and rooming houses were also built. Hotel rooms cost ten dollars to twenty dollars per week, and rooms at the cottages, with parlor privileges, were seventy-five cents a night.

A post office was opened in 1878 and the name was changed from Sea Grove (there is another near Asbury Park) to the enduring Cape May Point.

Lots, fifty-by-one-hundred feet, sold on easy terms, including an annual West Jersey Railroad pass for each thousand dollars expended. Ministers were given a five-hundred dollar lot without charge.

John Wanamaker was postmaster general in Pres. Benjamin Harrison's cabinet. As a founder of the Point, Wanamaker built a comfortable cottage there. Harrison visited the Point at Wanamaker's urging and established a summer White House in Cape May's Congress Hall Hotel. Wanamaker and a group of friends gave Harrison's first lady a cottage at the Point, where they spent that summer.

Three lighthouses have been built at the Point. The first, built in 1823, was nearly one-half mile south of the present one. The second was built in 1847, just one hundred yards north of the first. In 1859, the present lighthouse was placed in service. The first two have been washed out to sea.

A large military installation was built at the Point during World War II, as part of the anti-submarine battle to protect the vital shipping lanes from Philadelphia and along the coast. Secret equipment installations were located there. A gun emplacement that now serves as an observation point in the Cape May Point State Park, was built underground nine hundred feet away from shoreline. The gaunt exposed pilings and precarious thirty-foot height of the platform today provide stark evidence of the erosion that plagues the area.

Sea Grove's hotel and rental cottages were built along the beach as an enticement for tourists. Very few of these have escaped the ravages of the rampaging ocean. Private cottages were built farther inland and have fared better.

Across Sunset Boulevard from the entrance to Cape May Point are the relics of the Magnasite Plant, which

*The rustic bridge over Lake Lily (above) was a favorite promenade for the early residents of Cape May Point. It is obvious how Lake Lily came by its name. The ladies' shirtwaists and men's boaters were quite typical of the 1890s, when this picture was taken. The rustic bridge was matched by a rustic boathouse on the lake and a rustic entrance (below) to Cape May Point. The gateway was built very early in the history of the settlement and before the name was changed to Cape May Point. All the "romantic rustics" weathered away and were not replaced. Lake Lily is a duck and geese pond in the summer and a much used community ice skating center nowadays (below).*
*Photographs courtesy of: above—Jane Dixon, center—Harry N. Merz collection through Dr. John Siliquini, bottom—Herb Beitel*

closed in 1983. Prior to Magnasite, the Cape May Sand Company, an important operation, occupied the site.

South Cape May, located between Cape May and Cape May Point, was the site of several hotels and large cottages around the turn of the century. It was incorporated as a borough but after the ocean intrusion, what was left reverted to Lower Township. Cape May's famous Mt. Vernon Hotel, the world's largest in 1855, was built in what became known as South Cape May. Rafferty's wooden elephant hotel, Star of Asia, a sister of Margate's famous Lucy, was located here. South Cape May's buildings have all disappeared. Some have been moved to safer locations. Most have simply been claimed by the ocean. The 1944 hurricane and the 1962 nor'easter completed the devastation. The area is now open marshland. Cape May Point State Park and the Nature Conservancy area include most of the area now commonly called the Fow Tract.

Cape May Point was incorporated as a borough in 1878. When state laws governing the incorporation process were declared unconstitutional in 1896, the Point went back into the jurisdiction of Lower Township. It was reincorporated in 1908 and has remained a borough since.

Cape May Point is today a quiet small community. In spite of constant threats of the ravages of Mother Nature, the Point has become a popular place to live and has enjoyed a building boom in recent years. It is still a "dry" town and has almost no retail businesses.

*An intrepid crew of the Cape May Point Life Saving Station, pictured here in the 1870s. Seated, left to right, are Alex Church, Ton Van Winkle, and Bill Peterson. The sourdough cook, standing left, is believed to be Charles Rutherford. The other two members are unidentified. Courtesy of Dr. Irving Tenenbaum*

*The Cape May Delaware Bay & Sewell's Point Railroad operated from the steamboat landing at Cape May Point through Cape May to the Sewell's Point amusement complex. Horse drawn cars were replaced by steam engines (including "Dummies"), and later by electric cars. The railroad merged with the Pennsylvania Railroad in 1901. Part of the loop that was built to circle back to the Point was used for freight traffic from the Cape May Sand Plant on Sunset Boulevard. The end of the steamboat runs to Cape May, coupled with increased auto use and declines in tourist traffic, led to the demise of this line. The final run was made on October 14, 1916. One of the later electric cars is pictured here, circa 1910. The Cape May Point lighthouse is in the background. The motorman and conductor are not identified. Courtesy of Dr. Irving Tenenbaum*

One of the first improvements built by the founders was an octagonal shaped pavilion, one hundred feet in diameter. The amphitheater, with a raised pulpit, seated fifteen hundred people. A magnificent tower rising eighty-five feet in the air topped the structure. An observation deck around the tower afforded an excellent view of the surrounding area. Stained-glass windows depicting the four seasons were hung in the upper portion of the tower. The pavilion was torn down in 1913 and the tower moved to Cape May City where it became a sign for a garage. Engravings of the tower can easily be found but the authors have been unable to find a single photograph of the structure.
*Engraving photograph courtesy of Cape May County Historical Museum*

"St. Peters by the Sea" was retained as part of the centennial buildings in Philadelphia's Fairmount Park after the 1876 celebration closed. The church was purchased by the Episcopal congregation at the Point and moved here in 1879. The first services were held on July 25, 1890, and they have been held "in season" ever since. The church has been moved several times to protect it from the ocean's advances. Today, it is again very near the ocean's edge. Still another site is in reserve if needed in the future. This photo was most probably taken circa 1890 of the church on its first Cape May Point location.
*Courtesy of Jane Dixon*

John Wanamaker (1838-1922), famous Philadelphia retailer (left), was one of the founders of Sea Grove, later Cape May Point. He built a cottage at the Point (below) which may still be seen. Wanamaker joined Pres. Benjamin Harrison's cabinet as Postmaster General. Harrison and Wanamaker were very good friends, and the Harrisons delighted in the Cape May area as guests of the Wanamakers. Soon they became cottage owners through the gift of a home from Wanamaker and other wealthy summer residents who apparently wanted the prestige of having the president vacation among them.
Courtesy of: right, E. G. Williams, below: Harry N. Merz collection through Dr. John Siliquini

*The Harrison Cottage (below) was a gift, in June 1890, to Caroline Lavinia Scott Harrison (left), wife of Pres. Benjamin Harrison. It was presented to her by John Wanamaker, postmaster general under President Harrison, and William V. McKean, editor of the Philadelphia* Public Ledger. *Mrs. Harrison fell in love with the area during a visit with the Wanamaker family at their Point retreat. Three weeks after receiving the deed, First Lady Harrison moved into her cottage and spent the entire summer there, from June 20 to August 28, 1890. President Harrison joined her for several weeks during her stay. The first Mrs. Harrison died during President Harrison's tenure. He later sold the cottage.*
*Courtesy of, left: Harry N. Merz, collection through Dr. John Siliquini, below: Benjamin Walker*

The third Cape May Point lighthouse, built in 1859, is viewed, in this 1984 photo, through the remnants of the base of the second lighthouse, built in 1847. The base and site of the second lighthouse are now underwater. The first lighthouse, built in 1823, disappeared into the ocean well over a century ago. The present lighthouse has been leased by the Mid-Atlantic Center for the Arts, through a complex arrangement with the U.S. Coast Guard, which still owns property and operates the beacon, and the New Jersey Parks Department. The Mid-Atlantic Center (MAC) is restoring the lighthouse. After spending over $200,000 in safety improvements and restoration, the lighthouse was opened to the public for the first time in the summer of 1988.
*Courtesy of Cape May County Library*

*The first Cape May Point lifesaving station was built in 1849. The keeper was Lewis Stevens. The location was moved several times because of erosion. The station buildings shown here in 1940 were built in 1896, and used until 1948 when the activity was moved to West End Station at Villas. This building was abandoned and became a popular place for exploration by children and picnickers. Ocean tides gradually claimed it, and it finally disappeared. The West End Station at Villas was demolished to make room for the ferry terminal. This photo was taken from the top of the Cape May Point Lighthouse. Courtesy of Harry N. Merz collection through Dr. John Siliquini*

*The Carlton House, first called the Sea Grove, opened in 1876. It offered 125 guest rooms, and the main dining rooms which could accommodate 350 people at a sitting. A billiard room, bowling alley, and skating rink were in a building nearer the ocean. Located one-half mile from the steamboat landing and just a ten-minute ride from Cape May was the hotel's own railroad station. The Carlton was a very convenient and popular hostelry. Some pictures show a circular drive in front of the hotel; however, this 1890s artist's rendering does not. The Carlton stood empty for a number of years after it was closed in 1910. The Sisters of the Immaculate Heart of Mary purchased it and operated it as a summer retreat for sisters of the order. After the expenditure of hundreds of thousands of dollars in efforts to protect it from erosion, it was decided to demolish part of the old hotel. The storm of 1962 accomplished the final destruction. All that was left of the once glorious Carlton, after the pummeling by that nor'easter, was the fireplace and chimney shown below.*
*Courtesy of, above—Jane Dixon, below— the Harry N. Merz collection through Dr. John Siliquini*

*The Villa Lankenau (above), one of the famous hotels located in South Cape May, was built in 1890 by Dr. John D. Lankenau, founder of the Lankenau Hospital in Philadelphia, for the use of the nurses and employees of the hospital. Additions were made in 1909. The unusual towers at the front and back were part of that remodeling. Both the sand street and the Villa were claimed by the 1962 storm. The picture below is all that was left of the Villa Lankenau after the March 1962 storm.*
*Courtesy of Harry N. Merz collection through Dr. John Siliquini*

*The Shoreham, pictured here circa 1913, built on the ocean front close to the lighthouse as part of the early development, has survived the storms and erosion that have ravaged much of Cape May Point. The structure was sold to the Sisters of the Convent of the Sacred Heart and turned into a summer retreat. It is still used by them under the name of St. Mary's by the Sea.*
*Courtesy of Harry N. Merz collection through Dr. John Siliquini*

The Cape May Sand Plant (below), across Sunset Boulevard from the entrance to Cape May Point, was operated by George and Betty Patinee for many years. It closed down in the 1920s. The sand was in great demand because it was uncontaminated and the grains were uniform in size. Cape May sand had a ready market and the supply was inexhaustible. Inventory control was automatic—dig the sand and carry it away and the next tide would renew the supply. On a site overlapping the old sand plant works, Harbison-Walker Refractories, a division of Dresser Industries, built the "Magnesite Plant" (above). This plant extracted the mineral from sea water. Magnesite is used in making firebricks and important exotic metals needed by today's technology. The plant opened on December 1, 1941, and was closed on July 31, 1983. Remains of this operation are quite prominent along Sunset Boulevard. The next use of this valuable site is currently a matter of growing controversy. The Municipal Utilities Authority has expressed interest in it as a site for a trash or sewage processing plant. Some builders are seeking to build housing developments. The state of New Jersey is considering it as a nature conservancy. As of this writing, no determination of the future has been made. Courtesy of, above: H. Gerald MacDonald below: Ray McCoy

*Star of Asia* (above) was a hotel built by James Lafferty as a tourist promotion in 1884. Guests could travel light because the hotel came complete with its own trunk. Climbers to the "howdah" were treated to a panoramic view of the surrounding area. The overall height was fifty-eight feet, two inches. It was located at 15th Avenue and the beach, right behind the new Mt. Vernon Hotel. Never a commercial success, it stood empty for several years and vandals extracted a heavy toll from the structure. A drive to restore it in the later 1890s met with failure, and the Star was demolished in 1900. Her sister, Lucy, in Margate, New Jersey, was much more successful with her restoration. The new Mt. Vernon was moved back from the beach to save it from the ocean, and it was renamed the Cape May Hotel. It was severely damaged by storms. Part of the top two floors were moved to the corner of 9th Avenue and Sunset Boulevard, where it remains today as a private home (lower). Lafferty built three elephant hotels. The first, Lucy, at Margate, was twenty-two feet tall. It has been restored and is a national landmark and tourist attraction today. Star of Asia, also called Jumbo was his second. The third, Elephantine, was built in 1885 at Coney Island in Brooklyn, New York. It was destroyed by fire in 1896.
*Courtesy of, above—Harry N. Merz collection through Dr. John Siliquini below—by Vance Enck*

In spite of the appearances, these two houses were salvaged following a severe storm. Both were moved to Broadway, between Mt. Vernon Avenue and Beach Drive in Cape May City. Both still stand and can be recognized by their unique towers. The last of the houses was moved by 1917, according to later owners.
*Courtesy of Harry N. Merz collection through Dr. John Siliquini*

## WEST CAPE MAY

West Cape May is, and always has been, a small community adjoining Cape May City. Early settlers were whalers moving inland away from the eroding shore areas of the bay.

A colored population settled here early in West Cape May's history. One of the first of these was a pirate, John Batteast. He was born in the Cold Spring area in 1761 and returned to settle in West Cape May after turning states evidence to escape the hangman's noose and gain his freedom at a trial in Gloucester County of other pirates. He reportedly dug up some of his buried treasure to finance a church for colored families. His repentance apparently worked, for he died in 1866 at the ripe old age of 105. Batt's Lane in Lower Township is named after him.

Goldbeating was West Cape May's only industry. This refers to a process of beating ½-inch-thick strips of gold with hammers to produce gold foil 1/200,000th of an inch thick, most commonly known today as "gold leaf."

At no time were more than one thousand gold-beaters in the United States. Increasingly, mechanical rolling operations have replaced the older hand-beating methods. At its heights, the operation, located on Goldbeater's Lane, employed nearly seventy people. The business was started in 1864 by George Reeves in a two-story factory situated behind his home, located at the corner of York Street and Broadway. Theodore (Dorey) Reeves, George's son, continued the operation after his father's death. Mrs. James Glase took over on Dorey's death. Ultimately, the only part of the beating process done at the Reeve's factory was assembling the finished foil sheets in booklets. The factory was closed in 1961 after nearly a century of operation.

A new $1.5 million borough hall, facing Broadway, was built in 1986 which houses the borough offices, volunteer fire company, and recreational facilities.

*The West Cape May Volunteer Fire Department pictured with their fire truck, circa 1925. Unfortunately, none of the volunteers were identified. Judging from the bunting and flags, this formal photo was probably taken in conjunction with a 4th of July parade. The picture was posed in front of Cape May's Star Villa complex on Ocean Street.*
*Courtesy of Harry N. Merz collection through Dr. John Siliquini*

*William J. Moore was one of West Cape May's most outstanding residents. Raised in West Chester, Pennsylvania, Mr. Moore had the distinction of being the first black graduate of West Chester High School. After graduating from West Chester Normal School and Howard University, he located in West Cape May and began teaching there in the late 1890s. Following many years as an effective and highly respected educator, he retired, only to continue teaching. This time it was tennis at the Cape May Tennis Club. Mr. Moore is fondly remembered by many tennis buffs for providing their early training and by the citizens of both West Cape May and Cape May City for his warmth, impeccable character, and many accomplishments. The Cape May Tennis Club named their courts after him and they hold an annual luncheon honoring his August birthday. Mr. Moore lived to reach his one hundredth birthday.*
*Courtesy of William J. Moore Family*

*The 1917 sixth, seventh, and eighth grades at West Cape May's colored school. Students, left to right, are Harry Williams, James Moore, Weaver Howard, Frank Moore, Russell Lewis, Frank Williams, Elizabeth Robbins, Ruth Bythewood, Hattie Howard, Lillian Maples, Rachel Tranks, Alda Leach, Mamie Hunt, and Ethel Finnimen. In the rear is William J. Moore, teacher and school principal. Pupils James and Frank Moore were his sons. Courtesy of William J. Moore Family*

*The 1939 graduating class from the two grammar schools in West Cape May assembled for this pre-graduation ceremony formal picture. The class picture was traditionally taken by the fishpond in Ottier Howard's garden. The two schools were segregated and stood side-by-side on 5th Street and Columbia. The separation reflects in the positioning for this photo. The graduates are: girls, left to right, Ruth Brown, Frances Blakely, Bertha Markley, Catherine Lepor, Helen Norris, Virginia Shaw, Grace Wood, Clara Williams, Martha Wise, and Agnes Hicks; boys, left to right, are Robert Lemunyon, Cecil McCullough, Howard Ewing, Robert Pearson, Robert Leaming, Harry Hunt, Francis Hunt, Arthur Timmons, David Knight, and William Thaxton. Courtesy of William J. Moore Family*

*In full dress and ready for a Sunday afternoon spin in the family roadster, in this circa 1920 picture, are Linda Fow (center), "Uncle Gus" Clarence Fow (right), and an unidentified friend. They are standing in front of the Fow homestead. The Fow Tract encompassed much of South Cape May when it existed. The current bird sanctuary and open meadow at the end of Cape May's promenade is a part of that tract.*
*Courtesy of Daniel Ness and Robert Guldin*

*Christmas just would not be Christmas in the lower end of the county without West Cape May's annual Christmas Parade on the first Saturday in December. The first parade in 1965 was the inspiration of Charlotte Daly. She is still the driving force behind the parades, organizing and obtaining the funding each year. The parade of bands, marching groups, dancing schools, clowns, floats, and, of course, Santa Claus, originates in West Cape May and wends its way into Cape May. Since white Christmases are unusual in the Cape May area, Santa switches from his reindeer-drawn sleigh to a horsepower-driven fire truck. Here in 1971 we see Lou Crouch standing in for Santa Claus who was forced to cancel his personal appearance due to demanding Christmas production schedules at the North Pole. The helpful volunteer elves in the truck are Al Noble, Joe Roth, and Bob Hedley.*
*Courtesy of Charlotte Daly*

## CAPE MAY CITY

Cape Island, now named Cape May, claims to be the nation's oldest seashore resort, with good reason. The first resorters were Kechemeche Indians, a branch of the Lenni-Lenape tribe, that fished and dug mollusks during their summer sojourns.

First landowners in the area purchased their tracts from Dr. Daniel Coxe in 1689. They were William Jacocks, 340 acres, and Humphrey Hughes, 206 acres. Rendell Hewitt later bought an interest in the lands. They owned all of the island until 1700. The land was long cultivated as farmland and ownership was fragmented over the years. Cape Island shows as an island on maps in the late 1600s. It was separated from the mainland by Cape Island Creek and marshes. The narrow creek gradually filled in and Cape Island ceased to be an island long before it lost that name in 1869.

Cape May launched on the route to becoming a full-fledged resort area with the arrival of the first regular summertime visitors in 1796. Commodore Stephen Decatur, father of the famous naval hero, was joined by Captain Josiah of the East India service and Herr Fuller, a German businessman. Each man brought his own retinue of servants, and since space was limited, each stayed at a different "inn." Hunting and fishing were their main amusements. Commodore Decatur often cooked chowder on the beach for his companions. Ellis Hughes operated the first public house beginning in 1791. It was later moved to Jackson Street and the beach and was named Atlantic Hall. Commodore Decatur started taking measurements of the distance from Atlantic Hall to the ocean in 1804. In 1829 the hotel had to be moved back because the ocean was at its door. Erosion had claimed 334 feet of land in just

*An artist's conception of the Cape May Beach in the 1840s. By this time many rooming houses and hotels were being added to house the rapidly increasing numbers of visitors.*
*Courtesy of Virginia Walsh*

twenty-five years.

The MacMakin brothers bought the Atlantic Hotel in 1839. They built the one hundred foot-long New Atlantic on the east side of Jackson Street in 1842. The building burned in 1869. A second New Atlantic, built on the west side of Jackson Street, was destroyed by the Great Fire of 1878.

The first Congress Hall was built in 1816 by Thomas Hughes. It was first named "the Big Place," but many local residents called it "Tommy's Folly." Hughes served as congressman for the district from 1829 to 1833.

From the first settlers and the first construction, Cape May's development and interests have been unabashedly commercial.

The hotels, large crude rectangles, built prior to the 1850s, were multi-story boxes with gabled roofs. One author referred to them as having "all the grace of tobacco sheds." Verandas around the buildings were supported by tall slender pillars. Paint was practically unknown, until the early 1840s when the New Atlantic was painted white. Interiors consisted of large barn-like public areas on the main floor with small bedchambers on the other floors. The unfinished back of the clapboarding formed the interior walls. Plastered walls were introduced when the Mansion House was built in 1832. Cape May was popular because of its climate, beaches, and availability. It was not elegant, but it was busy. In 1840 there were three hotels and three boarding houses in Cape Island. Increasing stagecoach runs and the added push of regular steamboat service brought ever-increasing streams of visitors to the cape. Competitive pressure resulted in more comfortable, more elegant hotels. The Mansion House set new standards. By 1850 there were nearly two dozen hotels

*An Atlantic Hall existed in Cape May from 1800 onward. At first it was little more than a large room used for dining and then divided into women's and men's sections by sheets at night. In 1829 because the ocean was lapping at the porch, it was moved back and enlarged. Benjamin and Joseph McMakin, both pilot boat captains, bought the property in March 1839. They built a new house, a four-story one hundred-foot long hotel on the east side of Jackson Street at the ocean, which would accommodate three hundred lodgers. The new Atlantic was destroyed in the 1869 fire. A second New Atlantic was quickly built just across Jackson Street only to fall victim to the 1878 fire. This ended an eighty-year reign, since the Atlantic was not replaced. McMakin's was always the livelier of the major hotels. This picture was probably taken before the 1869 fire. Note the costumes of the women and children.*
*Courtesy of Jane Dixon*

*Cape May beach scene in the 1840s. The "bathing wagon" was standard for the times. Modest ladies, not wishing to bathe in public, would change to their bathing attire in the wagon, which would then be pulled into the water. They could then enjoy the pleasures of bathing in their own private ocean.*
*Courtesy of Virginia Walsh*

*Congress Hall as it appeared just before the Great Fire of 1878. The Miller family who owned it remodeled the hotel in 1874, adding a new wing and replacing all the old porches with new ones of uniform design.*
*Courtesy of Jane Dixon*

*An 1870 illustration appearing in* Harper's Bazaar *magazine depicts trendsetting styles of pre-Civil War Cape May. The bathing wear was made of wool, perhaps giving rise to the idiom, "getting the itch."*
*Courtesy of Jane Dixon*

*This photo of the Ocean House, looking north on Perry Street, was taken sometime in the 1870s. The ladies are quite fashionably dressed. The two-horse team wagon may very well have been headed for an excursion to Cold Spring. The 1878 fire started in the Ocean House.*
*Courtesy of Harry N. Merz collection through Dr. John Siliquini*

1.

2.

3.

The Mansion House (1), built in 1832 by Richard Smith Ludlam, was the first hotel in Cape May to have lathed and plastered walls. The front part shown here faced south along Washington Street. The 128-foot-long Kursaal, added in 1847, extended along the west side of Jackson Street. The Mansion House could accommodate three hundred guests. The Kursaal, with its seventeen-foot ceiling, was used as a dining room, ballroom, and concert hall. On June 16, 1847, Henry Clay (2) arrived for a two-week stay. It is reported that he was regularly pursued on the beach by ladies armed with scissors seeking locks of his hair as souvenirs. While this may have saved barber bills, it was the cause of much humor at his expense on his return to Washington. On July 31, 1849, Room 24 was assigned to A. Lincoln and wife (3). It was here that Lincoln received word from Pres. Zachary Taylor that he was being offered the post of governor of the Oregon Territory. Mary Todd Lincoln, his wife, adamantly refused to go. Lincoln declined the offer and left Cape May to return to Illinois. This set his course on the path that led to the White House and immortality.

Photographs courtesy of: (1)—Harry N. Merz collection through Dr. John Siliquini (2) & (3)—Cape May County Library

within four square blocks at the center of Cape Island.

Cape Island incorporated as a borough on March 8, 1848. Rapid growth led to the incorporation of Cape Island City on March 10, 1851. Isaac Miller Church, a Baptist minister, was the first mayor. The name was changed to Cape May City in 1869.

The Columbia House on Ocean Street, built by Capt. George Hildreth in 1846, and the elegant United States Hotel, built for Ayers Tomkins in 1849, at Decatur and Washington streets, were opened. In 1853 work started on the Mt. Vernon, located at the west end of Cape May. The Mt. Vernon became the world's largest hotel and it was the first hotel in Cape Island to have running water in every room.

By the mid-1850s, tourists were arriving by steamboat to Cape May at the rate of three thousand a day. Franklin Pierce, the first sitting president to visit Cape May, came to town on June 28, 1855. Pres. James Buchanan followed suit in 1858. Cape May County's first newspaper, *The Cape May Ocean Wave*, started publication in 1855.

Destruction by fire of the Mt. Vernon on September 5, 1856, and the Mansion House on June 8, 1857, reduced Cape

*The Mt. Vernon, during its brief existence, was the world's largest hotel. Located on the beach west of Broadway, it was to have twenty-one hundred guest rooms, with a dining room that seated three thousand people at one time. It opened in 1853, and was still not fully completed when fire destroyed it on September 5, 1856. Fortunately it was closed for the season; still the manager and five others employees perished in the conflagration.*
*Courtesy Jane Dixon*

*Horse-drawn trolley on the Cape May, Delaware Bay, and Sewell's Point Railway, circa 1879s. This trolley ran from the steamboat landing to Cape May. It is winter, indeed, with snow on the ground. The horse seems to be better protected than the driver and conductor. It is not surprising that business was poor on this run. Who would want to ride in an open car, along the beach, in the dead of winter?*
*Courtesy of Dr. Irving Tenenbaum*

Island's tourist capacity by one-half.

Tourist traffic and Philadelphia capital investments followed the railroads to Atlantic City. Cape Island fell on hard times, until the West Jersey Railroad completed an extension of its line from Millville to Cape May in 1863. The first train cautiously puffed into the city over tracks that had been completed just a few hours before. Arrival of the first train caused great celebration as Cape May anticipated a rebirth of its tourist industry. Leading the first wave of new capital to arrive with the railroad were Philadelphians John C. Bullitt and Frederick Fairthorne. They bought the Columbia House and hired famed architect Stephen Decatur Button to design an improved facility. Button's designs quickly revolutionized Cape May's architectural style. A large number of buildings he designed still exist in Cape May. In 1869 Bullitt completed construction of the palatial Stockton Hotel, named in honor of Senator Stockton, with rooms for one thousand guests.

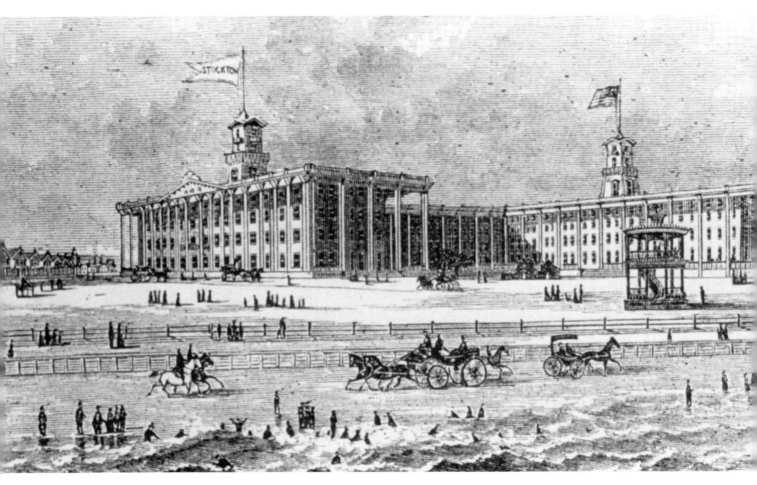

*The Stockton Hotel was dedicated on June 27, 1869. Built by Philadelphia lawyers John C. Bullitt and Frederick Fairthorne, on filled-in marshes at Gurney and Howard streets on the ocean front. The hotel was to be a major part of Cape May's skyline for forty-two years. Bullitt planned the hotel as an anchor for his ambitious project to develop other marshlands to the east. The small building in front was the summer house—an observation tower to better enjoy the ocean breezes and views. A large complex of bath houses facing on the ocean were built across Gurney Street. The Stockton operated until it was demolished in 1911. A movie theatre and small shops are located on Beach Avenue at the site today.*
*Courtesy of Jane Dixon*

The Sea Breeze was built by the Pennsylvania Railroad in the winter of 1867-68, adjacent to the Grant Street Summer Station which opened in the summer of 1867. The Sea Breeze was designed with the "day-trippers" in mind, having included changing rooms and day rooms.

While new hotels built during the post-Civil War boom restored the hotel capacity lost with the Mt. Vernon fire, the most significant change in Cape May came with the erection of many private cottages. Bullitt developed a large residential area between Columbia Avenue and the ocean. In 1869 Bullitt's petition to extend Beach Avenue to Madison Avenue was denied by the city, causing him to sustain substantial losses on the properties he owned in the area. Other than rebuilding the Stockton bathhouses after the 1878 fire, Bullitt ceased his activities in Cape May after the 1869 denial.

*The "summer station" (above) at Grant Street and the ocean was built by the Pennsylvania Railroad in 1863. It was indeed a summer station, open during the summer months only. Service reverted to the Jackson Street freight and winter station after the summer season. The railroad built the Excursion House across Grant Street from the station, to serve the "day-trippers" or "shoobies" who arrived here by the hundreds each day during the summer. Courtesy of Jane Dixon*

*Hotels and rooming houses in Cape May featured wide verandas, porches, and small bedchambers. People came to sit on the porches to see and be seen. Bedchambers were only for sleeping. The other hours were for bathing, sitting on the porches, and dining. Pictured here is Congress Hall's veranda in 1877. Note the gentlemen's hats and the full-skirted ladies. Courtesy of Harry N. Merz collection through Dr. John Siliquini*

1.

*Ocean piers, extending from the shore long distances over the ocean and providing amusements along the way, were Cape May's unique contribution to the shore's architecture. The most famous was the Iron Pier (1), near Decatur Street and Beach Avenue, built for Victor Denizot in 1878 across the street from his Lafayette Hotel. The building at the end of the pier included an opera house and amusement areas. The entrance was enlarged over the years to include shops (2). After weathering storms and tides for twenty-eight years, the pier succumbed to fire in 1907 (3).*
Courtesy of,
(1) Harry N. Merz collection through Dr. John Siliquini,
(2) Jane Dixon,
(3) Dr. Irving Tenenbaum

2.

3.

In the midst of the euphoric post-Civil War boom, a suspicious fire erupted in the Pearl Diver on Washington Street. The ensuring conflagration burned the district between Ocean and Jackson streets and from Washington Street to the ocean. Lost in that 1869 blaze were some of the city's oldest structures: the United States, the American House, and the New Atlantic hotels, the post office and many stores and offices on Jackson Street, which had become a secondary business district. Only the Columbia House was spared because the wind shifted and blew the fire back over the burned-out area. Some of the businesses were rebuilt. The hotels were not.

The national financial panic of 1872, cause by the collapse of Jay Cooke's financial empire, slowed Cape May's recovery from the 1869 fire. Emergence from the slowdown in building activity was sparked by J. C. Knight's purchase in 1876, and remodeling of the Atlantic Hotel. Colonel Sawyer built his rooming house, the Chalfonte, in 1875; John Kromer built the Arlington House in 1878; the Emlen Physick House was built in 1879-1881; and the city built a water pumping station in 1869.

In the 1870s, Cape May's ocean piers appeared, initiating an entirely new type of seashore structure. The piers, extending great distances over the ocean, were

*On November 9, 1878, a suspicious fire flared in the Ocean House on Perry Street. It quickly jumped the street to Congress Hall. Before it was controlled, over thirty acres, including most of Cape May's prized buildings, had been destroyed. These views are west (above) from Ocean Street and south (right) from Lafayette Street.*

*Looking west in the foreground is the site of the Columbia House. Looking south the lonely structure standing vigil over the charred wasteland is probably Congress Hall's "Summer House," the name applied to these elaborate observation gazebos. Courtesy of Jane Dixon*

designed to take the fullest advantage of the cooling breezes, provide amusement areas and panoramic views of the city, and serve as landing areas for pilot boats that were still bringing visitors to the city.

Gen. Ulysses S. Grant, as president, visited Cape May during four different seasons, staying at the Stockton Hotel and Congress Hall.

Again, in the midst of the economic resurgence, fire struck a major blow to Cape May. Starting in the recently remodeled Ocean House, on November 9, 1878, the fire spread to the remodeled Congress Hall. From there it spread south and east. The magnitude of the holocaust quickly overwhelmed the local fire department. Only with the help of firefighters from other areas, some brought in by train from Philadelphia, was the fire brought under control three days later. The area from Congress Street to Ocean Street and from Washington Street to the ocean was completely destroyed. Hotels lost were Congress Hall, the Columbia, Centre House, Ocean House, Merchants, Knickerbocker, Centennial House, Avenue House, Bowlings Saloon, and thirty boarding houses. Many new cottages and businesses were reduced to ashes. The heart of Cape May was a charred wasteland.

*Congress Place as it appeared in the early 1880s. To the left is the new Congress Hall Hotel, built in 1879. The first house on the right is the Eldridge Johnson House, better known today as the Pink House, which was moved across Perry Street to the corner of Carpenters Lane in 1969 to make way for a new motel. The second building, which was demolished, is the Oberon, a rooming house. Next to that is the Dr. Henry L. Hunt House, built in 1881. Next are the almost twin E. C. Knight and J. C. Evans houses, built during the winter of 1881-82. The house with the belvedere at the end of the street, facing on Congress Street, is the Jacob Neafie House, built in 1865-66. It survived the 1878 fire which stopped at Congress Street. Congress Place, which is only one block long, was opened between Perry and Congress streets after the 1878 fire. It was laid out across the Congress Hall property. The hotel that burned in 1878 sat where the street and some of these houses are now located. The authors, who own the Dr. Henry L. Hunt House, found remnants of an old Congress Hall patio and broken dishes when expanding their basement in 1971.*
*Courtesy of Jane Dixon*

In the wake of this disaster, Cape May once again began the task of rebuilding its economy and its inventory of physical buildings. This time however, the real shift was from hotel-dependent tourism to cottages; summer homeowners became the real heart of the refurbishing of Cape May. The only hotel rebuilt in the burned district was Congress Hall (of brick), but on a reduced scale of its former palatial proportions. Smaller hotels were built over the ensuing decades. The Carroll Villa on Jackson Street was built for George Hildreth in 1882. Stephen Decatur Button, at age seventy-one, designed the Lafayette Hotel for Victor Denizot, which was built on Beach Avenue in 1882. The Star Villa, a small rooming house, was built on Ocean Street in 1883. The Baltimore Inn, built for Emma Harrison, went up on Jackson Street in 1894-1895. It is reputed to have been the Swiss Pavilion at the Chicago World's Fair and to have been transported here by train. There is no record to support this story. Also in 1894-1895 the Colonial Hotel on Beach Avenue at Ocean Street was designed and built by the owner, William Church. The last hotel before the motel age dawned was the cedar shake Macomber on Beach Avenue, built in 1921 for Sara Davis.

*Probably the best-known of all Cape May Victorian buildings is the Chalfonte. Built for Cape May's Civil War hero, Col. Henry Sawyer, near the corner of Howard Street and Sewell Avenue, the first section was completed in June 1875. To the initial structure, an extension, along Howard Street to the corner, was built in 1876. This addition included the now familiar belvedere. Another one hundred-foot extension, containing the dining room, was added in 1879. Further extensions were added along Sewell Avenue in 1888 and 1895. This picture, taken after the 1895 additions, shows trees and a fence that no longer exist. Articles concering the Chalfonte and its role in Cape May have appeared in* The National Geographic Magazine *and numerous other major publications. Each spring for the last few years, work seminars/parties of University of Maryland students and other volunteers assemble for "paint up, fix up" sessions. These have been responsible for much restoration work throughout the hotel and for the addition of a cocktail lounge, made possible, under state law, after the room count exceeded one hundred. Annual pilgrimages of a number of loyal guests have made the Chalfonte a true landmark. The current operators have added an extensive array of music soirees, lectures, and entertainment programs to enhance the Chalfonte's genteel Victorian ambiance. Courtesy of Harry N. Merz collection through Dr. John Siliquini*

1.

*The saga of the Lafayette Hotel. It was built for Victor Denizot in 1882 and is shown (1) as it appeared circa 1910. A festive and curious crowd gathered to see Gov. Woodrow Wilson (2) (standing on a second floor balcony to the left) during his visit to Cape May on August 14, 1911. The pillars and overhanging roof were removed in the early 1920s (3), exposing the basic rectangular box design of Stephen Decatur Button (4). The hotel was demolished (5) in the late 1970s to make room for the construction of a condominium hotel complex.*
*Courtesy of,*
*1—Jane Dixon,*
*2, 4—Virginia Walsh,*
*3—Harry N. Merz collection through Dr. John Siliquini,*
*5—B. W. Palmer*

2.   3.

4.   5.

167

*The Colonial Hotel, recently renamed the Cape May Inn, was built by its owners, William and C. S. Church, who were contractors, in 1893. The wing to the right, which contains the dining room, was added in 1905. The low building at the right is Smith's photography gallery. The gentlemen at the right were probably waiting for the Ocean Street trolley after having Smith prepare their personalized picture postcards. This picture was taken from a 1900 postcard.*
*Courtesy of Virginia Walsh*

*John Philip Sousa, in 1881, led the Marine Band in a series of seven concerts on the Congress Hall lawn. The first performance, on August 12, drew an audience of three thousand people. The band performed in the temporary bandstand shown here. Sousa composed the "Congress Hall March" and dedicated it to the management of the hotel. He also paid tribute to the city by composing the "Cape May March." Neither of these marches ever achieved the martial music hit parade.*
*Courtesy of Cape May County Historical Museum*

*The trolley stop at Jackson Street on the Boardwalk, circa 1905. Arnold's Cafe is across Beach Avenue, and the Lafayette Hotel is in the background. The lighted arches, which extended the entire length of the Boardwalk, fell victim to a storm in 1921. An early version of Charles Atlas does not seem to be having much success at the moment in attracting the attention of the coy young maidens.*
*Courtesy of Virginia Walsh.*

*A quiet relaxed afternoon at the bar in the Capitol Hotel, in 1905—until the photographer arrived. The Capitol Hotel building, at Jackson and Washington streets, is now occupied by Barry's Clothing.*
*Courtesy of Harry N. Merz collection through Dr. John Siliquini*

Many cottages went up after the 1878 fire in the burned-out district. One-block-long Congress Place was opened between Perry and Congress streets, extending across the old Congress Hall property. The E. C. Knight House, the J. R. Evans Houses, the Dr. Henry L. Hunt House, the famous Pink House, among others, were built along the street in the 1880s.

Cape May slipped into the comfortable but static rut of a family-oriented seashore city that came to life on the July 4 weekend and closed down on Labor Day.

The next economic flurry came with the 1901 announcement of plans for a major development project at the east end of Cape May. J. Pemberton Newbold bought a large tract of land east of Madison Avenue for $100,000. After a desultory start, Peter Shields and Pennsylvania senator William Flynn took over the project in 1904, with plans for a $3 million development. Central to the plan was construction of the brick Hotel Cape May. A construction mishap delayed the opening of the hotel until 1905. Ownership changed hands in attempts to salvage the project, but it finally went bankrupt in 1916.

Cold Spring Inlet Harbor, an artificial harbor, was dredged and enlarged in 1912. Two long jetties were built. It is ironic that dredged material was used to fill the marshlands of east Cape May, making that land usable for the East Cape May project, but the jetties blocked the alluvial sand flow to Cape May beaches, accelerating their erosion. The wide beach in front of the Hotel Cape May, on which Henry Ford raced in 1903, is completely gone today, requiring a bulkhead to protect Beach Avenue from flooding at high tide. Erosion is threatening the future usability of the Coast Guard base farther east.

In the endeavors to make the East Cape May project a success, the Fun Factory amusement area was built at Sewell's Point in 1913. The boardwalk with its lighted arches extended all the way to the park. Boats docked there, carrying fun seekers from surrounding areas. The rail-streetcar tracks made their east-end loop past the Fun Factory.

Auto races were run in the summers from 1903 through 1905 between Sewell's Point and Madison Avenue, attracting early auto pioneers Henry Ford, Louis Chevrolet, Walter Christie, and others, and large crowds. All this hype, however, did not attract enough buyers to save the East Cape May projects.

World War I produced a burst of activity with the opening of three military bases in the area: the converted Fun Factory, the naval base on Cold Spring Harbor, and Camp Wissahickon at Cold Spring.

After the war building continued at a leisurely pace. East Cape May saw more, but modest, homes built in the vicinity. Other homes sprung up on various vacant lots and open areas. The municipal services buildings continued to cluster at the intersection of Washington and Franklin streets.

*In May 1906 during construction, the center section of the seven-story Hotel Cape May collapsed. Fortunately, this happened during hours when no construction workers were on the job and there were no fatalities. The collapse seemingly was triggered by faulty engineering, resulting from inexperience with building on Cape May's sandy soil. Opening of the hotel as a showcase of the East Cape May Real Estate Company's development, was delayed for two years. This catastrophe only added to the accumulating woes of the project. The anticipated development of east Cape May was not to be realized for several decades. Courtesy of Harry N. Merz collection through Dr. John Siliquini*

*Henry Ford, second from left (above), raced on Cape May beach in 1905. He was winning over Louis Chevrolet and Walter Christie when a wave hit his racer and knocked him out of the race. Unable to pay his hotel bill after losing the race, he sought a loan. He finally sold the touring car he had used to tow his racer to Cape May to Daniel Focer, an engineer for West Jersey Railroad, for four hundred dollars. Although Focer would not buy stock in the Ford Motor Company because he considered it too risky, Ford did pledge to make Focer the first dealer for his new car when it was ready for market. Ford kept his word. Focer, pictured below with the touring car he bought from Ford, did very well in the auto businesss. The car was on display in his Washington Street showroom (where Victorian Towers Apartments building now stands) for many years.
Courtesy of,
above—Dr. Irving Tenenbaum,
below—Tony Bevevino*

*The Windsor Hotel (1) pictured here, circa 1900 was built for Thomas Whitney in 1879. His house reportedly was the central part of the building to which two wings were added. Around 1900 a fourth floor and an elevator were added to the central portion. The E. C. Knight house, facing Congress Street, was then incorporated into the hotel. The Windsor was destroyed by a spectacular fire (2), of undetermined origin, in the spring of 1975. The Regency Beach condominiums now occupy the site. Courtesy of,*
*(1)—Virginia Walsh,*
*(2)—Tony Bevevino*

World War II again brought substantial military activity to the Cape May area. The navy joined with the Coast Guard at the Cold Spring Harbor Base. An extensive military encampment was built at Cape May Point, with radio relay towers, top secret operation centers, and gun pillboxes. A naval air station, NAS Wildwood, was built at Erma. It is now the Cape May County Airport.

*Moons' Drug Store at the corner of Perry Street and Congress Place offered a dazzling array of fine perfumes, cosmetics, and patent medicines, as well as a soda fountain for a refreshing phosphate, in 1910. Yes, Virginia, there was a five cent cup of coffee. The sign on the counter under the lamp says so.*
*Courtesy of Harry N. Merz collection through Dr. John Siliquini*

*An excellent portrait (above) of Cape May's volunteer fire company. Unfortunately, the picture was not dated, nor are any of the firefighters identified. It is only certain that the photo was taken before the company was motorized. It is possible that the picture above was taken at the same time the test of the steam pumper on Beach Avenue was captured on film.*
*Courtesy of Harry N. Merz collection through Dr. John Siliquini*

*Cape May City Hall and fire station, built in 1899, at the corner of Washington and Franklin streets. Two of the "engines" for the fire equipment are out for their morning exercise. City hall later moved to the former high school building, one-half block west of here. This structure was demolished and replaced by a modern brick building on this same site in 1975. The new fire museum was then built as part of the complex, on the corner shown in this photo. The building immediately behind the fire house was Cape May's colored school.
Courtesy of Jane Dixon*

*Smith's Photo Studio, in the Stockton Baths complex, advertised "postal cards taken by the painless method." It was apparently the first stop for new car owners after leaving the dealer's showroom. Pictures were printed on postcards so the proud new owners could show off their latest acquisitions to all their friends. The photos are excellent and copies are to be found in many postcard collections. This one, taken in the early 1920s, seems to have included all the men in the family. The studio apparently went out of business in the 1920s. The building was used as a souvenir shop for some time; later, it was moved to the grounds of the Winchester restaurant, on Lafayette Street, where it now serves as their gift shop.
Courtesy of Harry N. Merz collection through Dr. John Siliquini*

The old Hotel Cape May, now the Admiral, became a hospital and rest and recreation center. It also housed a command center complex and bachelor officers' quarters and family housing. The Cape May Canal was dredged across the cape, making Cape May truly an island again. During this time, Cape May was virtually an isolated military enclave. Blackout restrictions and gasoline rationing put shore excursions on hold until VJ-Day in August 1946.

After World War II, Cape May was caught up in the explosion of recreation, construction, and auto travel.

Motels sprung up along Beach Avenue like mushrooms. Housing development appeared. Most notable of these was the Village Green complex, built on parts of the old East Cape May development area, aptly named Frog Hollow because the filled-in marshland is prone to flooding. Extension of that development continues today despite the controversy that has surrounded it from its inception.

More recently, the condominium concept has captured the hearts and capital of developers. Regent Beach on Beach Avenue and Congress Street rose over the ashes of the Windsor Hotel which perished in a mysterious fire in 1979. Other condominium enclaves have sprung up in scattered locations around town. Some older buildings, including the Hotel Devon built in the 1890s have become condominiums.

Washington Street, which has been the main business street of Cape May since the mid-1800s, was converted into a highly successful pedestrian mall, extending three blocks between Ocean and Perry streets. It was dedicated in 1971. A number of older structures were demolished to make way for the service roads around the mall.

The mall condemnation, combined with the large scale demolition of older buildings to produce new "rateables," raised the hackles of conservationists among the residents, as well as the summer home property owners.

Conflicts simmered for most of the 1960s decade. Federal designation of a historic district covering the heart of Cape May, without the knowledge or consent of the city administration, and the formation of the Mid-Atlantic Center for the Arts in 1970 to save the Emlen Physick Cottage from demolition, led to a classic confrontation between the forces of the "rateables" and the conservationists.

In the 1972 municipal elections, Bruce M. Minnix, a television director who split his time between New York and his home on Jackson Street in Cape May, was elected mayor with control of the three-member city council. His bid for reelection in 1976 failed, but by then the die was cast. Cape May, with its 676 surviving Victorian structures, was declared a National Landmark City in 1976, becoming one of a very select group in the nation and the only one so honored in New Jersey.

With these developments, Cape May turned away from following the route of other shore communities into constant polyglot architectural change. Instead, Cape May has proceeded to capitalize on its role as a Victorian historic treasure.

In 1971 the first Bed and Breakfast hostelry was opened at the Mainstay on Jackson Street. Although Cape May had always had boarding houses and American Plan hotels, the idea of gracious, small rooming houses with gourmet breakfasts was new to Cape May. Providing an ideal commercial adaptive recycling of Victorian structures that would otherwise be white elephants because of the maintenance and restoration costs, the bed and breakfast concept has flourished, attracting to Cape May numerous new young entrepreneurs and visitors.

*Cape May High School had a small student body, but a strong basketball team. Unfortunately, their home games were played in a gymnasium too small to accommodate any spectators. The 1922 contenders are, left to right: W. Lynne, Oscar Tenenbaum, M. Cherry, J. Chambers, and Virgil Marcy. Standing are Lester Rhodes, principal of C. M. H. S. and Sam Eldredge, coach.*
*Courtesy of Dr. Irving Tenenbaum*

*The Cape May High School girls' basketball team was an active contender in 1927. Gathered on the steps of the school are (first row, left to right) Alice Reeves, Mildred Van Gilder, Bernice Hand, Barbara Roseman, and Helena Mills; (second row) Jenny Reeves, Coach Ruth Hines, Florence Cassidy, Catherine Campbell, and Burnice Wilson; (third row) Lennea Edholmes, Frances German, and Hilda Koula.*
*Courtesy of Julia Ginder*

*Charlotte Daly, founder and organizer of the annual West Cape May Christmas Parade, came by her love of parades very early. In her Swan Boat (with frog handle) she appeared as "Lake Lily Sprite" in a Cape May children's parade. To give the year of the parade would be unchivalrous. The "47" is just her parade entry number—not the year.*
*Courtesy of Charlotte Daly*

*Congress Place on the "morning after"...Hurricane Hazel blew portions of the roof from Congress Hall onto the Evans and Dr. Hunt houses in 1954. The houses have been restored to their original state.*
*Courtesy of* Cape May Star and Wave

*The moon, high tide, and a raging nor'easter at vernal equinox in March 1962, were positioned to cause the storm of the century. Before the storm was over, the Boardwalk and much of Convention Hall had been strewn across Beach Avenue (1), and most of Cape May was under water (2). The ocean and the bay merged on Cape May streets. The tides were so strong that lifeboats were carried several hundred feet inland and left high and dry on Franklin Street when the waters receded (3).*
*Courtesy of,*
*(1) Charles Bernard,*
*(2) & (3) Harry N. Merz collection through Dr. John Siliquini*

Fundamentalist minister Dr. Carl McIntyre was an important influence in Cape May's evolution in the 1960s and 1970s. Under his direction, the *Christian Beacon Press* purchased Congress Hall, the Windsor, and Admiral (now the Christian Admiral) hotels. In addition, his group bought a number of other properties in the city. He saved the Lafayette Cottages and the Morning and Evening Star Villas from destruction by acquiring and moving them to an enclave in East Cape May, near the Christian Admiral. Unfortunately, they are deteriorating rapidly because of a lack of use and maintenance and storm damage.

McIntyre endeavored to operate Shelton College on the grounds behind the Christian Admiral but gave up after failing to obtain accreditation from the state of New Jersey. The college was moved to Cape Canaveral, Florida. Classes were offered again in 1988, under the aegis of the Florida accreditation. Although Dr. McIntyre's role has been controversial, his efforts have greatly aided the preservation of Cape May's historical heritage.

The driving forces in the three centuries of Cape May's history and development have been its climate and the ocean. The salt hay, low dunes, and the modest overgrowth of brambles, vines, and trees made the area preferable to the Barrier Islands for cattle grazing and for farming. Very early visitors were attracted by the refreshing breezes, the soothing constant sound of the surf, the abundant wild and marine life, and the temperate waters. The first visitors were more interested in the hunting and fishing. Fishing tournaments are held at various times for the fish that are currently running. Commercial fishing is Cape City and Cape May County's second largest industry.

Although Cape May's development motivation has been principally commercial, the end result is a community that has charm, vitality, and strength. All of the city's assets have come together in recent years to restore Cape May to its rightful place among the most famous resort areas of the world.

*Dr. Emlen Physick (1858-1916), scion of a famous Philadelphia medical family, was an early city drop-out. He moved here with his mother and aunt while the Emlen Physick House was being built. Dr. Physick never practiced medicine. He was an avid dog breeder and hunter. He is pictured here circa 1890, with one of his dogs. Although some local guides might foster the myth that he was a Victorian playboy, there is ample evidence that he was an active real estate speculator. At various times he owned all of the land where North Cape May is now located and a large tract that is now part of the Wildwoods. At his death in 1916, he was negotiating with the city of Cape May to sell it beachfront land as a site for a convention hall. The sale was completed through his heirs and Convention Hall was built. Dr. Physick saved a historic oak tree on Bayshore Road near Tabernacle Road by providing money to move the road right-of-way away from the tree. He is buried in the family plot in Old Brick Church Cemetery.*
*Courtesy of Cape May County Historical Museum*

*The first act of Mayor Minnix's administration in 1972 was to approve acquisition of the Emlen Physick estate on Washington Street by the city of Cape May. The sixteen-room "cottage," designed by Frank Furness, was destined for demolition. The city leased the estate to the Mid-Atlantic Center for the Arts (MAC), which had been formed specifically for the purpose of saving and restoring the historic property. The cottage had become Cape May's very own haunted house, apparent from this "as is" photo taken in 1971. Vandals had done considerable damage to the structure. Through funds raised by volunteer activities and tours, MAC has restored the property and turned it into one of the finest museums in New Jersey, with a nationally acclaimed collection of Victoriana.*
*Courtesy of Virginia Walsh*

*A guard house, obtained from Philadelphia's Fairmount Park, was moved to Cape May. The Victorian architecture made it an ideal information booth at the Ocean Street end of the Washington Street Mall. Volunteers from the Coast Guard base restored and repainted the house. Mayor Bruce Minnix (second from the right) was on hand to express the city's gratitude for the volunteers' contribution. The house is still in active use and guards against any visitor entering the area without information on the city's many activities.*
*Courtesy of Bruce Minnix*

*Current building activity in Cape May includes widespread restoration of historic buildings, such as the cedar shingle roof replacement on the Dr. Henry L. Hunt house, right, and new condominiums complexes, such as those on Beach Avenue, shown above left.*
*Photographs by Vance Enck*

## THE WILDWOODS

Five Mile Island and Two Mile Island, originally separated by Turtle Gut Inlet, provide the sites of four separate communities, each with its own government. While each was established at a different time by a different group, they are generally considered as one unit today because of the interlocking economy, connecting streets, and common land mass.

Five Mile Island was a favorite summering place of the Indians because of the wide beaches and abundant food supply. Major Indian traces ran across the island and were so carefully established that their courses are pretty much that of the major streets through all of the communities. New Jersey Avenue follows the main trail.

In contrast to the other barrier islands, Five Mile Island had four owners at the outset, rather than the usual single proprietor. They were Aaron Leaming, Humphrey Hughes, David Wells, and Jonathan Swain; all are famous names in Cape May history. The island could not be farmed and was difficult to reach, so that it was distinguished for much of its history as a grazing area for the owner's cattle. In fact, those first four owners carefully portioned out the use as to the number of cattle that each could graze and the natural products that could be removed. At one time, John Taylor, who had inherited the property from his father in the late 1700s, attributed so little value to the land that he sold it for nine pounds to buy his wife a calico dress.

The first settlement was Anglesea (now North Wildwood) at the northern end of the island. The first settlers were fishermen. The lifesaving station established in 1849 was one of the most active because the shoals of Hereford's Inlet were the site of many shipwrecks. The Hereford Lighthouse was built in 1874 and the community began to grow around it. West Jersey Railroad opened a spur from Cape May Court House in 1884, providing the best access to the island. This spur was the runway for probably Cape May County's most famous train, affectionately called the "Mud Hen" because it derailed so often and sank into the mud. The first tracks were laid on cedar limbs placed on top of the sand. Tides had a habit of washing the tracks to new locations, requiring the train crew, and frequently the passengers, to nudge the tracks back into place. In bad storms, the Mud Hen was usually stranded on the Grassy Sound trestle.

In 1880 Frank Swope and a number of associates bought the land at Anglesea from Humphrey Cresse and laid out a town. They built the fifty-room Hotel Anglesea at Walnut Avenue and the ocean. The hotel burned in 1895 and the site of the building is now under water.

Holly Beach Improvement Company was formed on April 12, 1882, by Aaron Andrew and Joseph Taylor for the purpose of building a settlement on Five Mile Island. The original Holly Beach was located between Cedar Avenue and the present Morning Glory Road. Even though access to this portion of the island was very difficult, a number of houses and cottages were built. The area could only be reached by boat, across the marshes, or by an Indian trace through an extensive growth of bushes and vines that was a favorite haunt of snakes.

*Robert W. Ryan, who opened the first store in Wildwood at 137 East Wildwood Avenue, is shown here at the famous "W" tree with his son, Norman. Norman Ryan was the first child born in Wildwood. The Ryan's posed for this photo in September 1897.*
*Courtesy of Wildwood Museum*

*Philip Baker was one of the founders of Wildwood borough, and later of Wildwood Crest. He was the first elected mayor of Wildwood Crest after the borough was incorporated. Baker had been active in development of Vineland before transferring his energies to Wildwood.
Courtesy of Wildwood Museum*

*Aaron Andrew was one of the founders of Holly Beach. He was originally from Vineland, but became enamored with the Wildwood area when he brought his wife to the shore for health reasons.
Courtesy of Wildwood Museum*

*Water was a precious commodity in the early days of Wildwood. The first waterworks, shown here, was "the Public Drinking Pagoda," in the Cedar Park area at Oak and New Jersey avenues. The water was yellowish in color and brackish in taste, but it was drinkable. This 1890 photo shows a variety of visitors to the pagoda.
Courtesy of Wildwood Museum*

181

A post office was established in 1883 and the community was incorporated as a borough in 1884. The name has been changed to North Wildwood, but many still refer to it as Anglesea. The Hereford Light is still operating. It has been moved to prevent it from going under water.

Holly Beach was incorporated as a borough in 1884. Franklin J. Van Valin was the first mayor. A severe storm in 1889 washed away almost all of the buildings. The borough was rebuilt and went on to expand. In 1912 Holly Beach and the borough of Wildwood merged to form the present Wildwood City.

Philip Baker and his brothers, J. Thompson and Latimer R., formed the Wild-Wood Beach Improvement Company in 1885. Philip Baker had earlier purchased the Wales-Physick tract, which was nothing more than a thickset forest of cedar, maple, and oak trees tied together with massive grapevines. With indefatigable energy, the Bakers set about developing Wildwood. When there were only three houses in the settlement, Baker convinced Reuben Ryan to settle there. Ryan built the first store and went on to build a chain of five stores. He served as the first stationmaster when the trains arrived from Anglesea; he was also the first postmaster. He was co-founder of the Marine Bank and held many offices in service organizations.

A major attraction of earlier days in Wildwood was Magnolia Lake (the second in the county by that name), surrounded by a park located at Wildwood and New Jersey Avenue. The famous "W" tree grew here. That strangely distorted tree grew to become the symbol of Wildwood. When it had to be cut down, the "W" section was preserved and may still be seen in Wildwood City Hall.

Visiting dignitaries were typically photographed at the tree, including Pres. Benjamin Harrison, the only president to visit Wildwood. The lake has since been filled in to make room for a housing development and the park has met the same fate.

Wildwood was incorporated as a borough in 1895. The first and only mayor, prior to the merger with Holly Beach, was William Zeller. A road was cut through from Holly Beach to Wildwood in 1891.

In 1898 the Bakers purchased the 110-area Cresse tract, adding the area from Pine Street north to the Anglesea line, which doubled the size of the borough. A road was built over the marshes connecting Wildwood with Rio Grande in 1903.

After several years of agitation, the voters of Holly Beach and Wildwood voted to merge their boroughs into Wildwood City in 1912.

The last year cattle grazed on the island was 1888. However, wild cattle and horses plagued the residents for

*Very popular attractions in Wildwood's early days were Cedar Park and Lake Magnolia, located at Oak and New Jersey avenues. Boats could be rented for rowing around the waterways in the park. A famous Swan Boat carried passengers along the streams. The boat's "swan song" came when the park was closed and the lake filled-in for housing developments. Courtesy of Wildwood Museum*

years. Professional hunters were hired to eliminate the herds. In one year, reportedly, five hundred head of cattle were killed.

Wildwood's boardwalk began with planks being laid on the sand. In 1903 an elevated walk was constructed east of Atlantic Avenue. The boardwalk is a considerable distance from the ocean today because of beach additions by the ocean currents, in contrast to the erosion on other barrier islands.

Jeanette DuBoise Meech founded Wildwood's first newspaper, the *Holly Beach Herald*, in 1885. The first newspaper actually printed on the island was by Jed Dubois in 1895, and was the forerunner of *Gazette Leader*.

In 1905, Philip Baker turned his attention to the development of the area south of Holly Beach. He leveled dunes and pumped sand from Sunset Lake to prepare building sites. The first home in what became Wildwood Crest was built in 1905. The borough of Wildwood Crest was incorporated in 1910 and Philip Baker was unanimously elected by all twenty-nine voters.

West Wildwood was founded by Warren D. Hann, who bought the property in 1899. Actual building, however, did not begin until 1916. By 1918 there were sixty houses in the settlement. A casino was also built across the inlet. West Wildwood became a borough in 1920. The town has remained at virtually the same size since its peak in the early 1920s.

Today, the combined population of the communities on Five Mile and Two Mile Islands is about the same as Ocean City, and if combined, would be the second largest in the county. There are numerous motels and hotels in the area and many homes, both large and modest. During the summer season, the Wildwoods attract many resorters. The year-round population is steadily growing, and local businesses are increasingly staying open beyond the summer season.

*A rainy afternoon on the Wildwood boardwalk in the early 1900s. Hunt's Comique Theatre, on the right, is probably full of wet and disgruntled resorters. The Hunts operated several theatres in the county. Sagels fudge and lunch shop appears to be doing its biggest business, at the moment, protecting promenading ladies from the rain.*
*Courtesy of Wildwood Museum*

*The Hereford Lighthouse, built in 1884, was the anchor of the development of Anglesea. However, the lighthouse itself was not that well-anchored. It had to be moved because of the erosion that threatened its foundations, as is evident in this picture.*
*Courtesy of Harry N. Merz collection through Dr. John Siliquini*

*Wildwood was the first place in the United States to celebrate Memorial Day by tossing flower wreaths onto the water to commemorate men who died at sea. This picture was taken at the first ceremony on May 31, 1894.*
*Courtesy of Wildwood Museum*

*Holly Beach School at recess time in April 1909. The school was enlarged three times. At the time of this picture, Principal Chalmers had recommended that classes be held in the basement of the building because of overcrowding in the classrooms. Courtesy of Wildwood Museum*

*Capt. Joy Bright Hancock, a member of the prominent Bright family in Holly Beach. She entered the service in 1918. In 1948 she became the first woman captain in the regular United States Navy. She was later named the first director of the WAVES after their formation during World War II. This picture is of a painting by David Komuro which is hanging in the Naval Museum in Washington, D. C. Courtesy of Wildwood Museum*

*Cornerstone laying ceremony for Wildwood High School in 1915. Proposals to build a high school had been the center of bitter controversy for six years. There were strong forces opposing the high school, who felt an advanced school was not necessary. Many of the officials on the scaffolding are wearing top hats and dress Masonic aprons. Courtesy of Wildwood Museum*

## STONE HARBOR

Stone Harbor received its name from an English sea captain who managed his way in a severe storm through the treacherous Hereford Inlet to find shelter behind Seven Mile Island.

The island was purchased by Aaron Leaming in 1723. The Leaming family sold 2,575 acres to Joseph Silver in 1854. He in turn sold it to Henry B. Tatham, and he to George Tatham. Seven Mile Beach Company bought the island in 1887, but first proceeded to develop Avalon and did little about the area that became Stone Harbor. Through a series of transitions, the land that is Stone Harbor was acquired from Avalon Development Company in 1907 by South Jersey Realty Company. Horace Risley and his family, who controlled the company, engineered well-planned and steady growth for the development.

*Beginning with the tract they had just purchased (right), the Risley brothers tackled the massive job of transforming the rugged landscape into a bustling resort (below). Streets were laid out and graveled, curbs were built, boat channels were dug, and a turnpike carrying rail and auto traffic was built to Cape May Court House. Courtesy of Cornelia Corson Brown*

West Jersey Railroad had been granted property for a right-of-way in 1889. The first train arrived at the station between 88th and 89th streets in 1892. When the Risley's appeared on the scene, the railroad turnaround at 117th Street got a lot of use. The Risley's ran excursion trains to bring prospective buyers to town. A unique promotion that gave bond purchasers a free lot was also introduced.

The founders put in carefully planned gravel streets, complete with curbs and sidewalks. Utility lines were installed. Artesian wells were sunk to a depth of 862 feet to tap into clean fresh water aquifers. Three boat channel basins were dug.

Next came a road connection to the mainland. This was accomplished in 1911, over the jealous opposition of other developing Barrier Island resorts. Gov. Woodrow Wilson drove the gold spike to symbolically complete the rail line that ran alongside the turnpike connecting Stone Harbor with Cape May Court House.

The Stone Harbor Life Savings Station was authorized in 1854. A permanent station building, referred to as Tatham's Station, was built in 1872. This was replaced by a larger building in 1895. It remained in service until 1947. The American Legion purchased the building in 1948 and has used it as a lodge hall since that time. The first school opened in 1910. A 1.5-mile long boardwalk was built in 1917. Replaced after a number of storms, the boardwalk was permanently destroyed by the 1944 hurricane. The townspeople determined not to replace it; the beach is just fine.

Like nearly all shore communities, auto races were promoted in the early 1900s, but went flat in Stone Harbor.

*Bathers flocked to the beach during the summer of 1924. The boardwalk, shown here, was built in 1917 and damaged by several storms and finally destroyed completely by the 1944 hurricane. It was never rebuilt.*
*Courtesy of Jane L. Scott*

Stone Harbor was incorporated as a borough on April 28, 1914. A small tract was added from Avalon in 1947.

Stone Harbor has steadily developed a thriving business community. Special open houses are held during the Christmas season by retailers to assist and encourage local shoppers.

Residential growth has also been slow and steady over the years. Population figures were nearly static for the 1970s decade.

The nationally famous bird sanctuary, located between 2nd and 3rd avenue and 111th and 117th streets is the only one in the United States located within the city limits; and one of only two in the world. The other is in Japan. The twenty-one acre tract is alive with nesting egrets, herons, and ibises that may easily be observed between March and October. It is on the Registry of Natural Landmarks of the National Park Service.

Although not technically within the city limits, the Wetlands Institute is located on marshlands alongside Stone Harbor Boulevard. The institute undertakes research and sponsors lectures, exhibits, and tours concerning the salt marsh and salt water ecology. The building, donated by World Wildlife Fund International, was dedicated in September 1972 by the fund's president, Prince Bernhard of the Netherlands.

*Samuel E. Herbert became mayor of Stone Harbor when he was selected to fill the unexpired term of Howard Risley. He was later selected for a full term. He founded and ran the S. E. Herbert and Sons plumbing business at 385 96th Street for several years.*
*Courtesy of Marian Hornsby*

*The dedication of the Stone Harbor Turnpike, connecting Stone Harbor with Cape May Court House, was a local major event. The ceremonies on July 3, 1911, featuring a speech by New Jersey Gov. Woodrow Wilson, was attended by a large crowd (above). After Governor Wilson spoke, he drove the traditional gold spike in the last rail (in this case it was actually just a shiny nail). A two-mile parade followed, leading the way across the new connecting link (below).*
*Courtesy of, above—Leahy Real Estate Company, below—Jane Letzkus Scott*

*A group of refreshed resorters waiting for the train to return them to the hot inland cities. Beaver hats and derbies certainly topped the men's styles in the 1890s when this picture was taken at the Stone Harbor station.*
*Courtesy of Wildwood Museum*

*The volunteer fire company band was a source of great pride for Stone Harborians. This picture was made sometime in the late "teens." Unfortunately, the members are not identified.*
*Courtesy of Marian Hornsby*

*Stone Harbor's baby parades are big events. This 1930s entry doesn't seem to be the least bit intimidated by his elaborate floral boat.*
*Courtesy of Cape May County Historical Museum*

## AVALON

Seven Mile Beach, the barrier island on which Avalon and Stone Harbor were established, was purchased by Aaron Leaming in 1723. Access to the island was only by boat. Leaming used the island for grazing cattle in the summer and for hunting. Extensive marshes separated the island from the mainland and covered much of it. "Fast land," or dry land, included several high dunes that looked down on groves of cedar and holly trees. A few hunters' shacks existed but little else.

The Tathams purchased the island in the early 1800s.

*The Tatham family, who lived in this farmhouse, owned the land of Seven Mile Beach from the early 1800s until it was bought by the Seven Mile Beach Company in the 1880s. There are accounts of picnickers boating to the island and using boathouses operated by the Tatham family. Courtesy of Wildwood Museum*

*Old Limerick, the first house built on Seven Mile Beach, stood between 30th and 31st streets in present Avalon. Gilbert Smith, on the left, is holding Avalon Corson, the first child born on the island. The third person is not identified. The growth of the house, from the larger section to the left, is immediately evident, and interesting to study...design by necessity? Courtesy of Wildwood Museum*

They built a few beach houses for the convenience of the intrepid excursionists who boated over to the island.

Seven Mile Beach Company, headed by Philadelphian Frank Sidall, purchased three thousand acres of fast land in 1887, with the objective of founding a resort colony. Charles Bond, secretary of the company, chose the name Avalon from Welsh mythology, being the place for dead heroes, where King Arthur was carried.

The first deed for the founding company was to West Jersey Railroad for a right-of-way running the whole length of the island. The deed includes plots at Eighth, Eleventh, Twentieth, Twenty-second, Thirty-fifth, and Sixtieth streets in Avalon for station stops and service buildings. The company built twelve "sample" cottages and the Hotel Avalon in response to the railroad's refusal to run trains until there were buildings to show people. The railroad was put to the test, as well. Four attempts were required to build a trestle across Townsend's Inlet to Sea Isle City where a rail line was already operating. The first structure washed away before it could be used. The second washed away in an autumn storm. The third was washed away with equipment still on it, before it could be completed. The fourth one "took," and regular (in those days, it meant "erratic") service was put into effect as far south as Thirty-seventh Street.

The Hotel Avalon was built at Fifth Street and Avalon Avenue in 1887. The hotel had to be moved in 1891-1892 to save it from the ocean's encroachment.

For the first few years, colonists had to collect rain water for drinking and cooking. During one dry summer, a tank car of water had to brought in and was parked at Thirteenth Street for community use. A well was dug and water works built in 1898. Water pipes were extended to the Peermont section in 1901. A stand pipe was constructed in 1911.

*This motor train in the late 1890s is probably carrying an excursion group, since all the passengers are men and boys. Note the open car with canvas side curtains, "in case there's a change in the weather." And the man standing left is taking no chances, obviously.*
*Courtesy of Wildwood Museum*

*One of the regular excursion trains to Peermont, circa 1890. This was probably a posed photo session after the train's arrival. Note the lady hanging onto the side of the engine cab. Everyone looks much too clean to have traveled very far on those precarious perches. Also note the roughhewn and irregular size and shape of the railroad ties on which the track is laid.*
*Courtesy of Wildwood Museum*

There were still cattle and sheep on the island for many years. One woman's cows broke out of their pen and left their hoof prints in freshly poured concrete sidewalks at the Avalon Methodist Church; they are reportedly still there.

The area north of Forty-second Street was originally known as Townsend's Inlet, as well as Avalon.

Peermont Land Company bought six hundred acres of land to layout and develop Peermont, which extended from twenty-fifth to Forty-second Street. The Peermont Community Church was built at Thirty-second Street and First Avenue. It later became the United Methodist Church. After the congregation moved to a new church building in 1960, the old church became a private home.

For many years, Avalon and Peermont were separate communities with different schools and fire departments. Avalon opened a post office in 1888 and Peermont opened one in 1907. There was reason for the separation. The only usable access between the two, because of the high dunes and dense foliage, was by train or along the beach. The roads were built and Peermont became a section of Avalon. The area south of Thirty-seventh Street remained largely undeveloped for many years.

Avalon became a borough in April 1892. Land was annexed in 1910. The border between Stone Harbor and Avalon was finally settled at a line across the island at Eightieth Street.

A lifesaving station was established in 1895 between Fifteenth and Sixteenth streets, near Avalon Boulevard. There were only two keepers, John W. Swain and Frank Nicols, Jr., before the lifesaving service merged with the Coast Guard in 1913. Surfmen (crew members) patrolled the beaches for about three miles until they met their counterparts from the next station. They would exchange medallions as proof that they had completed their patrol. The building was abandoned in 1948 and boarded up. It was acquired as a private home by John Millar in 1968.

Avalon, by 1905, had two churches, a school and seventy-five houses. Avalon had developed twenty years ahead of its neighbor, Stone Harbor to the south.

A 1.25-mile boardwalk between Twenty-first and Thirty-second streets was dedicated in May 1913.

A dune protection program has been developed to protect the section where the few remaining high dunes exists. The World Wildlife Fund has purchased 953 acres in the Old Man's Creek area.

*A festive and fully dressed group of visitors to the beach at Peermont. The ladies' costumes are particularly noteworthy. One is caused to wonder if perhaps this is the annual family portrait, or are they posing for the "great American painting?" Courtesy of Wildwood Museum*

## SEA ISLE CITY AND STRATHMERE

When Joseph Ludlam purchased the island where Sea Isle City and Strathmere are now located early in the 1700s from the West Jersey Society, it was covered with meadows, large red cedars, and native holly. For nearly two centuries there were very few residents on the island. The most numerous visitors were cattle and sheep that grazed here during the summer months. Cattle swam over from the mainland and back. Sheep, who are non-swimmers, enjoyed the luxury of a barge trip for the annual migration. There were cattle on the island as late as 1895. Ludlam's herds spent the summer here and were identified with earmarks (Cape May's contribution to the widespread cattle branding in the far west) of an "L" on the underside of the left ear and a slit in the right ear. The Corsons and Townsends, who owned the mainland tracts adjacent to the island, also grazed their herds here for a fee.

Whalers often used the beach for harvesting their kill. Strathmere, in fact, is located on an area known as Whale Beach. Whalers probably used temporary settlements during their hunting periods. Apparently they also availed themselves of the local cattle for food supplies, according to some recorded complaints. The last recorded whaling lease in Cape May County was for Whale Beach in 1777.

Popular belief holds that pirates used the coves and bays to lie in wait for hapless victims and as a safe haven during the raging storms. It is also suspected they were "beefeaters," enjoying locally supplied roasts, judging from muzzle-loaded pistols found in the dunes.

Numerous ships have come to grief along the island beaches. An early disaster was the grounding of the British merchant ship, *Guatamoozin* in 1807, whose survivors were found by Nathaniel Stites, Zebulon Stites, and Humphrey Swain at a hunting shack on the island. Local residents enjoyed the bounty of tea, silk, and china salvaged before heavy seas destroyed the ship. That hunting cabin was the first permanent structure on the island.

The numerous shipwrecks led to the founding of the lifesaving stations along the Jersey Coast in 1871. However, stations at Corson's Inlet and Sea Isle City had been authorized in 1849. Sea Isle City's station ceased to operate by 1939, and Corson's Inlet facility was closed down in 1964.

*Members of the Sea Isle City Life Saving Station are identified in this summer 1918 picture are: 1—Fred Parker, 2—Richard Sutton, 3—Frank Clark, 4—Frank Cooper, 5—Walter Wright, 6—John Roche, 7—Patrick Cremmer, 8—John Sutton. Courtesy of Cape May County Historical Museum*

*Corson's Inlet Life Saving Station, June 1958, looking at Strathmere from the bay side. The first station built in 1849 was north of here on the Peck's Beach (Ocean City) side of the inlet. Although records are vague, the station was moved at least three times to locations in both Strathmere and Ocean City. This Strathmere station, probably established in the late 1920s, continued operations until closed by the Coast Guard in 1964. Most of the buildings in the background were demolished or badly damaged in the March 1962 storm. This neighborhood looks much different today. Courtesy of H. Gerald MacDonald*

Serious settlement began in 1880 with the laying out of the town of Sea Isle City by Charles K. Landis, Sr. Landis, who already had founded Vineland, set about developing Ludlam's Beach. The original plan extended 6.25 miles along the ocean and from .25 mile to 1.75 miles across the island to Ludlam's Bay, Corson's Inlet, and the navigable channel, called "The Thorofare." There were five houses in the early 1880s. Landis became enamored of Venice during the visit to the canal city and set about making his town an American version. He had canals dug and decorated the area with classical sculpture pieces. The beachfront was deeded to be "forever free." To connect Sea Isle City to the mainland, he had a log road with wooden bridges built from Ocean View across the marshlands.

*Charles K. Landis, Sr., founder of Sea Isle City, was the driving force behind SIC's miraculous growth from cattle grazing land in 1880 to a bustling resort and incorporated borough with train service, hotels, a post office, and several homes by 1882. Landis, fresh from his success in developing Vineland, planned and executed every detail of this rapid development, including classic statuary decoratively punctuating the carefully laid-out streets.*
*Courtesy of Cape May County Historical Museum*

*The first Sea Isle Turnpike Bridge, shown in this "pieced together" snapshot, was built in the early 1880s as part of Charles Landis' development program of Sea Isle City. Crawford Buck was the first bridge tender. The date of the picture is unknown, but is believed to be around 1885.*
*Courtesy of Cape May County Historical Museum*

1882 was a banner year for Sea Isle City. It became an incorporated borough and Martin Wells was elected the first major. A post office was established on June 20, with George Whitney serving as the first postmaster. Also in June, the first rail line, a 4.8-mile extension from the junction near South Seaville to the borough, begun in May 1881, was completed and the first train arrived amidst much fanfare.

Development began to move at a fast exciting pace. By 1885, the population had expanded rapidly to 558. Lewis Stevens reports in his 1897 *History of Cape May County, New Jersey* that:

> Sea Isle City is brilliantly illuminated at night with electric light, and the cottages and hotels are lighted by electricity. As to good water, Sea Isle City is supplied from an ever-flowing well of water. All cottages are supplied with this water.
>
> Two systems of railroads, West Jersey and Seashore and South Jersey.
>
> It has thirty hotels, an electric railroad, ice plant, schoolhouse, a Methodist church built in 1888 and a Catholic church built in 1890.

To set the stage for Stevens' glowing inventory, many interesting events occurred.

The first trolley was pulled by donkeys, in 1887, over tracks laid through Sea Isle to Townsend's Inlet. Donkey power was later replaced by the "The Dummy," a steam locomotive.

School classes were held in the dining room of the Aldine Hotel until 1893 when the schoolhouse on Forty-fourth Street was built. That school building is now used as the nunnery for St. Joseph's parochial school teachers.

The "thirty hotels" indicated by Stevens were of relatively modest proportions. However, the largest and most lavish was the five-story Continental which boasted Cape May County's first and only steam-powered elevator. The Continental was never a financial success and was demolished in 1921. Excursion houses, which Stevens did not mention by name, were Sea Isle's unique contribution to the shore's tourist attractions. They were, essentially, grandstands facing the beach and used as gathering places for "Shoobies" and hotel guests. Excursion House, the most famous of this style, was three stories high, with an enclosed first floor and open second and third floors. From these pavilions, patrons watched races on the beach— horses originally and later, in the 1920s, motorcycles.

*The "Yellow Kid," engine No. 6043, a "Dummy," was used by the Western Jersey & Seashore Railroad from Stone Harbor through Sea Isle City to Ocean City's Second Street wharf, connecting with boat excursions. Dummy engines bore a cover resembling a streetcar in order to appear more pleasing to people and be less frightening to horses. Four Dummy engines were used by W. J. & S. from 1895 to 1903, when they were replaced by standard steam engines. Note the tall smokestack on the front of the engine and the open-sided passenger car with bench seats. The crew in this 1900 photo is casually posing while waiting to start their run on schedule, as this was a very punctual line.*
*Courtesy of H. Gerald MacDonald*

*Excursion House, the large enclosed building in this 1920s beach scene, as originally built in 1882, had three stores and a skating rink on the enclosed first floor. The second and third floors were open pavilions where resorters might eat their lunches and watch the races and activities on the beach. Before destruction by storms, the Excursion included a ballroom that occasionally staged boxing matches. The first building to the left of Excursion House was the home of the Sea Isle City's Women's Club, the most active social activity center in the town. These two buildings and the boardwalk were all victims of the violent storms that have plagued SIC in this century.
Courtesy of Cape May County Historical Museum*

*Motorcycle races were held regularly along the beach in the early 1920s. But more appealing were the Bathing Beauties contests held along with the races. Daredevil groups from many areas of the region and the country thronged here for the sport, and each brought a curvaceous entry for the swimsuit contests. Pictured here are the lovely entries from about 1921. Their escorts and sponsors are understandably in the background.
Courtesy of Cape May County Historical Museum (from the Sea Isle City's* Centennial Book

The first newspaper in the borough (and the county's fifth), the *Cape May County Times*, founded in 1884, was printed in German for the benefit of German emigrees who resorted or settled here. A fishing fleet operated by fishermen of Italian descent who settled along the canals and lagoons added to the cosmopolitan atmosphere of Sea Isle City.

Many buildings from the Philadelphia Centennial Exposition were floated here for use as private dwellings, making Sea Isle City a long-running replay of the World's Fair's display of the latest architectural styles.

Sea Isle's boardwalks have come and gone. The first, from Twentieth to Sixty-third streets, built in 1907, was destroyed by the 1928 storm. In the 1930s, a new one was built from 32nd to 49th streets and was lost in the 1944 hurricane. This was rebuilt two years later only to wash away during the 1962 storm. A new $1 million paved promenade was dedicated on June 15, 1968, and still serves the city.

*There is no explanation of the occasion for this celebration nor any identification, except for "Mr. Brooks" who is standing to the far right, wearing the grey Fedora. Note the preponderance of derbys and three-piece suits and the young boys formally decked-out in their knicker suits and caps. Trolley cars ran the full length of S. I. C. and Strathmere, providing a very pleasant, scenic ride down the main streets of both towns. Taken in 1900, this picture is a postcard and is assumed to be one of the vanity cards popular as mementoes at the time.*
*Courtesy of H. Gerald MacDonald*

*Margaretta Pfeifer and her brother, John, were winners in Sea Isle's first Baby Parade in 1916. Local residents, Margaretta owned the famous Cronekers Bellevue Hotel and Restaurant until her death. John operated a department store in the city and was a member of First National State Bank's board of directors.*
*Courtesy of Cape May County Historical Museum (from the Sea Isle City* Centennial Book*)*

A sign of the times was the formation of the Sea Isle Yacht and Motor Club in 1905. The "motor" part overwhelmed the trolley line, constructed in 1896, that ran the full length of the island. It was closed down in 1916 and replaced with a wide roadway, named Landis Avenue in Sea Isle City and Commonwealth Avenue in Strathmere. Ocean Highway, which connects Sea Isle with Ocean City to the north and Avalon to the south, incorporates this road. Another road connects Sea Isle to the Garden State Parkway at Ocean View on the mainland.

Strathmere, built on Whale Beach at the northern end of the island, has never been incorporated and is a part of Upper Township, which leads to some jurisdictional confusion. The town can only be reached overland via Sea Isle City or over the Ocean Drive bridge from Ocean City.

Sea Isle City and Strathmere were devastated by three major storms in a span of eighteen years. The 1944 hurricane which ravaged the entire Cape May coast destroyed much of Sea Isle's beachfront area and flooded the city and Strathmere. The November 25, 1950 storm completely covered the island with surging tides. The March 6-7, 1962 "nor'easter storm of the century" destroyed or severely damaged most of the buildings on the island and again spread flood waters over the entire island.

Both Sea Isle City and Strathmere have rebuilt and returned as active communities. In 1946 shortly after the 1944 hurricane, Dr. Francis A. Dealy built Surf Hospital in Sea Isle City. The Catholic Sisters of Mercy purchased it in 1953 and operated it until 1969 when it closed. Closing at the same time was the Sea Isle City Hospital Training School, opened in 1926 and closed in 1958 and sold to the Sisters of Mercy who used it until 1969.

Sea Isle City has earned its nickname, "The city that refuses to quit." Since the 1962 devastation, many new, safer buildings have been constructed, including high-rise condominiums and apartment units. In 1987 alone, building permits were issued for construction totaling $17 million, including 121 new duplexes, five stores and one tennis court.

Through the good and bad years, Sea Isle City and Strathmere have been blessed with strong, dedicated residents whose optimism will not be daunted.

*How many fair damsels were snatched from the "jaws of death" (whether they really needed it or not) by this early corps of handsome SIC lifeguards? The only hero identified is Walter Wright, on the far left, in this early 1900 picture. Courtesy of Cape May County Historical Museum (from Sea Isle City's* Centennial Book*)*

*Beach exercises for beauty, health, and fun were a favorite activity for distaff resorters. Note the bloomers and skirted swimsuits in this fitness class picture on the SIC beach in the "teens."*
*Courtesy of Cape May County Historical Museum (from Sea Isle City's* Centennial Book*)*

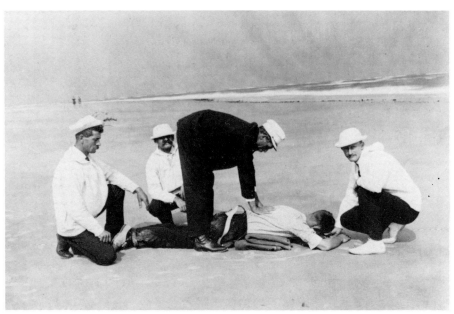

*Regular practice drills were held by the Sea Isle Life Saving Station members, covering all phases of lifesaving procedures, from sounding the alarm for a ship in distress to artificial resuscitation shown here. It seems certain this was a drill because the crew members' natty attire shows little evidence of a struggle with the raging surf in a wildly tossing boat. The hapless "victim" did, however, have to clean his outfit of all the wet sand collected in this prone position. Unfortunately, none of the intrepid crew members are identified in this 1918 picture taken on the S. I. C. Station Beach.*
*Courtesy of Cape May County Historical Museum*

*Townsend Inlet section of Sea Isle City from a postcard view, dated August 31, 1907. In the background are the railroad tracks crossing the inlet to Avalon. Authority to build the Avalon connection by rail was granted in 1889.*
*Courtesy of Bill Robinson*

## OCEAN CITY

Ocean City is built on an island long known as Peck's Beach. Although the source of the name is uncertain, the best conjecture is that it came from a whaler by that name, who operated in the area and may have used the beach for processing whales he had harvested.

In 1695, apparently, Thomas Budd acquired the northern part of the island. He used the land for grazing cattle until 1750. A 500-acre tract was acquired by John Somers that same year. Richard Townsend, one of the county's very earliest settlers, in 1726, purchased the 663 acres of land covering the southern portion of the island, from Corson's Inlet to what is now Twenty-ninth Street. Through a series of transfers, these properties ended in the hands of the Ocean City Society.

Three Methodist ministers, S. Wesley Lake, Ezra B. Lake and James E. Lake, determined to found a religious community. Their first attempt in the area of Margate fell through. A visit to Peck's Beach on September 10, 1879 ended with the decision to build their religious community here.

To insure that certain standards were maintained in the community, the founders controlled all deeds for properties in Ocean City, and inserted restrictive covenants that forbade the (1) conducting of business on the sabbath and (2) the sale of alcoholic beverages on any property. The "blue law" and prohibition restrictions, they set in this manner have withstood court tests and referenda to remove them and remain in force today. They proceeded to survey the entire island to clear up many confused and conflicting claims through lawsuits and negotiations. Before the work was finished, all titles were cleared and clarified forever. The founders insured their restrictive covenants would last.

An area for a tabernacle was set aside between Fifth and Sixth streets and Asbury and Wesley avenues. By 1880 the area was cleared and an open pavilion erected; and by the end of that year, thirty-five dwellings, a hotel, bath houses, and an association office at Sixth and Asbury had been constructed.

Ocean City was incorporated as a borough on April 30, 1884; it became an incorporated city on March 25, 1897.

*Ocean City has a long-standing reputation for strict enforcement of its "blue laws." This 1922 photo is a case in point. Beach officer Bill Norton is measuring the distance from the knee to the bottom of the bathing suit to make sure that the young lady is not violating the city ordinance covering the subject.*
*Courtesy of Sarah Pringle McKinley*

*When it was built in 1881, the first place of worship in Ocean City was named the Auditorium. Today, it is the Tabernacle. It was builllt on the campgrounds between 5th and 6th streets and Asbury and Wesley avenues. The frame structure was badly damaged in the 1944 hurricane, but it was rebuilt. A new brick tabernacle replaced it in 1957. The cannon, to the left, was jettisoned by the British brig Delight in 1779 in an effort to lighten the ship when it ran aground on Peck's Beach. After various travels, the cannon was brought to the campgrounds in 1906.*
*Courtesy of Bill Robinson*

One of the first borough councilmen, Parker Miller, elected in 1884, moved here as a maritime insurance agent in 1859. He built a house for his family near what is now the southwest corner of Eighth and Asbury. They were the only residents on the island until 1879.

The first jail was a small frame building at Fourth Street and Asbury Avenue, where the present city hall stands. It was called "the Naley," after the first prisoner.

*The Sentinel,* the first newspaper, was a crude handbill published by two brothers, William and Albert Boyle, in 1880. It grew into a full-fledged printing and newspaper operation. A former rival, *The Ledger,* merged with *The Sentinel* to become the *Sentinel Ledger* in 1923. It is the oldest private enterprise in Ocean City. A number of rivals have come and gone over the years but none have survived.

The first school was established in 1881. Classes were conducted by Mattie Boyle, the first teacher, in the association offices at Sixth and Asbury. A school building was erected on Central Avenue between Eighth and Ninth streets. The first high school diplomas were awarded in 1904 to graduating members Lyndon Ang, Morgan Hand, Harriet Schurch and Hiram Steelman. The newer school buildings were constructed in 1906 and 1913, and the present high school building opened in 1924. The school system has continued to expand with new schools being built to meet student population needs.

Railroads did not play as strong a role in Ocean City's development as they did in other barrier island developments. The first line opened in 1882, connecting through Sea Isle Junction, to Sea Isle City, then north to Ocean City. The Pleasantville and Ocean City Railroad, founded in 1880, ran from Pleasantville to Somers Point and connected by ferry to Ocean City. South Jersey built a spur from Tuckahoe to Ocean City in 1898. An electric rail line, later named the Shore Fast Line, began interurban car operations in May 1911, running from Eighth Street and the Boardwalk in Ocean City to Virginia Avenue and the Boardwalk in Atlantic City. This line operated over wooden trestles built from Somers Point. The Pennsylvania tracks, running along West Avenue, were abandoned in 1933, and the tracks were paved over to widen the avenue. Rail service gradually disappeared as it was replaced by bus lines.

A fire on October 11, 1927, originating in trash under

*As early as 1926, Ocean City High School students were taking a "winter break" (even if they couldn't get to Ft. Lauderdale). This high school building was opened in 1924. Courtesy of Cornelia Corson Brown*

the Boardwalk at Ninth Street, wiped out two blocks of the Boardwalk and spread as far west as Wesley Avenue. Two hotels, an amusement pier and several businesses and homes were destroyed. Burning embers were carried as far west as Somers Point by the high winds.

A hurricane in 1944 tore up four blocks of the Boardwalk, which were never replaced, and damaged the Music Pier and several other buildings along the ocean front.

The "storm of the century," 1962's nor'easter, washed out and damaged much of the Boardwalk. Six homes were washed away and 300 more damaged when flood waters were two to four feet deep on the streets. Martial law was declared in the southern section of the city for two weeks until clean-up operations could be completed.

Ocean City's population was the largest of all incorporated areas in the county for several decades. Lower Township moved into first place with the 1980 census.

Although technically a part of Cape May County, Ocean City is more closely associated with nearby Atlantic County communities and Atlantic City. The city extends north of the county. Business and social activities of Atlantic County are much closer at hand than other comparable Cape May County communities.

Ocean City's population continues to grow. Its business community is solid and progressive. The increasing affluence of the surrounding areas, sparked by Atlantic City's casinos, is favorably affecting the economy of Ocean City, as well as Upper Township communities. The future seems bright.

*The Music Pier in Ocean City is an institution. Concerts, beauty pageants, meetings, dances, and a wide variety of other activities are held here. Located on the boardwalk, it is a convenient gathering center for Ocean City and surrounding communities. It has survived through storms and, most recently, old age. The pier was renovated in 1988 to repair rusting girders and structural members. It was back into full swing before the summer season was over. This postcard photo was taken in 1910.*
*Courtesy of Cape May County Historical Museum*

*Early in the morning of December 15, 1901, the* Sindia, *on its way to New York from the Far East, was blown ashore near 17th Street. By the time a tug could arrive to pull the hulk off the sand, it was too late—the ship had settled to the bottom, as pictured here. Very little cargo was salvaged, although many items, scattered around the county, are claimed to have come from the wreck. As one historian commented, if all the things that are claimed to have come from the* Sindia *actually did, the ship would have to have been three times the size listed on the registry. For many years the hulk was a landmark and tourist attraction along the Ocean City beach. The metal hull slowly rusted away. The 1962 storm finally removed all traces of the ill-fated ship.*
*Courtesy of Jane Dixon*

*Aerial views of 1926 Ocean City, looking north along Asbury Avenue (left) and looking south along Asbury (below left).*
*Courtesy of Cornelia Corson Brown*

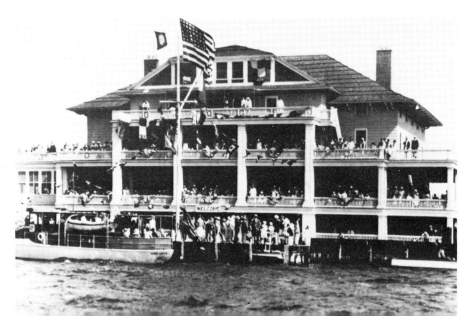

*Spectators gathered at the many excellent vantage points on the Ocean City Yacht Club to watch the weekend races during the 1926 season.*
*Courtesy of Cornelia Corson Brown*

*Captain Beam and his "Beaming Beauties" are out for their morning exercise class on the beach. Beam was a regular feature of the beach for many years. His trim students were the envy of many other beachgoers. Exercise classes on the beach during the 1920s and 1930s could be seen on most Cape May County beaches. Summer 1988 found that once again it is the "in thing" to do each morning.*
*Courtesy of Cornelia Corson Brown*

*The entire contingent of Ocean City's lifeguards, in 1926, line up in front of the Flanders Hotel for this group picture. Reassured that the beaches were safe, after seeing the morning lineup above, the swimmers rushed to the waters by the thousands (right). This photo, also taken in 1926, shows the Flanders again in the background.*
*Courtesy of Cornelia Corson Brown*

*Ocean City's Fire Department equipment and drivers pose beside city hall along 9th Street. The 1926 equipment was state-of-the-art.*
*Courtesy of Cornelia Corson Brown*

*The first Pet Parade on the boardwalk in the 1930s. Even though it became an annual event, the parade was short-lived because other parades and fairs awarded bigger prizes.*
*Courtesy of Bill Robinson*

# A MOVING EXPERIENCE

It seems that Cape May has been moving not just people but its buildings as well, almost from the day the first settlers arrived in its precincts.

Dr. Coxe's grand hall was disassembled and divided, with the three resulting sections ending in different areas of the county as parts of other structures. When the whalers were forced to move away from Town Bank, not only were some of their houses moved to various new locations, gravestones from their cemetery were rescued and relocated to the "Old Brick Church" cemetery in Cold Spring.

Some of the historical accounts indicated that building owners moved them around on their lands much like chess pieces. In some instances, there are reports that some, not pleased with the new locations, moved their buildings to still another spot and, in one case, back to the original site. The lone resident of Peck's Beach (Ocean City) for many years is reported to have made his kitchen from the wheelhouse of a wrecked ship that he moved inland to his building site.

Early Cape May settlers were a very frugal lot and moved their buildings to avoid the expense of buying new materials (or making them from "scratch") or hiring carpenters, as was probably the case with Coxe Hall. Others may have just been so attached to their homes that they wanted to take them with them, which may have been true for some of the whaler's cottages.

All through the history of the county, instances are recorded of buildings being moved to save them from the ravages of the ocean or the bay. Hotel Avalon was moved to save it from the ocean. According to one witness, that huge structure was pulled to its new location "by one horse."

In more recent times, many buildings have been moved to save them from destruction as progress with its itch for new buildings moved in to take over their locations. The "Lafayette Cottages" and both Star Villas, saved by Dr. McIntyre are examples, as is the Lower Township Municipal Hall that was moved to Historic Cold Spring Village. Still others were moved from distant locations just to have them in Cape May. St. Peters-by-the-Sea in Cape May Point is a classic example. It was moved here from Philadelphia. The owners of the massive Baltimore Inn in Cape May stoutly maintained that that building was disassembled and moved here from the Columbian Exposition in Chicago.

Whatever the reason, Cape May has moved and is still moving. The techniques for accomplishing these seemingly impossible tasks have been ingenious and often simple. In the early days, they were pulled over logs laid down in the path as rollers, and some were placed on large-wheeled platforms. In many cases oxen were used; in others horses were the muscle. Today, the buildings are, indeed, mounted on platforms and pulled by trucks to their new sites.

Some examples of Cape May's moving experiences are shown here for everyone to see with the same wondrous awe as the eyewitnesses at the time.

*An old toll house in Mayville sports a sign proudly proclaiming its move of approximately ten miles by a member of an early Cape May County family. Many other Cape May County buildings qualify for similar signs, boasting of their sojourns to new locations. The common practice of packing up and moving (one's building) has often caused confusion and consternation for historians trying to "get the facts."*
*Photograph by Vance Enck*

*Destined for demolition in downtown Cape May was the Star Villa complex on Ocean Street near the beach. Rev. Carl McIntyre bought the buildings and had them moved to East Cape May. This 1967 photograph shows the Star Villa enroute to its new home. Actually, the building spent a few days at this spot, after breaking through the street surface and dropping into the city's drainage system. Movers of earlier times are quoted as boasting to have moved buildings "without breaking plaster or pane." One can wonder if they ever faced a challenge of this proportion. This photo clearly exposes the building's two major additions (the entire fourth floor and the large four-floor section behind the porch), to a building originally referred to as "a small hotel." A parking lot replaced these condemned, but moved, buildings. Courtesy of Jane Dixon*

*Among the buildings "almost lost" in Cape May City's 1960 drive for tax-rateables is the Eldrige Johnson House, more renowned as the Pink House. This moving day photo, in the fall of 1969, shows it waiting to be seated on its new Perry Street foundation, next to the old* Star and Wave *building. Thomas Hand, publisher of the paper, purchased and moved the structure to his lot. The Pink House was the only survivor of a group of Victorian buildings condemned to be replaced by a motel. Another piece of history is depicted here by the one-way street sign, indicating westbound traffic only on Congress Place. It was realized, in a few short months, that more problems were created than solved by that change. Courtesy of Jane Dixon*

*This house is not pulling off the parkway to avoid paying its toll. It is the Philip Godfrey house "on the road to its salvation." Built in Swainton in the early 1700s, the Godfrey house was deserted and condemned to demolition in 1962, when Jean and Lou Albrecht, who possess a dedicated interest in antiquity, saved it. They moved the building to its present site in Seaville in December of 1962. Part of that move, pictured here, included a seven-mile trip north on the Garden State Parkway...in the wrong lanes. The meticulously restored house is now home to the Albrecht's.
Courtesy of Jean and Lou Albrecht*

*This 1985 moving day on Seashore Road finds the fire-ravaged and condemned Lower Township Municipal Hall on its way to its new home and haven at Historic Cold Spring Village. The movers, pictured at their work, have successfully passed the crowd of spectators and the Old Brick church and will soon ease the hall onto the village grounds. Today, the restored building houses the county's whaling museum, in addition to hosting numerous county community functions.
Courtesy of Historic Cold Spring Village*

# FISHING—THE FIRST INDUSTRY

Cape May's fortunes have always been closely tied to the water which surrounds it, flows through it, and settles in it.

Indians, the first settlers, were attracted by the plentiful supply of food from the sea, as well as the wildlife and equable climate. Whaling brought the first foreign settlers, initiating Cape May County's heritage as a major fishing area on the east coast and providing a steady source of experienced and dedicated sailors who are a major asset in times of peace as well as war.

That Indians love shellfish is amply illustrated by the mounds of discarded shells scattered throughout the shore areas. Colonists followed suit. As early as 1758, Cape May shipped 6,000 bushels of oysters to other areas, producing one-third of the county's total revenues. This had grown to 2,300,000 bushels by 1887. Oyster harvesting in the Delaware Bay flourished until the MSX disease invaded the region in 1956, virtually destroying the industry. Clams, lobsters and scallops have developed as major commercial crops, as have a wide variety of fin fish. These include bluefish, flounder, croakers, porgies, weakfish, drum fish, tilefish, tuna and sea bass, among others. At one time, sturgeon was harvested for a thriving caviar export trade, and even porpoises were killed for their skins, strangely enough, to make shoes.

Cape May City's fishing port is the second largest on the east coast, surpassed only by Gloucester, Massachusetts. Seafood processing plants clustered around Cape May are a major source of supply for seafood products. Commercial fishing in Cape May County provides annual revenues of $30 million and employs over seven hundred people.

Sport fishing has been a major Cape May County attraction since Commodore Decatur chartered fishing boats as early as 1799. Charter boat docks and private marinas abound in every barrier island city along the coast, serving the needs of sport fishermen and yachters.

The fishing industry is second only to tourism in Cape May's gross annual revenues. Despite growing complications from massive harvesting by foreign ships, interfering with normal fish migrations, and diseases in the shell fish supply, Cape May's fishing industry has continued to grow. More recently, the "fishport" operation in New York City's harbor, which is heavily subsidized through the bi-state New York, New Jersey Port Authority, is posing a threat to Cape May's port. Controversy concerning this operation is rapidly evolving into a major confrontation in the interstate relationships between New York and New Jersey.

*Modern clammers dredge clams up from the ocean floor by mechanical means. Earlier clammers relied on rakes and baskets dragged along the bottom. Another early and primitive technique was employed to test the bottom conditions. A bar of Felsaptha soap was tied to a line, weighted, and dropped; then, the softened soap would pick up floor material samples which would help the fishermen determine what gear was to be used at that particular location.*
*Courtesy of Cape May County Library*

*Indians often shucked their shellfish in the water, in order to lighten the load in their dugout canoes. The white man developed mass-production techniques to increase volume. This is a mollusk plant on the Delaware Bay, in operation in the 1920s. Cape May's early Indians would have loved this pile of wampum.*
*Courtesy of Cape May County Library*

*Commercial fishing boats can harvest up to 1000 pounds a day in numerous varieties of fish that are shipped or processed through Cape May as their home base. Although the fish shown here are not flounder, it is interesting to note that flounder must be hand-sorted to insure the white side is the top side for storage in ice, because the flounder will copy the color of their surroundings which would reduce their appearance quality.*
*Courtesy of Cape May County Library*

*Creation of Cold Spring Harbor, by dredging in the early 1900s, opened the way for Cape May's fishing industry. The harbor provided the only port in Cape May County which could handle the large fishing vessels. Schellenger's Landing, shown here in 1912, was one of the early and busy fishing docks in the harbor, and is still in use today. Shipping traffic in the harbor is visible in the background.*
*Courtesy of Tony Bevevino*

*Fish processing is an important part of the home port activity for Cape May's fishing fleet. From here, fresh fish are shipped to all parts of the county.*
*Courtesy of Cape May County Library*

*Sport fishing recognizes no sex boundaries. The only differences that show up are in sizes, based on where the fish are caught. The lady anglers, Mrs. Nelson Mayhew and Helen Pringle (above), hooked their catch angling on the Ocean City beach. How could any poor fish resist those smiles—and those costumes? Former Middle Township Mayor Harry Eldredge (right) and friend went farther out to sea to hook these drum fish.*
*Courtesy of,*
*above—Sarah Pringle McKinley,*
*below—Vernon Eldredge*

211

## MOTHER NATURE'S REALM

By virtue of its location, jutting thirty miles out to sea, Cape May has always been one of nature's favorite places. The natural rest areas and food stops for migrating birds, the huge current patterns of the ocean that built the peninsula by depositing sand to form the alluvial barrier islands are wondrous examples of Mother Nature's intricate patterns.

Cape May was a forbidding place for man. It was a paradise for animals and birds, providing an ecosystem of prolific balances. The gentle Lenni-Lenapes unlocked the doors and carefully feasted on the county's bounty. The foreign settlers however, succeeded in eradicating buffalo, panthers, bears, and wolves that freely roamed the area before their arrival.

After decades of indiscriminate harvesting and killing there have been, in recent years, strong drives to conserve nature's carefully planned preserve. About one-third of Cape May's area is protected as conservancy areas. The Great Cedar Swamp, the Pinelands, Belleplain State Forest, McNamara Preserve, Higbee Beach Wildlife areas and several marshland tracts are actively protected.

Located on the major flyways for migrating birds, Cape May is known throughout the world as a birdwatchers' paradise. During birding season, avid visitors from many parts of the world make pilgrimages here to see what too many of us take for granted and sometimes consider a nuisance.

There are active programs to protect the great dunes that still dot a landscape that once was filled with them. The wholesale destruction of those dunes to create building plots took away much of the natural protection for the peninsula. We have periodically paid the price in storm damage and flooding, for that profligacy.

The wealth of natural abundance that remains has spawned all sorts of human support groups to assist and protect that legacy. The Avian Center dedicated to treating injured birds, the Wetlands Institute working to increase our knowledge and respect for the intricate estuarine system of the area, and the numerous bird and wildlife sanctuaries are outstanding examples.

It is certain that Cape May will see much more development and building. The population will increase, perhaps dramatically, in the future. This is not bad, as the care and feeding and preservation of humans is part of nature's plan as well. The increasing recognition that we must live with our environment in order to live in it is encouraging. In this respect, Cape May is and will continue to play a vital role...as Mother Nature's helper.

*Cape May County is a "world class attraction" in nature's realm. Located on several major migrating bird flyways, the vast areas of marshlands and forests offer vital resting and feeding areas for common and exotic birds on their travels. The autumn and spring seasons attract thousands of avid bird followers from around the world. "Cape May is for the birds" is a consummate compliment. Extensive national, state, and local support and resources are regularly invested in keeping the county just that way.*
*Photograph by Herb Beitel*

*Tidal waters weave an intricate and spectacular lace across the extensive marshlands that separate the barrier islands from the mainland. This 1988 aerial view, looking west across the Cape May peninsula from Five Mile Island (the Wildwoods), provides a panorama of nature's endowment not often seen nor appreciated by those rushing to the surf and sun or to work.*
*Courtesy of Robert "Skip" Berry*

*Cape May County's own "Walden Pond" opens up through a narrow break in the graceful line of trees along southbound lanes at milepost twenty on the Garden State Parkway. The sudden glimpse of this sylvan enclave is a constant reminder of the bountiful natural endowment that graces Cape May County. Egrets and herons regularly sun themselves on the branches here in the late afternoon, adding a special dimension to this pastoral scene.
Photograph by Vance Enck*

*The silhouettes of Avalon and Stone Harbor are dwarfed by the scale of the three-mile wide marshlands and mid-morning sky in this 1988 photo. Even so, mounting concern over the encroachment of developments on the wetlands and forest areas is leading to careful planning of future building activities along the barrier islands and the mainland borders.
Photograph by Herb Beitel*

## INTO THE FUTURE

Over the three centuries of its existence, Cape May County's development has been characterized by slow, gradual but solid growth. The one great exception to this pattern was the explosive and miraculous building of the Barrier Island resort communities along the Atlantic Ocean coastline, beginning in the early 1880s. From that hectic and pioneering period, tourism emerged as the county's largest industry by a wide margin.

Augmented by bursts of activity following World Wars I and II, tourism has established a solid base that has continued to follow the county's pattern of growth. In the 1980s, the county is experiencing another building boom of modest proportions that should continue for some time into the future. This flurry has been prompted by an increasing number of permanent residents joining the county's population ranks and a business building drive to provide the support activities that parallel an increasing population and tourist base. New shopping malls, offices and office complexes, retail business locations, and health care service facilities evidence this development.

Sporadic entrepreneurial activities in the past endeavored to establish an industrial base for the county. They lasted for varying periods of time, but ultimately became victims of advancing technology or depleted natural resources that made their products obsolete or too costly. The very earliest industries—fishing and farming—developed in spite of and because of the county's natural isolation and surrounding water and have survived over the centuries.

Cape May County is fortuitously located near the heart of the huge megalopolis, extending from Boston to Virginia, which houses nearly one-third of the country's population. The seeming remoteness and isolation from the mainstream of commerce that inhibited growth in the past are proving to be major assets today. Cape May's vast stretches of wide, safe beaches and well-preserved natural areas are easily accessible to millions of people. The county's natural assets of the waterways surrounding it and the special attraction of Nature's favoritism toward it attract not only those seeking relaxation and safe recreation but also many special interest groups among nature lovers.

The pleasant four-season climate because of its southern location, on a parallel with Washington, D.C., and northern Virginia, and the tempering thermostat of the surrounding waters, make the county a desirable place for recreation and permanent living alike. The county has long been a favorite retirement area. Increasing numbers of year-round residents are attracted to the county because of all the natural advantages and the close proximity to major cultural and commerce centers, as well as the rapidly growing base of the Atlantic City area. Cape May County, in the 1980s, became the second fastest growing area in the state.

Resort areas that used to go into hibernation between Labor Day and Memorial Day not many years ago, now stay awake and alive year-round. The Christmas season is especially punctuated by shopping opportunities and interesting tours and activities to brighten the season. The long, very pleasant, colorful, and unhurried autumn seasons at the Cape May Shore have become "not-to-be-missed" tourist attractions.

Cape May City, with its treasury of Victorian architecture, leads the way to developing year-round activities to attract thousands of visitors in off-summer seasons. Nearly all of the county's communities have emulated that aggressiveness and pride and are constantly expanding the menu of activities available for visitors and for enriching the lives of residents. What may have been considered a cultural desert at one time has blossomed forth with a full-season professional equity theatre at Somers Point, right on the Cape May County border. Symphonic concerts are performed regularly by the South Jersey Symphony and the South Jersey Pops orchestras, in addition to the New Jersey Symphony Orchestra's visits to Cape May County on their frequent statewide concert tours. A community concert series is offered by the Mid-Atlantic Center for the Arts in Cape May. The nation's oldest art league presents exhibits and year-round activities, centering at its Cape May City base on the Physick Estate. There are several galleries and active arts groups in practically every area of the county. The quality of cultural life in the county is on a decided upswing.

Despite recent setbacks from foreign pollution washing up on Jersey shores (almost none of which, it should be noted, came ashore on Cape May County beaches), the mysterious dolphin deaths of 1987, and the spotty epidemics of diseases in the fishing areas, Cape May has always been and remains one of the safest and most stable ecological areas in the United States.

Cape May County's future growth is assured by many converging factors. What is still to be determined is the character and strength of that progress. Long-range planning in the county has been spotty, at best, in the past. Zoning, planning, and preservation standards have been governed by exceptions rather than rules. New Jersey's heritage of "home rule" making county-wide planning difficult, if not impossible. Fortunately, the growing national and state concerns with the ecology and safer building practices are producing enforceable, more pervasive standards for developments that would encroach on existing natural areas and foul our environment. The county's ecosystem, even with its occasional violent shows of strength, is very fragile and can be disastrously altered. The county and its local governments are exercising increasing control over the character of their growth. More will be needed. Each year more farmland is used to cultivate shopping centers and housing developments. Congestion, pollution, and escalating needs for government services are problems that must be planned for and addressed affirmatively.

Cape May County is a "destination of choice" for visitors and permanent residents alike. As long as this remains true, the county has a bright and solid future. It may not reach the spectacular levels of many nearby areas, such as north Jersey or the Philadelphia environs, but maintaining an attractive quality of life may be the desirable alternative. Big is not always the best and small is not necessarily bad. Growth is inevitable. What type of growth will be determined by the residents and their leaders.

*"Shacks at the shore" have attracted thousands of part-time residents to the county for a century. Sports activities and just "getting way from it all" have lined the shoreline of bays and inlets with modest vacation homes. Waste and pollution problems may make these colonies history unless controlled by self-regulation, as well as government regulations.*
*Photograph by Vance Enck*

*Old and new will exist side by side, as this Cape May scene shows. Planning and zoning enforcement will be essential in establishing the patterns and objectives of each governmental sub-division. As the street sign indicates, it is "one-way" to development.*
*Photograph by Vance Enck*

*A building boom in Cape May County is consuming more and more farm acreage in housing and commercial developments. The acreage offered for sale (right) is in Lower Township, one of the fastest growing areas in New Jersey. The area in the picture below was an open meadow until converted to a housing development. Loss of farmland and encroachments on fragile, sometimes physically "unsafe," wetlands are matters of increasing concern for government bodies and citizens alike.
Photographs by Vance Enck*

*Cape May County Municipal Utilities Authority has had a relatively short but controversial career. It is responsible for providing services to help the county and its local governments meet state and federal standards for pollution and water quality control. A number of new facilities have been built and more are in the process. This sewage processing plant at Cape May Point began operating in 1987. Photograph by Vance Enck*

# Bibliography

Adams, James Truslo, Ed. *Album of American History* Vol. 1. Charles Scribner's Sons; New York, 1969.

Albrecht, Jean Morris. "The Philip Godfrey House." *Cape May County Magazine of History and Geneaology*, Vol. VII, No. 5, 1977.

Albrecht, Jean; Campbell, Clare; and Van Vorst, Joyce. "Tales and Legends of Upper Township and Its Villages." Collection of articles published in the quarterly *South Jersey Magazine* during 1986 and 1987.

Alexander, Robert Crozer. "Cape Island, New Jersey 1860-1869. *Cape May County Magazine of History and Geneaology* (*) Vol. 6, No. 6, 1969.

———. "Cape May County Census." *C.M.C.M.H.G.* Vol. 7, No. 3, 1975.

———. "The Cold Spring." *C.M.C.M.H.G.* Vol. 7, No. 3, 1975.

———. "Historical Notes on Cape May." *C.M.C.M.H.G.* Vol. 5, No. 9, 1963.

———. *Ho! For Cape Island*. Cape May, N.J.: R. C. Alexander, 1956.

———. "The Principal Settlements." *C.M.C.M.H.G.* Vol. 6, No. 1, 1964.

———. *Steamboat for Cape May*. Cape May, N.J.: R. C. Alexander, 1956.

———. "Steamboat Republic For Cape May." Vol. 5, No. 8, 1962.

———. *Avalon, The Jewel of the Jersey Coast*. Avalon, N.J.: Avalon Development Company, 1909.

Benckert, Frances D. "A Little Look at Old Cape May." *C.M.C.M.H.G.* Vol. 7, No. 1, 1973.

Block, Florence Leeds. "Seaville Meeting." *C.M.C.M.H.G.* Vol. 6, No. 2, 1965.

Boyer, George F. "Five Mile Beach Newspapers." *C.M.C.M.H.G.* Vol. 7, No. 2, 1974.

Boyer, George F. "Philip Pontius Banker." *C.M.C.M.H.G.* Vol. 6, No. 9, 1972.

Boyer, George F. *Wildwood, Middle of the Island*. Egg Harbor City, N.J.: Laureate Press, 1976.

Boyer, George F., and Cunningham, J. Pearson. *Cape May County Story*. Egg Harbor City, N.J.: Laureate Press, 1985.

Campbell, Clare. "Old Mill Stones, Their Story and Recollections of Early Grist Mills." Reprint.

———. "Princess Snowflower." *C.M.C.M.H.G.* Vol. 9, No. 1, 1987.

Champion, Thomas. "Belleplain State Forest." *C.M.C.M.H.G.* Vol. 8, No. 4, 1984.

Christine, John D. "West Cape May Gold Beaters." *Homespun*, Winter 1976.

Circker, Hayward & Blanche. *American Portraits*. New York, N.Y.: Dover Publications, Inc., 1976.

Clark, Emily. "To Cape May County Civil War Veterans." *C.M.C.M.H.G.* Vol. 8, No. 3, 1982.

———. Compendium of Articles and Notes from Bulletins of 1950 through 1961; *C.M.C.M.H.G.* Vol 7, No. 4, 1976.

Cook, George. "The Steam Dummy Era at Cape May." Reprint.

Cunningham, John T. *New Jersey: A Mirror on America*. Florham Park, N.J.: Afton Publishing Co., 1978.

———. *New Jersey: America's Main Road*. Garden City, N.Y.: Doubleday & Co., Inc., 1976.

———. *This Is New Jersey*. New Brunswick, N.J.: Rutgers University Press, 1987.

Darby, Bertram M. "Ocean City Story, Part VII." *C.M.C.M.H.G.* Vol. 5, No. 9, 1963.

DeSantis, Donald. "United States Life Saving Service in Avalon." *C.M.C.M.H.G.* Vol. 8, No. 4, 1984.

Dickinson, Karl A. "After Cedar Forests Were Felled, Shingle Mining Came To Dennisville." *C.M.C.M.H.G.* Vol. 7, No. 5, 1977.

———. "Cape May Diamonds." *C.M.C.M.H.G.* Vol. 7, No. 5, 1977.

———. "Fulling Mill Road's Namesake Was Located On Site Now Covered by Airport Runways." *C.M.C.M.H.G.* Vol. 7, No. 5, 1977.

———. "Historic Cape Island." *C.M.C.M.H.G.* Vol. 7, No. 5, 1977.

———. "Historical Account of Fishing Creek, Villas Long Ago." *C.M.C.M.H.G.* Vol. 7, No. 5, 1977.

———. "Two Hundred Fifty Years On the Romney Plantation." Vol. 7, No. 5, 1977.

Donovan, Oliver, and Parish, Howard. "Cape May County: Our Southern Peninsula." *South Jersey Magazine* Vol. 16, No. 2, Spring 1987.

———. Excerpts from the Commissioner's Report: Division of the Lands & Real Estate of Joseph Falkinburg." *C.M.C.M.H.G.* Vol. 8, No. 3, 1983.

Godson, Susan H. "Captain Joy Bright Handock and the Role of Women in the U.S. Navy." *N.J. History* Vol. 105, Nos. 1 & 2, 1987.

Goldy, Jim. "Thar She Blows—Whaling Off the South Jersey Coast." *South Jersey Magazine* Vol. 15, No. 1, 1986.

* All future references to this publication will be listed as *C.M.C.M.H.G.*

Hand, Amelia S. "Scrapbook of Amelia S. Hand." *C.M.C.M.H.G.* Vol. 6, No. 6, 1969.

Hart, Willard H. "Departs As Soon As Loaded." *N.R. H. Bulletin* Vol. 34, No. 4, 1969.

*History of Stone Harbor, 1914-1964.* Philadelphia, Pa.: Allen, Lane & Scott, 1965.

Hollemon, Kenneth C. *From Whence We Came—A History of the Coast Guard in Southern New Jersey and Delaware.* Cape May, N.J.: U.S. Coast Guard, 1987.

Hunter, William Garrison, II. *A History of Education in Dennis Township, Cape May County, N.J.—1664-1964.* Thesis for MA. Glassboro State College, N.J., 1965.

Johnson, Cathy. "The History and Establishment of Stone Harbor." *C.M.C.M.H.G.* Vol. 8, No. 5, 1985.

Kobele, Robert F. "A History of the Court Houses of Cape May County." *C.M.C.M.H.G.* Vol. 6, No. 4, 1967.

Lee, Harold. *A History of Ocean City, New Jersey.* Ocean City, N.J.: Harold Lee, 1965.

MacDonald, H. Gerald. "A Brief History of Railroads On Ludlam's Beach." *C.M.C.M.H.G.* Vol. 8, No. 2, 1982.

___. "History of Railroads on Five Mile Beach." *C.M.C.M.H.G.* Vol. 7, No. 3, 1975.

___. "The Pennsylvania Railroad in Sea Isle City, N.J." *The High Line* Vol. 5, No. 1, Autumn 1984.

___. "1926 Derailment at Erma, N.J." Reprint.

McMahon, William. *Historic South Jersey Towns.* Atlantic City, N.J.: Press Publishing Co., 1964.

___. *South Jersey Towns.* New Brunswick, N.J.: Rutgers University Press, 1973.

McLaughlin, Capt. James M. "Maritime History of Cape May County." *C.M.C.M.H.G.* Vol. 7, No. 7, 1979.

Mason, Bessie Bristol. "Recollections of Holly Beach and Wildwood." *C.M.C.M.H.G.* Vol. 6, No. 7, 1970.

Meader, Stephen W. "How Cape May County Fought For Independence." *C.M.C.M.H.G.* Vol. 6, No. 2, 1965.

Meech, Susan Billings, compiler. *A Supplement to the Descendents of Peter Spicer.* Boston, Mass.: Stanhope Press, 1923.

Merrill, John. "Jersey Cape Historically." Collection of weekly articles published in the *Herald-Lantern-Dispatch* newspapers from December 1985 to June 1988.

Miller, William J., Jr. *A Ferry Tale.* Wilmington, Del.: Delapeake Publishing Co., 1985.

Moore, Wendeline. "Recollections of Old Swainton." *C.M.C.M.H.G.* Vol. 8, No. 1, 1981.

Moore, William James. *Autobiography.* Cape May, N.J.: William James Moore, 1973.

New Jersey Office of Historic Preservation Sites Inventory—Upper Township, Cape May County. Princeton, N.J.: Heritage Studies, Inc., 1981-82.

Nomination Forms for Cape May County Register of Historic Structures and Sites. Cape May Court House, N.J.: Cape May County Planning Board, 1977-78.

Prince, T. T., M.D. *Historical and Biographical Atlas of the New Jersey Coast.* Philadelphia, Pa.: Woolman and Rose, 1878.

Prince, Carl E., Ed. *The Papers of William Livingston* Vol. 1. Trenton, N.J.: New Jersey Historical Commission, 1979.

Reed, Adella. "Dias Creek." *C.M.C.M.H.G.* Vol. 8, No. 6, 1986.

Richards, Horace G., Ed. *A Book of Maps of Cape May, 1610-1878.* Cape May, N.J.: Cape May Geographical Society, 1954.

Scattergood. *Delaware River Guide—From Trenton to the Sea* (brochure sold on boats enroute).

Smith, Gilbert. "My First Experience in Avalon." *C.M.C.M.H.G.* Vol. 7, No. 6, 1978.

Steven, Lewis T. "Cape May's First Land Purchasers." *C.M.C.M.H.G.* Vol. 2, No. 5, 1943.

Stevens, Lewis T. *The History of Cape May County, New Jersey.* Cape May, N.J.: Lewis T. Stevens, 1897.

Strum, Harvey. "South Jersey and the War of 1812." *C.M.C.M.H.G.* Vol. 9, No. 1, 1987.

Sullivan, Audrey G., Ed. *Nineteenth Century South Jersey Camp Meeting—South Seaville, New Jersey.* Ft. Lauderdale, Fla.: Audrey G. Sullivan, 1980.

Swain, Hannah Kimble. "Hildreth-Rio Grande." Vol. 9, No. 1, 1987.

___. "Indian Lore—Cape May County." *C.M.C.M.H.G.* Vol. 7, No. 7, 1979.

Taylor, R. Cordelia. "A History of Education in Lower Township, Cape May County, New Jersey. *C.M.C.M.H.G.* Vol. 5, No. 8, 1962.

Thomas, George E., and Doebley, Carl. *Cape May, Queen of the Seaside Resorts.* Philadelphia, Pa.: The Art Alliance Press, 1976.

Townsend, Everett B., Sr. "Some Random Thoughts About Clermont, Its Places and People." *C.M.C.M.H.G.* Vol. 6, No. 6, 1969.

Van Vorst, Joyce. *Cedar Swamp Creek.* Joyce Van Vorst, 1977.

Wheeler, Edward. *Scheyichbi and the Strand (or Early Days Along the Delaware).* Press of J. B. Lippincott & Co., 1876.

Wilson, Ruth Swain. *The Tip of the Cape.* El Paso, Texas: Complete Printing and Letter Service, 1976.

# Index

**A**
Albrecht, Lewis & Jean, 41, 46, 208
Alms House, 73
Andrew, Aaron, 180, 181
Anglesea, 180
Atlantic Hotel, 156, 157
Avalon, 72, 190-192
Avalon, Hotel, 191, 206

**B**
Baker, J. Thompson, 182
Baker, Latimore, 182
Baker, Philip, 181, 182, 183
Baltimore Inn, 166, 206
Barrier Islands, 18, 22, 28, 140
Batteast, John, 153
Beesley Point Ferry, 34, 127
Beesley, Thomas, 24, 34, 36
Beesley's Point, 26, 34, 35, 40, 129
Belleplain, 53
Belleplain State Forest, 50, 53, 212
Berkeley, Lord John, 20
Bethlehem Steel Corporation, 92
"Beulah Land," 106
Blackbeard, 18
Board of Chosen Freeholders, 22
Bradner, Rev. John, 106
Buchanan, President James, 160
Buck House, The Samuel, 81
Bullitt, John C., 121, 161-162
Burdette Tomlin Hospital, 74
Burleigh, 72, 79, 88
Button, Stephan Decatur, 161, 166
Byllynge, Edward, 20, 23

**C**
Cabot, John & Sebastian, 12
Cape May Canal, 90, 100, 101, 175
Cape May City, 140, 141, 156-179
Cape May County Airport, 104, 134, 173
Cape May County Art League, 63, 79
Cape May County Bridge Commission, 129, 130
Cape May County Historical Museum, 75, 110
Cape May County Zoo, 76, 77
Cape May Court House, 10, 72, 79-87

Cape May Glass Works, 86
Cape May-Lewes Ferry, 111, 127, 128
"Cape May Ocean Wave," 160
Cape May Point, 26, 27, 120, 142-152, 218
Cape May Point Lighthouse, 127, 142, 148
Cape May Sand Plant, 142, 151
Camp Wissahickon, 99, 114, 170
Carlton House, 149
Carman, Caleb, 22, 99, 105
Carroll Villa, 166
Carpenter, George, 107
Carteret, Sir John, 20
Cedar Shingles, mined, 68
Chalfonte Hotel, 164
Chattin, Capt. John, 34
Chattin, Joseph, 34
Cholera, 106
Chevrolet, Louis, 128, 170, 171
Christie, Walter, 128, 170, 171
Civilian Conservation Corps, 33, 53
Clay, Henry, 159
Clermont, 22, 50, 56
Church, William, 166, 168
Cold Spring, 10, 29, 105
Cold Spring Academy, 106
Colonial Hotel, 166, 168
Columbia Hotel, 160, 161, 164
Congress Hall, 141, 157, 158, 162, 164, 165, 166, 168
Corson, John, 22, 38
Corson, Peter, 22, 28, 40
Corson, Remington, 57
Coxe, Dr. Daniel, 20, 21, 22, 23, 50, 56, 72, 98
Coxe Hall, 21
Cresse, Arthur, 22, 72
Cresse, Humphrey, 180
Crest Haven, 72, 73, 80

**D**
Daly, Charlotte, 155, 176
Dawson, Isaac, 60
Decatur, Commodore Stephen, 156
Denizot, Victor, 163, 166, 167
Dennis Township, 22, 50, 70
Dennisville, 22, 50, 65-71

DeHirsch, Baron, 61
Del Haven, 92
Dias Creek, 10, 23, 72, 92
Diverty, Jesse, 66
Douglass, William, 26
Dixon, Jane, 24, 68
Ducks Unlimited, 33
Duke of York, 20

**E**
East Cape May, 170
East Jersey, 20
Eldoro, 50, 60
Eldredge, Eli, 26
Eldredge, Francis, 105
Eldredge, Jacob, 26
Erma, 104
Evans, J. C., 165, 170
Excursion House, 195, 196

**F**
Falkenburge, Joseph, 71
Fenwick, John, 20
Fishing Creek, 10, 110
Fire of 1869 (Cape May), 164
Fire of 1878 (Cape May), 165
Five Mile Island, 90, 141, 180, 183
Flanders Hotel, 204
Flynn, William, 170
Ford, Henry, 99, 128, 170
Franklin, William, 27
Friends Meeting House, 40
Fun Factory, 113, 170

**G**
Garden State Parkway, 37, 40, 99, 133, 137
Gandy, Isaac, 66
"Gazette, The," 84, 94
Godfrey House, Philip, 41, 208
Goldbeating, 153
Goldin (Golding), William, 22, 34
Goshen, 22, 30, 68, 92
Grace, Eugene, 93
Grace, John, 52, 56
Grant, President Ulysses S., 165
Gravelly Run, 79
Great Cedar Swamp, 8, 22, 48, 50, 56, 212

Green Creek, 22, 23, 87

**H**
Hamilton, Andrew, 22
Hancock, Capt. Joy Bright, 185
Hand, Daniel, 79, 82
Hand, Henry, 26
Hand, Jesse, 26
Hand, John, 26
Hand, Jonathan, 26, 82
Hand, Nathan, 26
Hand, Shamgar, 22, 72, 79, 88
Harrison, President Benjamin, 142, 146, 147, 182
Hendrickson, Capt. Cornelius, 12
Herbert, Samuel E., 188
Hereford Glass Co., 86
Hereford Lighthouse, 180, 184
Higbee Beach, 23, 98, 120, 212
Higbee's House, 23, 99
Higbee, Joseph, 99, 120
High Beach, 92
Hildreth, George, 108, 160, 166
Hildreth House, George, 108
Historic Cold Spring Village, 102, 105, 108, 109
Holly Beach, 180, 182
Holly Tree Inn, 56
Holmes, Gabriel, 83
Hotel Cape May, 170, 175
Howland, John, 14
Hudson, Henry, 12, 13
Hughes, Abigail, 26
Hughes, Ellis, 26
Hughes, Humphrey, 1st, 22, 156, 180
Hughes, Humphrey, 5th, 27
Hughes, Thomas, 157
Hunt House, Dr. Henry L., 165, 170, 177, 179

**I**
Indian Mills, 10

**J**
Johnson, Reuben, 104
Jones, John Paul, 81

**K**
Kechemeches, 10
Kidd, Capt. William, 18, 142
Kimbles Beach, 92
King's Highway, 22, 56, 90, 98
Knight, J. C., 164, 165, 170, 172

**L**
Lafayette Hotel, 166, 167
Lake, Ezra B., 200
Lake, James E., 200
Lake, S. Wesley, 200
Lake Lily, 26, 143
Lake Magnolia, 54, 182
Lake Nummy, 10, 53
Landis, Charles, 194
Leaming, Aaron, 26, 40, 72, 92, 180, 186, 190
Leaming, Christopher, 22, 72, 100
Leaming, Thomas, 26
Lee, Robert E., 29
Lenni-Lenapes, 8, 10, 11, 42, 88
Lincoln, Abraham, 29, 159
Littleworth, 48
Lower Township, 22, 98-103, 218
Ludlam, Henry, 51
Ludlam, Joseph, 65, 193
Ludlam, Thomas, 51

**M**
McIntyre, Rev. Carl., 178, 207
McNamara Wildlife Management Area, 33, 212
Macomber Hotel, 166
Magnesite Plant, 143, 151
Mansion House, 157, 160
Marcy, Alexander, 105
Marmora, 36
Marshall, Randall, Jr., 44, 47
Marshall, Thomas Chew, 44
Marshallville, 44-47
Matthews, Samuel, 72
Mayflower descendents, 14, 106
Mayville, 10
Mechanics Row, 79
Merrill, John, 107
Mey, Capt. Cornelius Jacobsen, 12, 13

Mid-Atlantic Center for the Arts, 148, 175, 178
Middle Township, 22, 72, 73
Millman, Joseph, 110
Minnix, Bruce, 175, 178, 179
Moon's Drug Store, 173
Moore, John, 61
Moore, William J., 153, 154
Mt. Vernon Hotel, 143, 160

**N**
New Atlantic Hotel, 157
Newbold, J. Pemberton, 170
North Cape May, 111
North Wildwood, 72, 180, 182
Nummy, King, 10, 88, 100
Nummytown, 10

**O**
Ocean City, 200-205
Ocean House, 158, 164, 165
Ocean View, 50, 54, 55
"Old Brick Church," 16, 98, 103, 106, 107
Old Limerick, 190

**P**
Palermo, 38
Peermont, 191, 192
Penn, William, 14, 16, 20, 23, 99
Petersburg, 22, 48
Pettifer, Donald, 109
Philadelphia Pickle Co., 60
Physick, Emlen, 106, 111, 178
Physick House (Estate), 164, 175, 178
Pierce, President Franklin, 160
Pierces Point, 22, 92
"Pink House, The," 165, 170, 207
Portsmouth, 16
Powell, Mary, 11

**Q**
"Quaker Cannons," 26
Queen's Highway, 22, 79

**R**
Railroads:
  Cape May & Millville, 35, 56, 61, 104, 121

Pennsylvania, 42, 121, 123
Pennsylvania-Reading-Seashore, 123, 124, 125
Philadelphia-Reading, 121
Philadelphia & Seashore, 121
Pleasantville & Ocean City, 121, 201
Reading, 42, 121, 123
South Jersey, 201
West Jersey & Seashore, 121, 161, 180, 186, 191, 195
Reed's Beach, 22, 26, 92
Reeves, George, 153
Reeves, Theodore, 153
"Republic, The," 116, 120
Rio Grande, 72, 90
Rio Grande Sugar Cane Co., 91
Risley, Horace, 121, 186, 187
Route of the Gull, 129
Ryan, Reuben, 182

**S**
St. Elizabeth's Catholic Church, 95
St. Mary's-by-the-Sea, 150
St. Peter's-by-the-Sea, 145, 206
Salvatore, Anne, 108
Salvatore, Joseph, 108
Schellenger, Thomas B., 105
Sea Breeze Hotel, 162
Sea Grove, 142
Sea Isle City, 50, 193-198
Seaville, 22, 40
Seven Mile Beach, 121, 186, 190
Shields, Peter, 170
Shoemaker Holly Tree, 40
"Shoobies," 125, 162, 195
Shoreham Hotel, 150
Sindia, 202
Shunpike, 98
Snowflower, 10
Somers Point Bridge, 35
Sousa, John Philip, 168
South Seaville, 50, 56, 121
South Seaville Meeting Association, 56, 57, 59
Spicer, Jacob, 11, 22, 26, 65, 105
Springer's Union Hotel, 84
Star of Asia, 152

Star Villa, 166, 206, 207
Steven, Lewis, 195
Stillwell, Enoch, 26
Stillwell, Nicholas, 22, 26, 34
Stillwell, Rebecca, 26, 34
Stites, Isaiah, 34
Stites Point, 34
Stites, Richard, 34, 35
Stockton Hotel, 161
Stone Harbor, 186-189
Strathmere, 50, 193, 198
Summer Station, 162
Swain, Ebenezer, 72
Swain, Jacob, 40
Swain, Jonathan, 72, 78, 180
Swain, Richard, 72, 78, 104
Swainton, 22, 23, 28, 72, 78, 104

**T**
Tatham, George, 186
Tatham, Henry B., 186
Todd, Lester & Sallie, 56
Town Bank, 14, 16, 98, 102
Townsend, John, 22, 50, 54, 56
Townsend, Richard, 40, 50, 200
Townships/Precincts, 22
Tuckahoe, 10, 23, 42, 121
Tuckahoe Indians, 10
Tuckahoe Inn, 34, 35
Turtle Gut Battle, 26
Turtle Gut Inlet, 180
Two Mile Island, 180, 183

**U**
U-Boats, 100, 101, 133
U.S. Coast Guard, 100, 101, 112-115, 134
United States Hotel, 164
Upper Township, 22, 32

**V**
Van Gilder, Abraham, 48
Van Gilder, John, 44, 48
Van Gilder, Thomas, 44, 48
Verazzano, John De, 12
Villas, 110

**W**
Wampum, 11
Wanamaker, John, 142, 146
West Cape May, 153-155
West Wildwood, 183
West Jersey, 20
West Jersey Society, 18, 20, 22
Whaling, 14, 15
Whilden, Alexander, 142
Whilden, Hannah, 14
Whilden, John, 14
Whilden, Matthew, 16, 104
White, George H., 96
Whitesboro, 72, 96
Wildwood, 10, 72, 182
Wildwood Crest, 183
Willett's Point, 34
Williamson, Rev. Moses, 106
Wilson, Woodrow, 87, 167, 187, 188
Windsor Hotel, 172
Woodbine, 50, 61-64
Woodbine Agricultural School, 62

# About the Authors

Collaborating in producing this history were Vance Enck and Herb Beitel, residents of Cape May City. Both moved to Cape May permanently a few years ago. Prior to that, they were weekend commuters beginning in the mid-1960s. They have owned homes in Cape May since 1966. Vance did most of the legwork and research as well as most of the contemporary pictures. Herb copied the pictures loaned for use in the book and did much of the writing.

Vance and Herb have collaborated in a number of Cape May activities. Vance served nine years as a trustee for the Mid-Atlantic Center for the Arts and served as chairman for initiating MAC's theatre and performing arts programs. He helped research and develop MAC's famous walking, trolley, and stained glass tours. Herb served as MAC's president for three years and as treasurer for two and one-half years. They are both currently active in the Cape May County Art League. Vance has chaired special events and Herb is treasurer.

Vance became a permanent resident in 1986 after retiring from a rewarding thirty-two year career as a drama, history, English, and speech arts teacher that took him to Maryland, Pennsylvania, and New Jersey. Since retiring he has been more than busy restoring his century-old classic Cape May home. He is a native of the Harrisburg, Pennsylvania area and a graduate of Indiana University of Western Pennsylvania.

Herb settled in Cape May in 1985 after being named managing director of South Jersey Regional Theatre in Somers Point, South Jersey's only full-time professional theatre. He has been a magazine publisher and editor, and earned the highest journalistic achievement award of the American Business Press. Herb has been a trade association executive and counsel, a savings and loan association officer, and a national officer of the Republican party. He is a graduate of the University of Chicago Law School and a member of the Illinois and Indiana bars. He was awarded Phi Beta Kappa for his engineering studies record at the University of South Carolina and Emory University.

Vance and Herb's love affair with Cape May County is apparent. They both agree, after residing in many other areas, that Cape May is the only place to live.

*Beesleys Point, Tuckahoe River, 1930s. Courtesy of Harry N. Merz Collection through Dr. John Siliquini*